HINDUISM

Second Edition

HINDUISM
A Cultural Perspective

David R. Kinsley
McMaster University

PRENTICE HALL
Englewood Cliffs, New Jersey 07632

Library of Congress Cataloging-in-Publication Data

Kinsley, David R.
 Hinduism: a cultural perspective / David R. Kinsley.—2nd ed.
  p.   cm.—(Prentice Hall series in world religions)
 Includes bibliographical references and index.
 ISBN 0-13-395732-2
 1. Hinduism. I. Title. II. Series.
 BL1202.K48 1993
 294.5—dc20   92-31484
                                                       CIP

Acquisitions editor: Ted Bolen
Editorial/production supervision: Bridget Mooney
Copy editor: Mary McDonald
Cover design: Patricia Kelly
Cover credit: Vishnu with His Wife on a Bird. Victorian Albert
            Museum. Scala/Art Resource, New York.
Prepress buyer: Herb Klein
Manufacturing buyer: Robert Anderson

 © 1993, 1982 by Prentice-Hall, Inc.
A Simon & Schuster Company
Englewood Cliffs, New Jersey 07632

Printed in the United States of America
10 9 8 7 6 5 4 3 2 1

ISBN 0-13-395732-2

Prentice-Hall International (UK) Limited, *London*
Prentice-Hall of Australia Pty. Limited, *Sydney*
Prentice-Hall Canada Inc., *Toronto*
Prentice-Hall Hispanoamericana, S.A., *Mexico*
Prentice-Hall of India Private Limited, *New Delhi*
Prentice-Hall of Japan, Inc., *Tokyo*
Simon & Schuster Asia Pte. Ltd., *Singapore*
Editora Prentice-Hall do Brasil, Ltda., *Rio de Janeiro*

*This book is dedicated to my professors
at the University of Chicago:
Edward Dimock, Mircea Eliade,
Joseph Kitagawa, and Charles Long*

Contents

Foreword

The Prentice Hall Series in World Religions is a new set of introductions to the major religious traditions of the world, which intends to be distinctive in two ways: (1) Each book follows the same outline, allowing a high level of consistency in content and approach. (2) Each book is oriented toward viewing religious traditions as "religious cultures" in which history, ideologies, practices, and sociologies all contribute toward constructing "deep structures" that govern peoples' world view and life-style. In order to achieve this level of communication about religion, these books are not chiefly devoted to dry recitations of chronological history or systematic exposition of ideology, though they present overviews of these topics. Instead the books give considerable space to "cameo" insights into particular personalities, movements, and historical moments that encourage an understanding of the world view, life-style, and deep dynamics of religious cultures in practice as they affect real people.

Religion is an important element within nearly all cultures, and itself has all the hallmarks of a full cultural system. "Religious culture" as an integrated complex includes features ranging from ideas and organization to dress and diet. Each of these details offers some insight into the meaning of the whole as a total experience and construction of a total "reality." To look at the religious life of a particular country or tradition in this way, then, is to give proportionate attention to all aspects of its manifestation: to thought, worship, and social organization; to philosophy and folk beliefs;

to liturgy and pilgrimage; to family life, dress, diet, and the role of religious specialists like monks and shamans. This series hopes to instill in the minds of readers the ability to view religion in this way.

I hope you enjoy the journeys offered by these books to the great heartlands of the human spirit.

ROBERT S. ELLWOOD, JR., editor
University of Southern California

Preface

This book has two aims: to present an overview of the Hindu religious tradition and to describe the essence of the Hindu vision of reality.

The book deals historically and analytically with many facets of Hindu culture: philosophy, art, mythology, ritual, and social structure. Detailed descriptions of specific rituals and extended portraits of important Hindu thinkers and saints are included. These descriptions permit readers to sense the distinctive textures of Hinduism for themselves.

The essence of the Hindu vision of reality is located in the persistent tension between dharma, or social duty, and moksha, or release from the material and social world. Throughout the book these two emphases are treated side by side; and at several points it is shown how they tend to conflict with one another, giving rise to a creative tension that is the heart of the Hindu tradition. In dealing with Hindu philosophy, mythology, ritual, and society, the book takes examples from both strands—the world-supporting realm of dharma and the world-denying realm of moksha—in order to show how the Hindu tradition insists upon both tendencies as essential in fulfilling human destiny.

Since 1982, when this book was first published, many excellent studies have been done on the place of women and goddesses and the centrality of gender in the Hindu religious tradition. Thanks to a vigorous feminist movement in religious studies, religionists increasingly are being forced to take into account the extent to which males have dominated written religious traditions (particularly scripture) and the extent to which scholarship has been preoccupied with questions and structures that exclude or play down the role of females in religious traditions. It was clear to me in thinking about the second edition of this book that the most important modifications to be made should be toward giving a fuller picture of the place of women and female imagery in the Hindu religious tradition. Hindu scriptures were almost all written by high-caste males (who were the only literate people in India for centuries), and it is easy to get the impression that there is little place for females except as supporters and nourishers of males in the Hindu tradition. That this is not actually the case is evident to anyone who spends a little time in India. This second edition, then, has been expanded to include an entire chapter on the place of goddesses and the roles of women in the hope of conveying a more complete picture of the richness of the Hindu tradition.

DAVID R. KINSLEY

HINDUISM

PART *I*

AN OVERVIEW OF THE HINDU TRADITION

1

Introduction: Varanasi

Even before the sun has risen, the streets and alleyways of Varanasi[1] leading to the Ganges River swirl with devout pilgrims making their way to the broad steps that lead down into the river. By the time the sun is up the steps teem with pilgrims and devout residents taking ritual baths in Mother Ganges' sacred waters, which are believed to cleanse one of all sins. Small shops specializing in religious paraphernalia crowd the area around the steps and do a thriving business. Hundreds of priests whose task it is to aid pilgrims are setting up their large umbrellas against the heat of the sun, and by midday the steps leading to the river look as if they are overgrown with immense mushrooms.

Dawn also signals the beginning of activity in the hundreds of temples and shrines throughout the city dedicated to the many gods and goddesses of the Hindu pantheon. In the impressive Vishvanath temple of the ascetic god Shiva, hereditary priests prepare to do puja (worship by personally waiting upon a deity), and devotees crowd the temple precincts to have a view of the image of the deity, a sight that is held to be auspicious, and to watch the colorful ceremony. Throughout the day devotees stream to the hundreds of temples scattered all over Varanasi to worship their favorite god or goddess. The variety of images from which they can choose reflects the extraordinary richness through which the divine has revealed itself in the Hindu tradition.

[1]Also known as Banaras or Benares.

2

   Enshrined in these temples is a veritable kaleidoscope of divinity: Vishnu, the great heavenly king who descends to the world from time to time in various forms to maintain cosmic stability; Shiva, the ascetic god who dwells in yogic meditation in the Himalayas, storing up his energy so that he can release it periodically into the world to refresh its vigor; Krishna, the adorable cowherd god who frolics with his women companions in the idyllic forests of Vrindavana; Hanuman, the monkey god, who embodies strength, courage, and loyalty to the Lord Rama; Ganesha, the elephant-headed god who destroys all obstacles for his devotees; Durga, the warrior goddess who periodically defeats the forces of evil in order to protect the world; Kali, the black goddess who dwells in cremation grounds and is served with blood; and many more.

   Dawn is a busy time at the cremation grounds on the Ganges too. A steady stream of funeral processions wends its way to a particular set of steps where several funeral pyres burn constantly. At the funeral grounds the stretcher-borne corpses are set down to await their turn in the purifying fires. The constant activity at this particular burning ground reflects the belief of pious Hindus that death in or near the Ganges at Varanasi results

FIGURE 1-1 India.

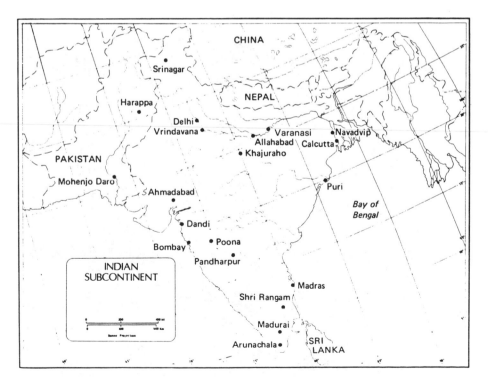

in moksha, the final liberation from the endless cycles of birth and rebirth that is the ultimate spiritual goal of most Hindus. Thousands of devout Hindus, in their old age, come to die in Varanasi, and many funeral processions seem joyous, reflecting the auspicious circumstances of the person's death. As one watches the crackling fires consume the corpse, the rising tendrils of smoke suggest the soul's final and longed-for liberation.

Varanasi is the center of several religious orders, and the city's population includes a great number of ascetics who have chosen to live in the holy city permanently or who are simply wandering through. It is not unusual to see several of these holy men or women sitting in meditation around the steps. The burning ground itself is an auspicious site to perform meditation, as the funeral pyres remind the ascetics of the transcience of the worldly life they have renounced. The appearance of these renouncers is striking. Ascetics often wear saffron-colored robes, a minimum of clothes, or perhaps are even naked. Their bodies may be smeared with ashes, sometimes taken from the cremation grounds. Their hair is long and matted, indicating their utter neglect of bodily appearance, or their heads may be shaven. Their only possessions are a water pot and a staff. In the midst of a bustling city like Varanasi, which like all cities caters to the inexhaustible worldly desires of its populace with markets, cinemas, shops, and so on, the

FIGURE 1-2   The bathing ghats at Varanasi. (Courtesy of Air India.)

FIGURE 1-3 Brahmin bathing at Varanasi. (Courtesy of Timothy Moody.)

ascetics look like wayfarers from another world. They are a common sight in Varanasi, however, and remind one of the importance of world renunciation and asceticism in the Hindu tradition.

Before the day is over, a visitor to Varanasi will have witnessed many scenes common to the Hindu tradition: Brahmins performing ancient Vedic rituals; devotees from Bengal performing communal worship to Lord Krishna with much singing and dancing; students at Banares Hindu University consulting an astrologer to determine if the day on which their exams will be held will be auspicious; a low-caste pilgrim making an offering at the shrine of a beloved saint who is little known outside the pilgrim's own caste; a traditional pundit, or teacher, expounding the ethereal subtleties of Hindu philosophy to students; a priest or storyteller telling stories from Hindu scriptures to groups of devotees in the precincts of a temple; a woman pouring sacred Ganges water on an image of Shiva; a pious person ritually worshiping a cow; and a woman performing a ritual for the well-being of her household.

By the end of the day the visitor to Varanasi seeking to discern the essential outlines of the Hindu religious tradition probably will be very confused and tempted to conclude that Varanasi, with all its diversity, is not the best place to look for the essential ingredients of Hinduism. Indeed, Hinduism itself, like Varanasi, tends to defy neat analysis and description and leaves the impression that what happens in the name of Hinduism is chaotic. Hinduism, it seems, eludes and frustrates attempts to summarize it neatly because it offers exceptions or even contradictions to what at first might seem essential or generally true.

For example, many Hindus in Varanasi say that ahimsa (noninjury) is essential to the Hindu vision of reality, and they will be able to cite count-less texts to support that view. They will mention Mahatma Gandhi as a recent example of the centrality of this theme in Hinduism, and possibly also the Hindu respect for cows and the emphasis on vegetarianism. You may be convinced that here, indeed, is an essential aspect of Hinduism. Thanking your informant, you will go on your way, only to come upon a temple of Kali or Durga, where worshipers are beheading a goat in sacrifice to the goddess. Or you might happen upon a copy of the *Artha Shastra* of Kautiliya, an ancient and authoritative text on Hindu political philosophy from around the fourth century C.E. You will look in vain for Gandhian political principles in this book, because the *Artha Shastra* is consistently ruthless and cunning in its approach to seizing and holding power.

You might, on the other hand, be told by an ascetic in Varanasi that Hinduism involves essentially the renunciation of society and all egotistical desires and the achievement of liberation from the lures of the world. But before long you would find a group of orthodox Brahmins performing an-cient rituals from the *Vedas*, also affirmed to be the essence of Hinduism, the explicit aim of which is the stability and welfare of the world, what the Hindus call *loka-samgraha*, one of the central teachings of Hinduism's most famous scripture, the *Bhagavad Gita*.

Who is right? The orthodox Brahmin who performs daily rituals pre-scribed by the ancient *Vedas*? The ascetic who performs no such rituals, who may even show disdain for them, and who denies any obligation to society? The low-caste farmer who daily praises the Lord Rama and celebrates his heroic exploits? The untouchable who makes a pilgrimage to Varanasi to honor a saint beloved by his or her entire caste but virtually unknown to most high-caste Hindus? Or the pious businessman who consults his astrol-oger before closing a deal? One must believe them all, it seems, for they are all Hindus undertaking common and acceptable Hindu practices. And this leads to our first generalizations about the Hindu religious tradition.

One cannot find the equivalent of a Hindu pope or an authoritative Hindu council in Varanasi. Historically, Hinduism has never insisted on the necessity of a supreme figure in religious matters and has never agreed on certain articles of belief as essential for all Hindus. Throughout its long history, Hinduism has been highly decentralized.

Another feature of Hinduism follows from this one, a feature reflected in both the caste system and the different paths one may take in the reli-gious quest. Hinduism affirms in a variety of ways that people are different from one another and that these differences are both crucial and distinc-tive. People have different *adhikaras*, different aptitudes, predilections, and abilities. What is natural to one person is unnatural to another. So it is that different ways are made available to different types. Some may have an aptitude for philosophy, and a path centering on knowledge is available for them. Others may be of a devotional aptitude, and so a path of devotion is appropriate for them. Over the centuries, then, Hinduism has accepted a variety of paths, spiritual techniques, and views of the spiritual quest that all succeed in helping humans fulfill their religious destiny.

On the social level the Hindu emphasis on differences manifests itself in the caste system. Human differences are systematically arranged in hierarchical order, and people are segregated into specialized cohesive groups called castes. Social contact with other castes is carefully circumscribed in such a way that the religious beliefs and practices of a particular Hindu often reflects his or her caste tradition and differs markedly from the religious practices of other castes. The philosophical ideas underlying the caste system are karma, the moral law of cause and effect according to which a person reaps what he or she sows, and samsara, rebirth according to the nature of a person's karma. The basic idea is that what one is now is the result of all that one has done in the past, and what one will become in the future is being determined by all one's actions in the present. In effect, a person's present caste identity is only a brief scene in an endless drama of lives that will end only with moksha, liberation from this endless round of birth, death, and rebirth.

Hinduism also affirms that during one's life a person changes, and different kinds of activities are appropriate to various stages of life. Traditionally four stages have been described, with different obligations for each one. The ideal was designed primarily for men, and only very rarely did a woman follow the pattern. Ideally, a high-caste male is to pass through these stages in the following order: student, householder, forest recluse, and wandering holy man. As a student, a male's duty is to study his tradition, particularly the *Vedas* if he is a Brahmin. As a householder he is to foster a family, undertake an occupation appropriate to his caste, and perform rituals, usually Vedic rituals, that help insure the stability of the world. As a forest hermit, he is supposed to leave his home, retire to the forest with his wife, continue Vedic rituals, and meditate on those realities that will bring about liberation from the world and rebirth. Finally, he is to abandon even his wife, give up Vedic rituals, wander continually, begging his food, and strive for the knowledge that emancipates him from the cycles of rebirth. Although this pattern is not always followed, it affirms the tradition's liberality in permitting a variety of approaches in one's spiritual sojourn: study; support of the world through rituals, work, and family life; meditation away from society; and renunciation of the world through extreme asceticism.

The Hindu insistence on differences between people, then, leads to the very common definition of Hinduism in sacred texts as varna-ashrama-dharma, which may be loosely translated as performing the duty (dharma) of one's stage of life (ashrama) and caste or social station (varna).

Hindus also have acknowledged that differences exist among the regional areas of the Indian subcontinent, and the Hindu Law Books accept regional customs and peculiarities as authoritative. These regional dissimilarities help us understand another aspect of the diversity of belief and practice among Hindus in Varanasi. Hindus from Tamilnad in the South

FIGURE 1-4   Woman greeting the dawn, Varanasi. (Author's photograph.)

have a cultural history that differs greatly from, say, Hindus from Bengal. Each region has its own vernacular tradition, its favorite gods and goddesses, its own distinctive customs and rituals. In Varanasi, where pilgrims from all over India congregate, these differences further complicate any attempt to discern common themes, patterns, and beliefs. The history of Hinduism is, to a great extent, the record of what has gone on in the regions of India and is therefore marked by much diversity in belief and practice.

On the other hand, a strong, articulate, and authoritative tradition, called the Great, Sanskrit, or Aryan tradition, has counterbalanced this diversity by imposing on it certain myths, beliefs, customs, and patterns of social organization. Dominated by a literate Brahmin elite, Hinduism over the centuries always has manifested a certain coherence because of the prestige of this tradition throughout India. Thus, today Hinduism is, as it always has been, the dynamic interaction of various regional traditions with an all-India tradition in which the particular beliefs and rituals of any given Hindu are a combination. For orthodox Varanasi Brahmins, very little if any of the regional traditions may affect their brand of Hinduism. For low-caste Bengali peasants, on the other hand, very little of the Sanskrit tradition may be a part of their religion.

All this adds up to what one might call a liberal tendency in Hinduism that permits and even encourages men and women to undertake their religious sojourns in a variety of ways. Some things, to be sure, are encouraged for all Hindus: caste purity (intermarriage between castes is discouraged strongly), respect for Brahmins, and life-cycle rituals, for example.

Certain ethical precepts also are encouraged for all, and certain underlying beliefs are accepted by most Hindus, such as karma, samsara, and moksha. In Varanasi, then, we find very general parameters defining Hinduism that for the most part are provided by the Sanskrit tradition and that permit a great diversity of belief and practice. What goes on within these parameters, finally, may be summed up as representing four accents within the Hindu tradition.

1. *The Vedic Tradition.* Historically, the Aryans, who composed the *Vedas*, were foreigners who succeeded in superimposing on the indigenous peoples of India their language, culture, and religion. This Vedic religion is still domi-nant in living Hinduism and is best represented by the orthodox Brahmins. One of the central aims of this religion is the stability and welfare of the world, which is achieved through a great variety of rituals. In Varanasi today this accent is represented by those Brahmins who study the traditional Law Books and sponsor elaborate Vedic rituals.

2. *The Devotional Tradition.* The Hinduism of the majority of people in Varanasi is devotional, and this accent within the tradition goes all the way back to at least the time of the *Bhagavad Gita* (around 200 B.C.E.). Devotion is of varying types and is directed to a great variety of gods and goddesses, but generally we can speak of three strands within this tradition: (1) devotion to Shiva or to one of his family; (2) devotion to Vishnu or to one of his avatars (incarna-tions), the two most popular of which in the Varanasi area are Krishna and Rama; and (3) devotion to one of the many manifestations of the Great God-dess, the Mahadevi. It is primarily against the background of the devotional tradition that Hindus identify themselves as Shaiva (devotees of Shiva), Vaish-nava (devotees of Vishnu), or Shakta (devotees of the Goddess). Devotion to all three manifestations of the divine is concerned with eternal proximity to the deity in his or her heaven or with liberation from the cycle of endless births (Moksha).

3. *The Ascetic Tradition.* The several thousand ascetics in Varanasi are the living representatives of a tradition that is probably as ancient as the *Vedas* and that has been highly honored in Hinduism for over twenty-five hundred years. The underlying assumptions of this tradition are that: (1) life in the world is a hindrance to realizing one's spiritual destiny; (2) renunciation of society, in-cluding family ties, is necessary to realize one's spiritual essence; (3) various kinds of austerities are the necessary means of purifying oneself of both ig-norance and attachments; and (4) the ultimate goal of this arduous path is complete liberation from the wheel of rebirth. There are various types of ascetics, ascetic orders, and spiritual exercises undertaken by ascetics. Gen-erally, though, they all share these ideas and emphasize the importance of the individual's emancipation rather than one's obligations to the social order and its maintenance. In this respect there has often been a tension between the Vedic tradition and the ascetic tradition, a tension we shall return to later.

4. *The Popular Tradition.* This tradition refers to all those other rites and beliefs of Varanasi Hindus that do not fit neatly under the other three traditions. The sanctity of Varanasi itself, and of the River Ganges that flows through it, points to the central importance of sacred places and pilgrimage in the Hindu tradition. For Hindus the entire subcontinent bubbles with sacred places where immediate access to sacred and purifying power is obtainable. Most

prominent geographical features, such as mountains and rivers, are sacred and are the focal points of pilgrimage. Most cities contain famous temples and are also sacred centers. In addition to geographical sites and cities, some plants are held to be sacred. To the worshipers of Vishnu, the *tulasi* plant is particularly sacred, whereas to many devotees of the Goddess, it is the *bilva* tree. Time is punctuated by auspicious and inauspicious moments that are determined by the movements of the stars, the planets, the sun, and the moon. Many Hindus are extremely sensitive to these rhythms and will undertake nothing of significance unless they have been assured by their astrologer that the time is auspicious. Most Hindus know precisely at what time they were born, because they, and their parents, need that information to determine the compatibility of marriage partners. We also include under the popular tradition the preoccupation many Hindus have with diet. Many Hindu scriptures give lists of pure and impure foods and characterize the different properties of foods according to the physical and spiritual effects they produce. The preoccupation of many Hindus and many Hindu scriptures with signs and omens is also part of the popular tradition, as are rituals that have to do with gaining control over enemies and members of the opposite sex. In short, the popular tradition refers to things that we might call magical or superstitious simply because we do not understand them fully; we are unable to do so because those who practice them cannot articulate in ways we can understand what these practices and beliefs mean to them or meant to their ancestors.

By way of concluding this introductory portrait of Hinduism, let me suggest an image that might be useful in thinking about its diversity. We all know someone who is a collector, who rarely throws anything away, whose possessions include the exquisite treasure, the tackiest bauble, the unidentifiable photograph, the neglected and dusty item, and the latest flashy gadget. The Hindu religious tradition has shown itself to be an incurable collector, and it contains in the nooks and crannies of its house many different things. Today this great collector may hold one or another thing in fashion and seem to be utterly fascinated by it. But very few things are ever discarded altogether, and this is probably one of the most interesting and distinctive features of Hinduism. Like a big family, with its diversity, quarrels, eccentricities, and stubborn loyalty to tradition, Hinduism is a religion that expresses the ongoing history of a subcontinent of people for over thirty-five hundred years. The family album is too immense to describe in a single book, but I hope that what follows succeeds in at least suggesting the extraordinary wisdom, richness, and beauty of that particular family of humanity we call Hinduism.

2

History

The Formative Period (2500–800 B.C.E.)

From the middle of the third millennium B.C.E. to the second millennium B.C.E. there was a thriving city civilization in Northwest India, the Indus Valley civilization, which was centered in two cities, Harappa and Mohenjo-Daro. This civilization undertook extensive trade with the city civilizations of the ancient Near East, was based on an agricultural economy, and seems to have had a complex, hierarchical social structure. Writing was known, but it has not yet been deciphered by scholars.

It is difficult to say anything definite about the religion of the Indus Valley civilization. Many female figurines have been found, and it is probable that goddesses were worshiped in connection with the fertility of the crops. The bulls depicted on seals, the intriguing scenes depicted in the art, and a variety of stone objects are tantalizing in suggesting possible prototypes of later Indian religion, but until the script is deciphered most aspects of the religion of this ancient culture must remain unknown or at best vague.[1]

---

[1]For a judicious account of the religion of the Indus Valley civilization, see Herbert P. Sullivan, "A Re-examination of the Religion of the Indus Civilization," *History of Religions*, 4, no. 1 (Summer 1964), 115–25.

The Indus Valley civilization came to an abrupt end around 1500 B.C.E. at about the time an energetic people known as the Indo-Aryans migrated into Northwest India. Although many aspects of later Hinduism may well have been inspired by the Indus Valley civilization or regional peasant cultures in India, it is the Indo-Aryans and their religion that Hinduism traditionally has looked to as its source and inspiration; the earliest scriptures of the Indo-Aryans, the *Vedas*, have been acknowledged for thousands of years to embody the primordial truths upon which Hinduism bases itself.

The *Vedas* represent a diversified and continuous tradition that extends from around 1200 B.C.E., the probable date of the *Rig Veda*, the earliest Vedic text, to around 400 B.C.E., the probable date of some of the late *Upanishads*. Generally, Vedic literature is of three types: (1) *Samhitas*, hymns in praise of various deities; (2) *Brahmanas*, sacrificial texts dealing with the meaning and technicalities of rituals; and (3) *Aranyakas* and *Upanishads*, philosophical and mystical texts dealing with the quest to realize ultimate reality.

The central figure of the *Samhita* texts is the rishi, a heroic visionary figure and poet who was able to experience directly the various gods and powers that pervaded the Vedic world. In the quest to commune with these sacred powers, the rishi does not seem to have employed ascetic techniques, as later Hindu visionaries were to do. The rishis did, however, employ a plant called *soma*, which was most likely a hallucinogenic mushroom.[2] Drinking soma, the rishi was transported to the realm of the gods. Having experienced the gods, the rishis subsequently were inspired to compose hymns in their praise. The Vedic gods themselves are said to enjoy soma, and one of the most popular gods, Indra, a mighty warrior, is often described as drinking soma and experiencing its exhilarating effects. The centrality of the rishis' quest for an unmediated vision of the divine in the earliest Vedic literature has persisted in the Hindu tradition to this day, although the means of achieving this vision and the nature of the vision itself have changed over the centuries. In the later Hindu tradition, asceticism and devotion replaced the use of soma, and the polytheistic vision of the rishis has been replaced by visions emphasizing the underlying unity of reality.

Complementing the visionary dimension of the rishis in Vedic religion is a priestly, sacrificial cult centered on the great Vedic god Agni. Agni represents fire and heat. He is present at the sacrificial fire, at the domestic hearth, in the primordial fire of precreation, in the digestive fires of the stomach; he pervades all creatures as the fire of life. In addition, Agni is the intermediary between humans and gods because he transmits their of-

---

[2]Soma has been identified with *Amanita muscaria*, the fly agaric, a hallucinogenic mushroom, by R. Gordon Wasson, *Soma: Divine Mushroom of Immortality* (New York: Harcourt Brace Jovanovich, Inc., n.d.).

ferings to the gods in the sacrificial fire. In general, nearly all Vedic sacrificial rituals aim at aiding, strengthening, or reinvigorating Agni so that the creative and vital powers of the world may remain fresh and strong.

At the daily and domestic level, the *agnihotra* ritual, performed by the head of most Vedic households three times each day, nourishes Agni in the form of the sun through simple offerings of clarified butter. At sunrise, midday, and twilight the householder makes offerings to Agni to help him in his perpetual and life-giving round. On a much more elaborate scale, such as the ritual of building the fire altar, a similar aim is clear. The sacrificer, with the aid of Brahmin priests, builds an elaborate structure infused with elements and objects representing Agni in his many forms that have been collected over a year's period. The resulting fire altar in the form of a bird represents the rebuilt, distilled essence of Agni before he diffused himself throughout the created order. Agni is put back together again, as it were, so that he can regain the strength necessary to reinvigorate the world. This ritual, and others like it, then, is part of a cyclical pattern. Initially, Agni, representing the divine forces generally, diffused himself into the creation for the benefit of humans. Humans in turn sustain and reinvigorate Agni and the gods through rituals that enable Agni to redistribute himself periodically in the creation. In this ritual scheme the gods and humans are partners in maintaining the ongoing creative processes of the world.

The Speculative Period (800–400 B.C.E.)

The sacrificial texts concern themselves to a great extent with the underlying potency of the rituals they describe and as such are metaphysical in nature. However, philosophical and metaphysical concerns only come to dominate Vedic literature in the *Upanishads*, in which we find a third dimension of Vedic religion.[3] This dimension may be described as the quest for redemptive knowledge, or the search for the truth that will make people free. The *Upanishads* are primarily dialogues between a teacher and a student, they usually take place away from society, and from time to time they criticize the performance of rituals as superfluous to the religious quest. Some of the texts extol the renunciation of society and the performance of austerities that in later Hinduism become increasingly important techniques for liberation.

Although the *Upanishads* are somewhat diverse in their teachings, all agree that underlying reality is a spiritual essence called Brahman. Brahman is One, is usually said to be without delimiting attributes, is impersonal, and is essentially present in all people in the form of the Atman, a

---

[3]For translations of the *Upanishads*, see Robert Ernest Hume, trans., *The Thirteen Principal Upanishads* (London: Oxford University Press, 1921), and S. Radhakrishnan, trans., *The Principal Upanishads* (London: George Allen & Unwin, 1953).

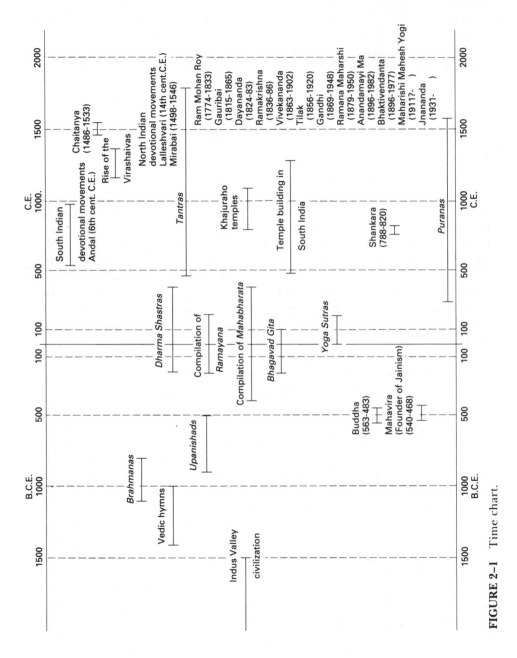

FIGURE 2-1 Time chart.

person's inmost self, or soul. The religious quest in the *Upanishads* involves realizing the fundamental identity of Brahman and Atman and realizing that one's essential self transcends individuality, limitation, decay, and death. The realization of this truth wins the adept liberation or release (moksha) from the shifting world of constant flux and the endless cycle of rebirth (samsara), which is perpetuated and determined by all one's actions (karma).

Unlike earlier Vedic texts, then, the *Upanishads* do not associate the religious quest with the vitality of the physical world but rather aim at a goal that transcends or overcomes the world. In later Hinduism moksha comes to represent the highest religious goal in nearly all texts, and the *Upanishads* are therefore important in the history of Hinduism as the earliest scriptures to describe the religious quest for liberation from the world. The *Upanishads* are also important because they are the earliest texts to advocate withdrawal from society and the use of ascetic and meditational techniques in this quest. In the *Upanishads* it is clear that the Aryan-Vedic tradition has been influenced by one that was probably indigenous to India, the ascetic tradition.

The earliest systematic presentation of the ascetic tradition is found in the *Yoga Sutras.*[4] Yoga is a technique of ascetic and meditational exercises that aims at isolating humans from the flux of the material world in order for them to recapture their original spiritual purity. Yoga seeks to disentangle the individual from involvement in prakriti (nature, matter, the phenomenal world generally) so that one may glimpse, and be liberated by, one's pure spiritual essence, purusha. Yoga represents an ancient Indian view of the world that emphasizes the transient nature of existence and seeks to overcome it by discovering and isolating one's eternal, unchanging, spiritual essence. Although this tendency is most clearly expressed in other Indian religions such as Jainism and Buddhism, it gains increasing importance in the Hindu tradition and remains central to that tradition to this day.

The Epic and Classical Periods (400 B.C.E.–600 C.E.)

The period from around 400 B.C.E. to 400 C.E. in Hinduism is known as the epic period. During this time the Indo-Aryans ceased to be a nomadic people. They settled into towns and cities, especially in the Gangetic plains of North India, and began to infuse their religion with elements of the

---

[4]Although the *Yoga Sutras* probably were not compiled until around the second century C.E., it is clear that the techniques described there are much more ancient. For translations of the *Yoga Sutras*, see James Haughton Woods, trans., *The Yoga-System of Patañjali*, Harvard Oriental Series, vol. 17 (Cambridge, Mass.: Harvard University Press, 1914), and Swami Prabhavananda and Christopher Isherwood, trans., *How to Know God, The Yoga Aphorisms of Patañjali* (London: George Allen & Unwin, Ltd., 1953).

religion of the indigenous peoples they had come to dominate. It was during this period that the two great Hindu epics were written, the *Mahabharata* and the *Ramayana*.[5] Both epics concern themselves with royal rivalries, perhaps reflecting political turmoil during this period, and exhibit, in their rambling ways, a tension between a religion aimed at supporting and upholding the world order and one aimed at isolating a person from society in order to achieve individual liberation.

As both epics are explicitly concerned with royal heroes, they have much to say about the world-supporting aspects of Hinduism. Vedic rituals, the ideal social system, and the preservation of order are essential concerns of the ideal king in Hinduism, and the heroes in both epics grapple with the subtleties and complexities of these concerns in their kingly roles. Rama, the hero of the *Ramayana*, for example, must come to terms with a dilemma that contrasts the written law (in this case, that the eldest son should inherit his father's kingdom) with the unwritten law of obeying one's father (for complicated reasons Rama's father commands him to exile himself to the forest for fourteen years so that Rama's half-brother may inherit the kingdom). Both epics emphasize that the king is a crucial figure in maintaining the harmonious realm of dharma (social and moral obligation) and rarely question the ultimate good involved in the preservation and refinement of the social order and those rituals and religious practices that insure it.

In the background of the epics, however, a host of characters call into question the ultimate good of the order of dharma. Called by a variety of names, these individuals have usually renounced the world, live in forests or small settlements, and are said to possess extraordinary powers. The epic heroes almost always treat these world renouncers with great respect and are often their students or beneficiaries.

The epics, like Hinduism itself, manage in various ways to hold together the tension between the aims of the royal heroes, which have to do with worldly order, and the aims of the world renouncers, which have to do primarily with individual liberation. On the narrative plane, first of all, both sets of epic heroes must wander for many years in the forest away from civilization and the realm of dharmic order among those who have renounced the world before gaining world sovereignty. In the disorder of the forest and from the teachings and examples of the world renouncers, the royal heroes acquire the knowledge and means to become rulers.

The epics offer a second solution to the tension between supporting

---

[5]For translations of the *Mahabharata*, see Pratap Chandra Roy, trans., *The Mahabharata*, 11 vols. (Calcutta: Oriental Publishing Company, 1927–32), and the incomplete translation of J. A. B. van Buitenen, trans., *The Mahabharata*, 3 vols. (Chicago: University of Chicago Press, 1973–78). For the *Ramayana*, see Hari Prasad Shastri, trans., *The Ramayana of Valmiki* (London: Shantisadan, 1953–59), and the as-yet-incomplete translation by Robert P. Goldman et al., *The Rāmāyana of Vālmīki: An Epic of Ancient India*, 7 vols. (Princeton, N.J.: Princeton University Press, 1984–).

or renouncing the world by defining the stages of life each person passes through. When Yudhishthira, the eldest of the five brothers who are the heroes of the *Mahabharata*, wishes to renounce the world because he is depressed at the slaughter that has taken place as a result of his desire to become king, his brothers and wife argue against him by saying that it is not proper to renounce the world until one has fulfilled one's social obligations. Increasingly this becomes the Hindu tradition's official position in seeking to wed the world-supporting and world-renouncing traditions. First one must fulfill one's obligation to society, and in performing this obligation the religion of the *Vedas*, with its emphasis on refreshing and sustaining the world, is appropriate. Second, there is one's ultimate obligation to achieve final liberation, and this may be pursued when it is timely, preferably after one's grey hairs have appeared and one has seen one's grandchildren. In performing this obligation asceticism and renunciation of the world are appropriate.

A third solution to the tension between these two religious aims is found in the *Bhagavad Gita*, which forms a part of the *Mahabharata*. The *Gita*'s solution is philosophical, suggesting that true renunciation involves the renunciation of desires for the fruits of actions and that this renunciation may be undertaken in the world while fulfilling one's social duty. Selfless action without desire for reward, action as an end in itself, is true renunciation for the *Gita*, and as such no tension need exist between one's dual obligation to support the world and to seek individual liberation.

Roughly contemporary with the epics is a whole genre of literature concerned with the ideal nature of society, the Law Books.[6] It is in this literature that the definition of the ideal society as varna-ashrama-dharma, the duty of acting according to one's stage of life (ashrama) and position in society (varna), is arrived at as most descriptive of Hindu society specifically and of Hinduism in general. The writers of these works have considerable respect for renouncing the world and seeking moksha in ascetic isolation, but they quite carefully relegate this aspect of the religious quest to old age. These works are concerned primarily with social stability, and underlying all the Law Books is the strong Hindu affirmation that an orderly, refined, stable society is to be cherished. Order, stability, and refinement have primarily and essentially to do with the proper functioning of the various castes and the proper observance of interaction among castes and among members of the same castes. Although the Law Books tolerate certain regional idiosyncrasies concerning social customs, all of them share a unified vision of society as hierarchically arranged according to caste. In the Law Books the social system has as its primary aim the support of Brahmins, who undertake Vedic rituals to maintain and renew the cosmic forces that period-

---

[6]The most famous Law Book is the *Manu Dharma Shastra*; see Georg Buhler, trans., *The Laws of Manu*, Sacred Books of the East, vol. 25 (London: Oxford University Press, 1886).

ically must be refreshed in order to keep the world bounteous and habitable. Beneath the Brahmins are the Kshatriyas (warriors) and Vaishyas (merchants). These three highest social groups (Brahmins, Kshatriyas, and Vaishyas) are called the twice-born classes, as they alone are permitted to perform the initiation ceremony of the sacred thread, which is believed to result in a second birth for the initiate. These groups alone, according to the Law Books, are qualified to study the *Vedas* and to undertake Vedic rituals. The serfs, or Shudras, are ranked below the twice-born classes, and their proper task is to support the higher castes by performing services for them. Beneath the Shudras, and barely even mentioned in the Law Books, are the untouchables, whose occupations are held to be highly polluting or who are so classed because they belong to tribal groups in India that are not yet acculturated.

Although the social ideal of the Law Books probably was never realized in the past, and although current Hindu society is quite different from this idealized model,[7] the ideal society of the Law Books has had a great influence on Hindu thought and does succeed in capturing its underlying hierarchical assumptions and the preoccupation with ritual purity in Hindu religious practice and social intercourse.

The Medieval Period (600–1800 C.E.)

The medieval period in Hinduism is characterized by three developments: (1) the rise of devotional movements with a corresponding outburst in the construction of temples; (2) the systematization of Hindu philosophy into six schools dominated by the school of Advaita Vedanta (nondualistic Vedanta); and (3) the rise of Tantrism, a movement employing ritual techniques to achieve liberation.

Although devotion (called *bhakti* in Hinduism) enters the Hindu tradition as early as the *Bhagavad Gita* (around 200 B.C.E.), it was not until about the sixth century C.E. that devotion began to dominate the religious landscape of Hinduism. Beginning in the South with the Nayanars, devotional saints who praised Shiva, and the Alvars, devotional saints who worshiped Vishnu, an emotional, ecstatic kind of devotion became increasingly central to Hindu piety. By the seventeenth century bhakti of this type had come to dominate the entire Hindu tradition. Devotion as described in the *Bhagavad Gita* was primarily a mental discipline aimed at controlling one's actions in the world in such a way that social obligations and religious fulfillment could be harmonized. In the later devotional movements, devotion is typically described as a love affair with God in which the devotee is willing to sacrifice anything in order to revel with the Lord in ecstatic bliss. The best example of this theme is the devotion to the cowherd Krishna, whose ideal

---

[7]For a discussion of the Hindu social order, see chap. 8.

devotees are married women who leave their husbands and homes to revel with Krishna in the woods. Unlike the *Bhagavad Gita*'s rather staid description of devotion, the later movements delight in describing the devotional experience as causing uncontrollable joy, fainting, frenzy, tears of anguish, madness, and sometimes social censure. Underlying most of these movements is the theological assumption that, although men and women may have differing inherited or ascribed duties and social positions, all creatures share the same inherent duty, which is to love and serve God. Although few devotional movements actually criticize the traditional social structure, it is sometimes the case that they are indifferent to traditional society, which they describe as confining when one undertakes the task of loving God. Two famous women devotees, Mahadeviyakka, a Virashaiva saint,[8] and Mirabai, a Rajastani princess and devotee of Krishna, for example, both chafed under traditional marriages and eventually left their husbands to devote themselves entirely to their respective gods.

Contemporary with the rise and spread of devotional movements, and perhaps reflecting their importance, was the rise of temples as important religious centers in Hinduism. Hindu temples, as the earthly dwelling places of the gods, are usually patterned on the model of a divine mountain or palace.[9] They are centers of worship, centers for religious instruction, and often the homes of devotees who have renounced the world to pursue their service to God. Traditionally some temples dominated by the high castes have excluded low-caste devotees, but Hindus of all castes take part in temple worship, either at grand temples famous throughout India or at village temples that may consist of nothing more than a mud hut.

At these temples a great variety of deities are worshiped. Generally, however, the deity belongs to one of three strands within the Hindu pantheon: the Shaivite strand, which includes Shiva and members of his family; the Vaishnavite strand, which includes Vishnu and his avatars (incarnations); and the Shakta strand, which includes Hindu goddesses. The worship may be elaborate or simple but usually consists of some form of puja,[10] a type of ritual service to the deity. This rite is normally performed by a priest, who is usually a Brahmin in temples frequented by high-caste Hindus but who may be a low-caste non-Brahmin in humbler temples used by the low castes.

The mythology of the deities worshiped, which is often portrayed in temple artwork, became systematized during the medieval period in a genre of works known as the *Puranas*, or "stories of old." As elsewhere in the

---

[8]For a discussion of the Virashaivas, see "Examples of Dissenting Movements" in chap. 3. For a discussion of Mahadeviyakka and Mirabai, see chap. 7, "Sacred Female Imagery and Women's Religious Experience in Hinduism."

[9]For a description and discussion of temples, see "Illustrations of Hindu Art" in chap. 4.

[10] For a discussion of worship in the Hindu tradition, see chap. 6.

Hindu tradition, the tension between *loka-samgraha*, supporting the world, and moksha, striving for release from the world, is reflected in these texts. Dominating the *Puranas* are two quite different manifestations of the divine: Shiva and Vishnu.

Shiva is the ascetic god, the great yogi who meditates in isolation on Kailasa Mountain in the Himalayas, who burns the god of love to ashes with the fury from his middle eye when the god tries to distract him. He is often portrayed as an outsider with matted hair, his body smeared with ashes and clothed in animal skins, with snakes and a garland of skulls as ornaments. Although a good deal of Shiva's mythology concerns his eventual marriage to the goddess Parvati and his most typical emblem is the lingam, the phallus, Shiva clearly embodies the world-renouncing tendencies of Hinduism and as such provides a model for this aspect of the tradition.

Vishnu, on the other hand, is usually described as a cosmic king who lives in the heavenly splendor of his palace in Vaikuntha. His primary role in the divine economy is to supervise universal order and prosperity. As the cosmic policeman he descends from time to time in various forms to defeat enemies of world stability, and as such he provides a model for supporting the world.

Turning to the second major development of the medieval period, the systematization of Hindu philosophical thought, we find a considerable diversity tolerated. The six schools that eventually came to be accepted as orthodox emphasize very differing points of view and reveal again the underlying tension between dharma, supporting the world, and moksha, release from the world. The tension is best seen in the rivalry between the Purva Mimamsa and Uttara Mimamsa schools. Although both schools emphasize the *Vedas* as their source of inspiration, the former preoccupies itself with the ritual aspects of the *Vedas* and affirms the centrality of Vedic rituals as the key to realizing both religious duty and personal salvation. For this school Vedic rituals are the most potent of all actions and are crucial in maintaining the world. One's ultimate duty, according to Purva Mimamsa, is continually to support the world by performing those rituals that are revealed in the *Vedas*.

The Uttara Mimamsa school, more commonly known as Vedanta, occupies itself with the *Upanishads*, which as we have noted emphasize individual release from the world by realizing the essential unity of Brahman, the Absolute, and Atman, the essential self in each person.[11] The most brilliant and systematic exponent of this school was the eighth-century South Indian, Shankara, whose particular school of Vedanta is known as Advaita Vedanta (the Vedanta of no difference, or nondualism).[12] For Shankara,

---

[11]The term *vedanta* means "essence of knowledge" (*veda*, "knowledge," plus *anta*, "end" or "essence").

[12]For a discussion of Shankara, see "Representative Thinkers" in chap. 5.

actions per se, whether good or bad, are of no ultimate significance in achieving liberation because they arise from a false sense of individuality. Knowledge alone, a transforming, experiential knowledge of one's identity with Brahman, is the goal of the religious quest and is not dependent upon social obligations. However, Shankara's own life is often taken as a model for adepts of this path, and as Shankara himself was a world re- nouncer, most followers of his philosophy extol renunciation as helpful, if not necessary, in achieving liberating knowledge. Although Shankara did not criticize traditional society and traditional religious practices that aim at supporting the world, he was clear that a person's ultimate spiritual goal is not achieved by or through them. Not surprisingly, Shankara is held by the Hindu tradition to have been an incarnation of the ascetic god Shiva.

The *Tantras*, the third major development of the medieval period, seem to have arisen outside the elite Brahmin tradition.[13] The *Tantras*, of which there are hundreds, often criticize established religious practices and the upholders of those practices, the Brahmins. In many ways, however, the *Tantras* express central, traditional Hindu ideas and practices. Underlying Tantric practice, for example, is the assumption that an individual is a min- iature or microcosm of the cosmos and that by learning the sacred geog- raphy of one's body one may, by means of various yogic techniques, bring about one's own spiritual fulfillment, which in most Tantric texts is the result of uniting various opposites within one's body/cosmos.

The *Tantras* claim to be appropriate to the present era, which is dec- adent and in which people are less spiritual and less inclined to perform the elaborate rituals prescribed in earlier ages. The *Tantras* claim to intro- duce techniques that lead directly to liberation without traditional practices and routines. Vedic study, Vedic rituals, pilgrimage, puja, and other tradi- tional practices, although not always disregarded in the *Tantras*, are often held to be superfluous in the present age. The *Tantras*, then, offer a variety of rituals that employ mantras (sacred formulas), mandalas (schematic dia- grams), and yogic techniques that are believed to achieve either complete liberation from the mundane world or extraordinary powers, such as om- niscience and the ability to fly.

The *Tantras* themselves distinguish between a right-handed path and a left-handed path. The right-handed path is for all adepts and consists primarily in the use of mantras, mandalas, and ritual techniques based upon Tantric sacred bodily geography. The left-handed path, appropriate only for those of a special heroic temperament, centers on a particular ritual in which the adept partakes of five forbidden things, thereby transcending the tension between the sacred and the profane and gaining liberation.[14] This

---

[13]For a thorough treatment of the *Tantras*, see Āgehananda Bharati, *The Tantric Tradition* (London: Rider & Co., 1965).

[14]For a description of this ritual, see "Examples of Dissenting Movements" in chap. 3.

left-handed aspect of Tantrism has been greatly criticized by the Brahmin establishment.

The Modern Period (1800 to the Present)

Increasing contact with the West, including the political and economic domination by England from the middle of the nineteenth century to the middle of the twentieth century, provides the background for three important developments in the modern period of the Hindu tradition: (1) the Hindu revival of the nineteenth century; (2) the independence movement of the nineteenth and twentieth centuries; and (3) the introduction of Hinduism in a variety of forms to the West, particularly to North America.

As early as the eighth century C.E. Muslims had entered India, and by the thirteenth century Islam had come to a position of political dominance in North India. Increasingly Hindus found themselves ruled by non-Hindus, and British domination, beginning in the eighteenth century, represented to Hindus a continuation of foreign rule. Although many Indians were attracted by the teaching of the equality of all believers in Islam and converted to that religion, the majority remained at least nominal Hindus and in various ways continued the traditions of the past. With the arrival of Western powers in the eighteenth century, however, both Westerners and Hindus began to articulate an increasingly vocal criticism of the Hindu tradition. Many aspects of traditional Hinduism were castigated, and in the nineteenth century Hindu reform movements arose that sought to meet these criticisms by distilling what was most central to the Hindu tradition and doing away with the rest. Two movements in particular gained all-India fame: the Brahmo Samaj, founded by Ram Mohan Roy, and the Arya Samaj, founded by Swami Dayananda.

Ram Mohan Roy (1774–1833) was a prominent citizen of Bengal, and before he founded the Brahmo Samaj (the Society of Brahman) he had considerable contact with Christian missionaries. He was acquainted with Western humanistic traditions and made a journey to England, where he became even more familiar with Western ideas. In 1828 he founded the Brahmo Samaj, which represented his vision of a reformed Hinduism. For Ram Mohan the essence of Hinduism was found in the *Upanishads*. There, he said, was revealed the One Nameless Absolute God of all people, who was to be worshiped through meditation and a pious life. Such Hindu customs as image worship, pilgrimage, festivals, and the rules of caste, he held, were superfluous in the service of this God. The Brahmo Samaj, then, instituted worship services and a type of piety that were rationalistic, humanistic, and devoid of distinctive Hindu symbols and customs. Many Westerners applauded this movement, but it never gained popularity among Hindus.

The Arya Samaj was founded in 1875 by Swami Dayananda (1824–83) as another attempt to restore Hinduism to its original purity. Like Ram

Mohan Roy, Dayananda found the essence of Hinduism in the *Vedas*, which he said taught monotheism and morality. Dayananda was particularly keen on abolishing image worship and caste discrimination. His basis for criticizing the Hindu tradition as it existed in his own day was the *Vedas*. He was suspicious of Western ideas and insisted that a purified Hinduism must involve a return to the *Vedas*. Although the Arya Samaj had a wider appeal than the Brahmo Samaj, it did not succeed in gaining a very wide audience either. Both movements, however, were important in revitalizing Hindu pride and helped to lay the spiritual groundwork for the independence movement, with its championing of Indian traditions and criticisms of Western values and domination.

A third important religious phenomenon of this time was the Bengali saint, Ramakrishna. Ramakrishna (1836–86) in most ways represented traditional Hindu beliefs and spiritual techniques. He was a temple priest of the goddess Kali, and though he found in this goddess his favorite object of devotion, he worshiped other deities as well in an attempt to discover the special blessing of each god. He also experimented with the different Hindu paths, such as Tantrism and the path of knowledge. His reaction to Western religions was simply to experiment with them in his own religious life. In these experiments he is said to have been successful, several times having visions of Muslim and Christian heroes. Ramakrishna sought, then, to incorporate Western ideas and religions into the expansive Hindu context and not to reform Hinduism by making it conform to Western ideas of monotheism or humanism. Unlike Ram Mohan Roy and Dayananda, Ramakrishna was widely considered a great saint by his fellow Hindus even before his death and probably represents the most typical Hindu response to foreign influence.

Ramakrishna's favorite disciple was Vivekananda (1863–1902), who is often considered the first successful Hindu missionary to the West. In 1893 he addressed the First World Parliament of Religions at Chicago and was enthusiastically received there and by many Americans in his subsequent travels throughout the United States. Returning to India a national hero, he instituted plans for fellow members of his movement to set up centers in the West to foster the teachings and practice of Hinduism. The Hinduism of Vivekananda was much less devotional than Ramakrishna's own piety and stressed the monistic teachings of the *Upanishads* and the Vedanta of Shankara. The Ramakrishna Mission was thus inaugurated in the West and became the first successful attempt to transplant Hinduism to that part of the world.

Both the persistence and modification of traditional Hindu themes are clear in the Indian independence movement, particularly in its two most famous leaders, Bal Gangadhar Tilak (1856–1920) and Mohandas Karamchand Gandhi (1869–1948). Both Tilak and Gandhi took the *Bhagavad Gita* and its teachings concerning *loka-samgraha*, supporting the world, as central to their positions, and both were considered karma-yogis, masters of disciplined action. However, the two differed considerably in their styles and provide a modern expression of the continuing tension between renunciation and support of the world.

Tilak's greatest work was his commentary on the *Bhagavad Gita*, the *Gita Rahasya*, in which he argued that the Hindu's primary responsibility is to work out his or her spiritual destiny while remaining in the world and acting without desire for the fruits of his or her actions. He systematically refuted all earlier commentaries on the *Gita* and saw in this most famous of Hindu scriptures the theoretical foundation of political activism. Tilak, opposing all Hindus who argued for gradual reform and eventual independence, advocated no compromise with foreign rulers. For Tilak the *Gita* was a manual for action that, given its context, the battlefield, permitted the use of violence in a just cause. Renunciation of the world was unpatriotic and a sign of weakness. In his many speeches and writings Tilak never tired of calling his fellow Hindus to responsible action in and for the world.

Gandhi, too, interpreted the *Gita* as teaching involvement in the world, and it was the *Gita* that provided the theoretical background for his teaching and technique of satyagraha, holding to the truth.[15] Satyagraha for Gandhi was the task of expressing the truth in every action, no matter what the result, the task of acting without regard for rewards. Gandhi, however, chose to read the *Gita* as a nonviolent text and refused to permit violence in his various political campaigns; he urged restraint, negotiation, and self-sacrifice instead. His style of life also differed from Tilak's and is reminiscent of the ascetic tradition in Hinduism. Although a householder, Gandhi early in his career practiced strict poverty, restricting his possessions to a few necessities, and later in life took a vow of celibacy. He wore little clothing and lived on a very restricted diet. Gandhi added to the role of the classic Hindu world renouncer, however, the element of community service. His asceticism was aimed at harnessing energy and vitality that would be used to support India's poor and oppressed. His spiritual mission, in addition to personal liberation, was the liberation of his fellow Hindus from ignorance, caste hatred, economic and political domination by foreigners, and material poverty. Gandhi's quest represented the inextricable combination of personal purification with the purification of the world.

In recent years varied expressions of Hinduism have found their way to the West, in a continuation of the precedent set by Vivekananda in 1893. Although Hinduism had moved beyond its own borders before the modern period, it was primarily a result of Indian emigration to other countries and the resulting establishment of Hindu culture in such places as Sri Lanka and Indonesia. In the modern period, however, beginning with Vivekananda, various Hindus have self-consciously sought to spread Hinduism

---

[15]For a discussion of Gandhi, see "Representative Thinkers" in chap. 5.

outside of India. These figures have been many and diverse in their interpretations of the Hindu religion.

Two recent gurus (spiritual masters) who have gained a degree of popularity in the West are Maharishi Mahesh Yogi (ca. 1911–), founder of the Spiritual Regeneration Movement, or Transcendental Meditation, and Swami A. C. Bhaktivedanta (1896–1977), founder of the International Society for Krishna Consciousness. Although both movements have begun to take on certain pragmatic aspects suitable to the West, by emphasizing the scientific laws underlying their teachings and the practical or emotional benefits obtained from them, both movements, especially in their early phases, represent authentic Hindu traditions. Transcendental Meditation looks to Vedanta for its theoretical basis, emphasizing each person's inner divine essence and the liberating powers that may be harnessed when one's true identity is known. Maharishi is a typical modern exponent, then, of the ancient tradition in Hinduism that emphasizes the inward search for liberating knowledge. The International Society for Krishna Consciousness, on the other hand, emphasizes enthusiastic devotion to Lord Krishna and is a direct descendent of the Bengali devotionalism of Chaitanya (1485–1536).[16] As such the movement expresses the kind of devotion to personal gods that has dominated Hinduism since the sixth century C.E.

HISTORICAL SCENES

Introduction

As with all religious traditions there is little doubt that Hinduism has been shaped and refined to its present form by momentous historical events and heroic individuals. Unlike other well-known religious traditions, however, Hinduism is neither a founded religion nor a historical one. That is, Hinduism does not acknowledge a historical founder, although it does revere a number of great saints and teachers, nor does it look to important historical events or periods in its development as significant to its essence. In Hinduism, as in some other religions of the East, historical particularity is not cherished and rarely is remembered. This has to do in great part with an underlying assumption of Hinduism, namely, that the truth is one, and when the truth is expressed concretely it always looks pretty much the same.

The tendency in remembering the past, then, is to make individuals and events conform to eternal models of the truth, to translate historical events and persons from the insignificant, fleeting, confusing realm of day-to-day history to the truly significant, eternal realm of myth. All great men and women in the Hindu tradition tend to be remembered as express-

[16]For a discussion of Chaitanya, see "Historical Figures" in this chapter.

ing the same, or similar, truths and as having led similar lives. The closer to the archetype a saint is, the more sacred his or her life is affirmed to be. So, in remembrance of such lives by pious Hindus, individual peculiarity and individuality are left behind as the saint's life increasingly is told according to the pattern of all great lives. Similarly, historical events or political events have little significance, religiously speaking, in themselves. Only as expressions of ideal types or ideal periods in mythological time are they remembered as important. Great kings tend to be remembered as conforming to the ideal first king, Prithu, who first ordered the world and the affairs of humankind by inaugurating varna-ashrama-dharma. Great kings identified themselves, or have been remembered by the later tradition, as incarnations of various gods whose task it was to combat cosmic evil. As such their lives and deeds tend to conform to the accounts of well-known incarnations of those gods. Cosmic significance is worth remembering; individual, biographical, or historical distinctiveness is not.[17]

In reflecting on which events and figures most significantly influenced the history of Hinduism, then, one is left with two kinds of choices: (1) events such as the Aryan migration into India, the Brahmanization of India by the Aryans, or the rule of the Imperial Guptas, events that certainly took place and influenced the development of Hinduism, despite the Hindu tradition itself scarcely mentioning them and few facts about them being available; or (2) legendary and mythological events such as the *Mahabharata* war, the life of Rama, or the life of Krishna, namely, events that the Hindu tradition has cherished and embellished, despite their seeming to have only a tenuous connection with historical events.

In describing momentous events in the Hindu religious tradition, I have decided to follow the preference of the Hindu tradition itself and shall focus on its two great epics, the *Mahabharata* and *Ramayana*. I shall also try, however, to suggest that these great epics deal with and reflect significant historical events in the life of the Hindu tradition and that they address certain questions arising from these events in their own ways. No attempt will be made to seek out the historical Krishna or the historical Rama or to try to determine some historical kernel in the epics. Rather, I shall try to show how certain concerns of the epics reflect changing social and religious conditions that were central in shaping classical Hinduism. I shall be interested primarily in showing how the epic visionaries reflected certain tensions of their times and how they sought to unify their tradition through the writing of the epics themselves.

---

[17]This idea has been nicely expressed as follows: ". . . if the life of an individual has cosmic significance, its particulars are unimportant, and if the particularities are important, the life is not worth writing." Edward C. Dimock, "Religious Biography in India: The 'Nectar of the Acts' of Caitanya," in Frank E. Reynolds and Donald Capps, eds., *The Biographical Process: Studies in the History and Psychology of Religion* (The Hague: Mouton, 1976), p. 109.

The *Ramayana*

The date of Valmiki's *Ramayana* is not known with any precision. Scholars usually date the epic sometime between the second century B.C.E. and the second century C.E. The Hindu tradition itself, however, says that the events of this epic tale took place at the close of the treta age, that is, long ago in a time before the evils and decadence of recent times befell the world.[18] The truth of the matter probably is that the *Ramayana* was not the original creation of Valmiki himself but represents the poet's polished and elaborated rendering of certain oral traditions that reflected idealized rememberings of a particular hero named Rama.

The central narrative of the *Ramayana* concerns a cosmic battle between Rama, the son of the king of Ayodhya, a city in North India, and Ravana, the demon king of the island of Lanka. In the *Ramayana* this battle is presented as a typical example of Lord Vishnu's ongoing struggle with the forces of disorder and irreligion. Rama is Vishnu's avatar (incarnation), and Ravana is the king of the race of Ashuras, or demons, and has been granted the boon of being immune to any creature but a human. The *Ramayana*, then, is cast in a familiar structure and reflects in theme and detail the recurrent truths of Vishnu theology.

It is impossible, nevertheless, to be unaware of the fact that this particular contest between Vishnu's avatar and the forces of evil opposes and contrasts North and South and that Rama's task is to subdue the South by defeating its powerful leader, Ravana. Throughout the epic the virtues of Rama and the perfection of Ayodhya in the North are contrasted with the wickedness of Ravana and the decadence of Lanka in the South. What has been ideally remembered in the *Ramayana*, then, is quite likely the process whereby the Aryans, who entered India in the Northwest in the middle of the second millennium B.C.E., eventually came to a position of cultural dominance in South India.[19] Historically the process of Aryan migration into and settlement of the South was gradual and took place over a period of centuries. It is unlikely that military excursions were undertaken by the North against the South. Aryan domination, rather, was established primarily through small settlements and the increasing influence of the Brahmin elite. It is also obvious historically that the Aryans themselves came to accept into their own tradition many Southern or indigenous traditions

---

[18]According to traditional Hinduism the world passes through four ages, each of which is shorter than the preceding age and each of which represents an increasing decline in virtue. The four ages and their durations are krita (1,728,000 years), treta (1,296,000 years), dvapara (864,000 years), and kali (432,000 years).

[19]Certain political parties in South India today interpret the *Ramayana* in just this way and have used it for propaganda in their campaign to achieve independence from North India. For the southern separatists, the villain of the traditional *Ramayana*, Ravana, is the real hero of the story, since he represents the indigenous people of South India, who were colonized and subjugated by the invading Aryans.

and cultural forms. The *Ramayana*, with its great battles, nevertheless takes place against the background of a North-South tension and undoubtedly commemorates an important event in the history of Hinduism, namely, the Aryan accommodation of a strong indigenous tradition that resulted in what came to be known as classical Hinduism.

In the imagery of the *Ramayana* this process is spoken of as the taming of the wilderness and the overthrow of demonic forces by the hero Rama. In his fourteen-year sojourn in the wilderness, Rama confronts and kills or subdues many monsters and demonic enemies. He is often requested by forest-dwelling sages to protect their communities from these destructive forces, and eventually he makes an alliance with a race of monkeys, who help him in his conquest of Ravana. Rama's forest sojourn, in sum, represents, at least in part, an ordering of chaos. Rama represents the infusion of the stabilizing influence of dharma to hitherto dangerous and chaotic realms. In the ancient Vedic ritual of the horse sacrifice, the grandest of all Vedic rituals, great kings, in order to demonstrate their power and right to rule over all others, were enjoined to let one of their horses wander wherever it wished for an entire year. If the wanderings of the horse went unchallenged during this period, the king had demonstrated his power to control the cosmos and was considered a preeminent king indeed. In a sense, Rama's wanderings, which no challenger is able to halt, represent his mastery of all environments, including the uncharted forests and foreign realms. By sojourning in untamed regions Rama tames them, bringing them under the control of a just, righteous king and within the secure, refined, redemptive sphere of dharma.

By the time Valmiki wrote his epic, the Aryan domination or accommodation of the South was undoubtedly well underway, if not complete, and other important concerns occupy the poet, particularly questions that concern Hindu self-identity rather than Hindu relations with non-Hindu traditions. The period during which the *Ramayana* was probably written (200 B.C.E.–200 C.E.) was a time during which many of the Law Books were also being written. A central concern of almost every Law Book is the proper conduct of a king and the king's duties and proper role vis-à-vis the various castes, particularly the Brahmins. Behind this preoccupation very well may have been tension between Kshatriyas (warriors) and Brahmins, between political and economic power, on the one hand, and ritual, sacred, priestly power, on the other. The Law Books, however, rarely pose the issue in these terms, nor is it presented in this way in the *Ramayana*. The role of the king in both the Law Books and the *Ramayana* is defined within a sacred whole, and in the latter this role is understood to reflect a divine model—Vishnu's establishment and maintenance of the cosmos. In the Hindu tradition Rama soon became the archetype of the ideal king, and to this day Hindus fondly recall an idealized past by referring to the Rule of Rama. A central concern of Valmiki's was to portray in Rama the ideal king who both expressed and protected the order of Hindu dharma.

In many Hindu texts the necessity for a king is justified by reference to the law of the fishes. Without discipline, order, and the administration of justice, humans revert to their natural state, in which the strong prey on the weak. Civilized society, according to most Hindu texts, presupposes stability and order, which are only maintained by the liberal use of just punishment. In the sections of many Law Books concerned with the duties of kings, and consistently in the *Artha Shastras*, books on power and wealth, the necessity for order and a strong ruler permits the use of a great variety of unjust means in maintaining that order. Cunning, deceit, betrayal, and ruthlessness are often stated to be prerequisites of an effective king.

The *Ramayana* undoubtedly shares the assumption that a strong king who institutes and maintains order is good for society. However, its portrait of the ideal king in the person of Rama departs from many other texts by depicting a ruler who recognizes differing but interconnected realms of order and who is not content to endanger one realm for the sake of the other, who is not content to justify evil means with reference to just ends, but who sees the implicit connection between methods and goals. For Rama certain kinds of actions are unthinkable for a king. To indulge in such actions under the pretext of maintaining order would only lead to disorder at a more fundamental level. It is Rama's ability to do the right thing in conflicts between contrasting responsibilities, and his ability to perceive a transcendent realm of order that impinges on the social order, that make him a great king. Two incidents in the *Ramayana* illustrate this aspect of Rama's character: his unquestioned obedience to his father when asked to undertake a fourteen-year exile and his abandonment of his wife in order to stop the gossip of his subjects concerning her chastity while under Ravana's control.

In the opening sections of the *Ramayana* Valmiki portrays Rama as having all those martial and ethical qualities that befit a prince who would become king. Rama is surpassingly adept with weapons. He is versed in sacred law. His beautiful physical appearance reflects perfected inner qualities such as truthfulness, benevolence, and honor. Valmiki states that Rama always puts the wishes of others before his own and that he is loved by all who know him. Rama alone among a gathering of princes is able to display the necessary strength to break a mighty bow and win the hand of the beautiful princess Sita, the daughter of Earth. Their marriage is ideal, the union of heaven and earth, and Rama, it seems, is clearly in line to inherit his father's kingdom. He is the oldest son, he excels his brothers in every way, and it is no secret that he is the favorite of his father, Dasharatha.

However, Rama's stepmother, Kaikeyi, the mother of Rama's half-brother, Bharata, is persuaded by her maid to put forth the claims of her own son. It so happened that Dasharatha, in a mood of generosity toward Kaikeyi in the past, had promised her a boon. She had not asked for one at that time, but now, desiring the promotion of her son to king of the realm, she asks Dasharatha to fulfill his promise to her and make Bharata king. Dasharatha, renowned for his truthfulness, cannot renege on his promise, and he accedes to Kaikeyi's wish even though it pains him greatly. She also asks him to exile Rama to the forest for fourteen years so that Bharata will be unchallenged. This Dasharatha agrees to also.

Now many Hindu books on kingship and politics warn rulers to eliminate possible rivalry from their own sons by exiling them or even arranging their demise. It is assumed in many of these texts that he who can grasp power will do so by any means and keep it at any cost. Neither Dasharatha nor Rama is tempted to follow this kind of advice. Dasharatha could have dealt with Kaikeyi and Bharata quite handily by reneging on his promise to his wife or by exiling Bharata and thus could have realized his own wish to have Rama succeed him. And Rama might well have simply ignored his father's request to exile himself and taken over the kingdom, undoubtedly to the delight of the people of Ayodhya, who were grief stricken at the turn of events. The justification for these actions would have been both credible and defensible: The best man should rule as king in order to bring about the most righteous ordering of society. Furthermore, traditional law held that the eldest son, if qualified, should inherit his father's kingdom. What, after all, is the mere whim of a woman when it comes to ruling a kingdom?

However, both Dasharatha and Rama recognize, and are unwilling to compromise, the more fundamental order of proper relations between father and son and ruler and subject and the order implicit in truthfulness. Truthfulness, since ancient times in India, has been honored as one of the fundamental virtues. Both order and power flow naturally from this virtue, which must be inviolable. Although severely tested, Dasharatha does not go back on his word. That would be to risk losing all sense of personal order and power. And Rama, because he too is truthful and understands the underlying necessity of a king's truthfulness, never questions his father's apparently unjust command. Rama understands that basic virtues reflecting the very fiber of a just society are at stake. He understands the proper ordering of human relations. A son is subservient and obedient to his father, and a subject is subservient and obedient to the king. If these fundamental relations are jeopardized, civil order also is endangered. To sacrifice orderly personal relations for the benefit of social order is fruitless, as social order depends upon the proper conduct of individuals toward one another. An orderly society presupposes orderly human relations. Truthfulness and obedience are the very texture of orderly human relations; to sacrifice them for social order in fact would be to destroy it.

Rama obeys and sets off for the forest with his wife, leaving behind apparent chaos. Dasharatha soon dies of a broken heart. The citizens of Ayodhya lament and wish to follow Rama to the forest, as do his brothers, including even Bharata himself. Rama's mother is grief stricken, and it is clear that the delicate Sita will suffer greatly in exile. In this heroic act of obedience and self-denial, however, Rama shows that he understands the deepest underpinnings of genuine order in human society. To the citizens of Ayodhya, who complain that the city will now become like a wild forest because of Rama's departure, it may appear that dharma (civil and cosmic order) has been ill served by these traumatic events. However, Rama has shown himself a truly great protector of order by providing the Ayodhyans with an exemplary model of dharma in human relations. Rama will go on to install cosmic order precisely as a result of his exile when he defeats Ravana, and he will return to Ayodhya as its king after severe testing and institute a golden age of dharma. But this is not the real point of his heroic renunciation, as neither Rama nor the Ayodhyans foresee these events. The point to be appreciated is Rama's ability to discern that society is founded on the proper ordering of relations between relatives and citizens, that social order can never be simply imposed by laws and punishment but must flow naturally from the example of the king and his family.

In the second incident that marks Rama as an exceptional ruler, he has been installed as king following his long exile. As master of his realm he finds himself receiving implicit obedience from his subjects. However, according to Valmiki and many Law Books, the king is by no means permitted to seek his own happiness at the expense of his subjects. Indeed, the great king is he who sees himself as the subject of his citizens. As the Law Books say, a king never sleeps when it comes to the welfare and happiness of his people. The king is attentive to their needs and in his own life must provide an example of social order. However, during Rama's exile, disorder impinged on his life, albeit because of circumstances beyond his control. The demon Ravana abducted Rama's wife, Sita, to Lanka, where he imprisoned her until Rama rescued her.

Although Rama himself is satisfied that Sita had remained chaste while under Ravana's control, when Rama returns to Ayodhya and is inaugurated as king, the Ayodhyans begin to gossip about Sita and publicly wonder what occurred when she was under the demon's power. In controlling his realm and his personal affairs, a king in ancient India was duty bound to control and protect his wife. This meant especially protecting her from the approaches of other men. For women chastity was a basic virtue, any compromise of which permanently flawed their character. Through her chastity, furthermore, a woman sustained her husband's reputation and magically empowered him with his prowess.[20] Rama's exemplary character as king, then, is called into question because of Sita's abduction. How may the situation be made right? Ignoring the citizen's complaints is out of the question. It is their right to question their king in such basic matters of morality and to wonder what kind of king Rama is if he cannot protect his own wife

---

[20]This belief is demonstrated clearly in the myth of the demon Jalandhara. When the gods are incapable of defeating Jalandhara, they seduce his wife, Vrinda, and thereby weaken Jalandhara himself. See *The Śiva-purana*, vol. 2 (Delhi: Motilal Banarsidass, 1975), pp. 904ff.

or continues to live with a woman whose character has been compromised. The reader of the *Ramayana* knows very well that Sita is blameless. Rama knows this too. We might expect, therefore, that Rama will make a spirited defense of Sita's chastity in light of her virtue and in light of his love for her. However, Rama does not entertain this possibility. His decision is immediate, decisive, and very painful to both Sita and himself. He banishes her from his kingdom.

Although this act may seem cruel and unfair and may suggest to modern Western readers a flaw in Rama's character, in the Hindu tradition it is seen as noble and self-effacing and marks Rama as a king of exceptional character. In giving up Sita, his beloved wife, Rama demonstrates his proper understanding of the king's role: Social order and the welfare of citizens are foremost; personal happiness and pleasure are secondary. In abandoning Sita, Rama subordinates personal happiness to the welfare of his people and the orderliness of his kingdom. As a model king in the Hindu tradition, Rama illustrates that every individual, no matter how powerful and preeminent, is called upon to control individual preferences for the good of society as a whole.

To modern readers, Rama may appear inhuman, without emotion, inner turmoil, or doubt. He may seem to lack individuality. Precisely in this respect, however, he is a model of Hindu dharma. What is crucial in the Hindu vision of the ideal society is the proper definition and functioning of various social roles in relation to each other. An individual *is* his role, as it were, and that role only has significance vis-à-vis other roles in society. For Rama to have kept Sita despite the complaints of his citizens would have meant his willful destruction of his role as king in favor of selfish, egotistical desires.

The *Mahabharata*

According to the Hindu tradition the events of the *Mahabharata* took place in the dvapara age, a time long after the events of the Ramayana. The dvapara age was a heroic one, superior in all respects to the present kali age, in which morality is in serious decline, but nevertheless a time of less perfection than earlier ages. The characters in the *Mahabharata* seem more human, more given to flaws and shortcomings, than the heroes of the *Ramayana*, and much of the appeal of the former stems from the characters' perplexities concerning the proper course of action in given circumstances. Rama always seems to know exactly what to do, and does it unhesitatingly. Many of the *Mahabharata*'s characters, however, wonder aloud what to do when confronted with hard choices and at times make devastatingly wrong decisions.

The historical background of the *Mahabharata* also seems different from that of the *Ramayana*, even though scholars estimate that it was compiled during the same period. The rivals in the *Mahabharata* are two related clans of North India. The issues that divide them have to do primarily with rules of inheritance, and the great battle that eventually is fought between the two clans and their allies does not oppose good and evil, the gods and the demons, order and chaos in the same unambiguous way as the *Ramayana* does. The struggle is between relatives, not between Aryans and foreigners. The historical setting is one in which rulers of settled peoples compete with each other for control of the North Indian plains. The Aryans had been settled for centuries by the time the *Mahabharata* was compiled, and the dominating issue of the day was not the conquest of foreign powers but the proper remolding of the Aryan religious vision in the context of a new life-style and a new environment.

The Aryan religion of the Vedic period focused on maintaining and periodically reinvigorating the cosmos through sacrifices. Ideally society was arranged to support the priestly class so that they, in turn, could perform rituals that would guarantee the continued fecundity and prosperity of the world, which flowed from the sphere of the gods. The focus of Vedic religion was very much on the material world, and spiritual fulfillment concerned primarily achieving a prosperous life in this world and gaining heaven after death. People's essential religious obligation was twofold: (1) service to the gods through sacrificial rituals and (2) support of society so that these rituals could be carried out regularly by the Brahmins for the welfare of the entire cosmos.

This vision of the religious quest was seriously challenged, however, by various heretical movements of the sixth century B.C.E., and is even called into question in the *Upanishads* themselves, which are a part of Vedic literature. Although several movements criticized the old Vedic view of reality, the two most famous dissenting groups of the sixth century B.C.E. were Jainism and Buddhism. For both of these religions the spiritual quest involved the renunciation of society. Life in the world was seen to be incompatible with the kind of life that must be led to achieve ultimate liberation. For Jainism, rigorous asceticism was necessary to disentangle oneself from the binding effects of karma, which Jains believed polluted the soul as actual physical matter.[21] For the Buddhists, life in a monastic community was believed necessary to overcome egotistical desires that obscured one's true nature. Both religions understood salvation as something that could be achieved only outside everyday society. Consequently, neither religion revered the Vedic insistence upon upholding society or respected the Brahmin class, whose primary task was to insure cosmic and social stability through Vedic rituals.

---

[21]For the Jains every action attracts karma in the form of subtle matter, and this matter pollutes the soul. Bad actions attract heavy, dark karmic matter, whereas good actions attract light karma. However, as all actions attract some matter, the aim in Jainism is to achieve complete inactivity in order to purify the soul entirely. The notion of karma as actual physical matter is rejected by Hindus and Buddhists.

Ever since Vedic times asceticism had been known to the Hindu tradition. Asceticism, however, did not seem to have been an important part of early Vedic religion, and Vedic texts, with the exception of the *Upanishads*, are either suspicious of asceticism or ridicule it. By the time of the *Mahabharata* things have changed. Throughout this epic asceticism is regarded with considerable respect, and it is clear that the Jain and Buddhist emphasis upon renouncing the world had begun to enter the mainstream of the Hindu tradition. Whenever ascetics appear in the epic they are depicted as powerful. They are usually described in positive terms, as truthful, self-controlled, and virtuous. The *Mahabharata* also includes sections that seem to call into question the ultimate efficacy of Vedic rituals. At the end of the great war, for example, when the heroes gather to expiate any sins they may have committed in the battle by performing the most elaborate of Vedic rituals, the horse sacrifice, they are criticized by a lowly mongoose. After the great sacrifice, which is described in glowing detail, the mongoose appears and contrasts the heroes' elaborate ceremony with the virtuous act of a starving householder who gave his last remaining food to a hungry visitor during a famine. That householder's act was more meritorious, he says, than the heroes' costly sacrifice. The importance of the ascetic god Shiva in the *Mahabharata* also attests to the increasing importance of world renunciation in the Hindu tradition. The old Vedic view of the world is seriously challenged by one that respects asceticism and emphasizes the transient nature of the world and a person's ultimate destiny to transcend it.

Underlying many sections of the *Mahabharata*, then, is a tension between differing world views and the attempt to reconcile two apparently contradictory ideals: the Vedic world-supporting view and the ascetic world-denying view articulated in the *Upanishads*, Yoga, Jainism, and Buddhism.

Two central scenes of the *Mahabharata* are set in the context of this tension and seek to provide solutions: Arjuna's reluctance to fight just before the great battle and Yudhishthira's dilemma whether to rule his kingdom or renounce society after the great battle. Both scenes picture the epic heroes as reluctant to persist in their social roles as Kshatriyas (warrior rulers) and as wanting to withdraw either from society as a whole or from particularly painful social duties. In both scenes the epic's authors have provided solutions that permit a balance between supporting the world, doing one's social duty, and renouncing the world in pursuit of individual liberation.

The Bhagavad Gita.   The heroes of the *Mahabharata* are five brothers, the Pandavas. Early in the story they become embroiled in a controversy with their cousins, the Kauravas, over who will be the rulers of North India. After many failed attempts to settle the question peacefully, the two sides prepare for war. Finally the two embittered factions, with their allies, gather at Kurukshetra, a famous battlefield, and confront each other. The most renowned warrior of the Pandavas is Arjuna. He is frequently described as equal to the gods in the martial arts; he has been given devastating divine weapons by Shiva and Indra, two mighty gods; he has never been defeated in battle; and to the reader of the epic, a Pandava victory in the battle seems assured because of Arjuna's prowess. Just before the battle is to begin Arjuna asks his charioteer, Krishna, to take him into no-man's land so that he can see the ranks of the enemy more closely. When Arjuna looks over those arrayed against him he sees old friends, relatives, and former teachers. Contemplating their slaughter, Arjuna loses heart, drops his weapons to the floor of the chariot, turns to Krishna, and says that he will not fight. No matter who wins, he says, the price will be too great.

Krishna's response to Arjuna's lack of resolve constitutes the *Bhagavad Gita*, the most famous of all the Hindu scriptures. In the context of the *Mahabharata* story, Krishna's aim is to change Arjuna's mind and convince him to fight. While doing so, Krishna discourses on various types of religious action and offers to Arjuna, and to the Hindu tradition as a whole, a brilliant compromise between two apparently conflicting ideals: the Vedic ideal of serving society in order to insure worldly stability and the renunciation of society in order to achieve moksha, release from karma and samsara.

In refusing to fight, Arjuna calls into question the virtue of his social role as a warrior and the importance of upholding social order. In the Vedic ideal his duty is clear: As a warrior it is his responsibility to combat those forces that threaten order even if he finds the task personally painful. Thinking about all the killing that will be necessary to accomplish the preservation of order, however, Arjuna is disheartened and suggests to Krishna that it would be preferable to withdraw from society altogether and to seek salvation in solitude and inaction. Arjuna, that is, offers renunciation of society as an alternative to his life in the world, which requires him to undertake painful actions. In effect, Arjuna tells Krishna: "Life in society is too painful. I want to renounce society and end my present way of life."

Krishna's response to this view is not sympathetic. Renunciation of society by itself, he says, solves nothing. Although one's basic dilemma is bondage to karma (actions and their consequences) and samsara (rebirth according to karma), complete inaction is impossible. Even those who have renounced the world, Krishna says, continue to act and therefore are still bound by their actions and liable to rebirth. The key to liberation from bondage to actions is not renunciation of actions as such, or of a particular set of actions (a social role), but the performance of any action with the proper understanding, attitude, or knowledge. Actions themselves, Krishna says, are not binding. It is the *desires* that prompt actions that cause bondage. Liberation from karma, then, involves the renunciation or control of those egotistical desires that prompt action in the first place. The ideal is to act without concern for the fruits of actions, to act without desire, to renounce one's ego in all of one's doings. The process of doing so is called *karma-yoga*, disciplined action. In effect, Krishna tells Arjuna that he should detach his inmost self, his eternal Atman or soul, from his social role and then play that role without concern for personal consequences. True renunciation involves not renunciation of one's social role and retirement from society but renunciation of desires for the fruits of actions. When Arjuna asks how this kind of action is possible, Krishna recommends that he perform every action as a sacrifice to the Lord Vishnu, of whom Krishna is an incarnation. By living one's life as an offering to God, by making of each action a sacrifice to God, one is able to act selflessly and disentangle one's soul from the binding effects of actions that are egotistically motivated. Freed from the bondage to actions, that person may be liberated. It makes no difference, according to the *Gita*, what a person's social role may be. Anyone may seek liberation while remaining in society if one disciplines one's actions and thus performs genuine renunciation.

The genius of the *Bhagavad Gita*'s solution to Arjuna's dilemma lies in the fact that it synthesizes the world-maintaining view of the Vedic tradition and the world-denying view of Buddhism and Jainism, which had come increasingly to influence Hinduism. By counseling Arjuna to stay at his post, to persist in his duty as a warrior and fight the battle at hand, Krishna upholds the Vedic view of supporting the world, *loka-samgraha*. By teaching that ultimate liberation involves freedom from karma and samsara and the renunciation of desires, however, Krishna accommodates the world-denying view. In short, Krishna expresses a central theme of Hinduism, namely, that each person has a double responsibility: (1) to maintain social order and (2) to seek individual liberation from karma and samsara. For the *Gita* the two obligations may be undertaken simultaneously while remaining in society and performing karma-yoga.

Yudhishthira's dilemma.   At the end of the great battle, which is won by the Pandava heroes, the tension between obligation to society and the desire for individual liberation is again expressed in Yudhishthira's dilemma.[22] Yudhishthira, the eldest of the Pandava brothers, is now undisputed heir to the kingdom of North India. The battle itself, however, and the subsequent butchering by a few Kaurava survivors of most of the Pandava allies while they slept have caused Yudhishthira so much misery and pain that, like his brother Arjuna earlier, he is disheartened to the extent of wanting to give up life in the world in order to seek peace and liberation in the forest.

---

[22]This scene is found in the opening chapters of the Shanti Parva of the *Mahabharata*. In Roy's translation the scene is in vol. 8, pp. 1–85.

Grief stricken, Yudhishthira complains that if he continues to live in the world as king he will inevitably have to inflict pain on others as part of his natural duty. To rule is to punish others in order to maintain order, and Yudhishthira is sick of violence and pain. Life in the world, he complains further, is governed by desires for material well-being, and as these desires are insatiable, worldly life is always painful. The pursuit of power and wealth, the dejected hero says, has only led to pain, grief, and death. The best path is to renounce worldly life, retire to the woods, and perform austerities. Tranquility, noninjury, peace of mind, and detachment from the world's cares can only be found far from his kingly duties. Someone who values gold and dirt equally, Yudhishthira asserts, is superior to someone who possesses the whole earth. And finally, only in a life of world renunciation may ultimate liberation from rebirth be gained. Giving up all bonds and obligations, one will become as free as the wind and transcend the wheel of endless lives.

Yudhishthira's brothers, his counselors, and his wife object to his desire to abandon the world, and they marshal many arguments against renunciation and for the merits of remaining in the world. His wife, Draupadi, accuses him of being inconsistent. Having gained the kingdom through violence, will you now give up violence, she asks? Your brothers, she continues, fought for you under the impression that their reward would be the kingdom. Will you go back on your word to them? She concludes by calling into question his manhood. Only eunuchs, she says, seek tranquility and are afraid of violence. Yudhishthira's brother Bhima takes up a similar theme. To refuse to accept the kingdom at this point would be unnatural and inconsistent. It would be like a man climbing a tall tree in search of honey and having found it refusing to taste it, or like a sexually aroused man finally finding a woman similarly inclined and then refusing to have sex with her. Others pick up the theme, saying that Yudhishthira should follow custom. It isn't proper or natural for warriors to refrain from action and the worldly life. That is, renunciation of the world is proper for Brahmins but not for warriors.

Arjuna objects to his brother's desire to renounce the kingdom by arguing that disorder would follow from this decision. Chaos would result, and because of it Yudhishthira would earn great amounts of bad karma, which would condemn him to hell and lowly rebirth. As for the use of violence being necessary in the administration of kingly duties, Arjuna argues, it is both natural and meritorious when undertaken by a king. Violence is the natural way of things in the world. Creatures feed upon other creatures to sustain themselves, and this is the way the world was made. For the king to use violence to maintain order is thus divinely sanctioned. The gods themselves, Arjuna points out, employ violence against their enemies to achieve their high status. Finally, violence properly administered is compared to a king's sacrificial ritual. The bow is the king's sacrificial stake, the bowstring is the cord that ties the victim, the king's arrows and sword are his sacrificial ladles, and the blood he sheds is the sacrificial butter. His chariot is the altar, and his wrath in battle is the consuming sacrificial fire. That is, to administer punishment and to fight in battle are sacred rites for a king and result in no sin or blame.

Others argue that a king's duty generates great merit and that the whole world, including the gods, depends upon the king doing his duty. Wealth itself may produce great merit when it is given away, it is argued, and many people, particularly the Brahmins, depend upon the king's generosity. The gods themselves prosper and are invigorated by the king's great sacrifices. In more general terms, Yudhishthira's brother Nakula argues that of all the four stages of life—student, householder, forest dweller, and wandering holy man—that of the householder is superior to all the rest. He tells his elder brother that once the four stages were weighed on a scale and that the householder stage outweighed the other three combined.

His counselors and brothers also argue, following the logic of the *Bhagavad Gita*, that true renunciation is the renunciation of desires. They argue that a good king must control his desires and practice disciplined action and in so doing earn the same merit and the same reward as a world renouncer.

Finally, one of Yudhishthira's counselors argues that renunciation of the world before fulfilling one's obligations to society, before old age and decrepitude, is unnatural and untraditional. Yudhishthira is counseled to put off his desire to abandon society until a later time, to follow the stage of life appropriate to his age. This is the solution of almost all Hindu Law Books, and it seems to be the solution that Yudhishthira finds most convincing. Although the story does not tell us exactly which arguments the dejected king finds most persuasive, he gives up his despair and ascends the throne. At the end of the *Mahabharata*, however, when he has grown old and ruled for many years, Yudhishthira abandons the world as he wished to do after the great battle. In effect, then, the king is not convinced of the superiority of the worldly life, only convinced of its necessity. Renunciation of society for him is still the ultimate path to liberation, and he is persuaded only that this path should be postponed until a more appropriate time.

The solutions presented in the *Mahabharata* to Arjuna's and Yudhishthira's dilemmas never dissolved the tension between the paths of dharma and renunciation. To this day the tension persists, and for many Hindus the two paths are seen as very different religious possibilities. The solution of the Law Books—namely, the four stages of life, in which renunciation is postponed until old age—is usually ignored. Most world renouncers in India leave the world while still young. Most famous Indian saints who renounced the world did so well before they had fulfilled their social obligations. On the other hand, the vast majority of Hindus who do not renounce the world as youths never renounce the world, preferring to remain in society during their old age.

The extent of the effectiveness of the *Gita*'s solution to the tension between dharma and renunciation is more difficult to assess. It seems unlikely, however, that a great many Hindus have found it possible to live in the world while remaining detached from it. The *Gita*'s solution is brilliant, no doubt, but the continuing tension between social duty and the quest for liberation outside society in the Hindu tradition suggests that karma-yoga, the way of desireless action, has been a difficult path for the majority of Hindus.

HISTORICAL FIGURES

Introduction

Although many people have made important contributions to the history of Hinduism or typify various aspects of Hindu religious life, we do not have much historical information about most of them. Biographies of famous religious leaders usually were not written until centuries after they had lived, and the biographers were more concerned with illustrating how their idealized subjects personified accepted models of spirituality than with recording information about their unique history. So although the Hindu tradition supplies us with an abundance of names of important religious figures, it gives us very little detail with which to construct a historical biography. Only in recent times, perhaps under Western influence, have biographies of religious figures become available, and we are therefore in a better position to study how the religious ideals of Hinduism are lived and expressed in persons whom the tradition considers saints in the modern period.

It would be fitting, given the double emphases in the Hindu tradition upon *loka-samgraha* and moksha, to describe the life of a great Hindu king as illustrative of the former emphasis and the life of a world renouncer as illustrative of the latter. However, insofar as we have already dealt with models of kingship in our discussions of the *Mahabharata* and *Ramayana*, I have chosen as examples of important figures in the Hindu tradition two famous saints who illustrate differing types of world-renouncing spirituality. The sixteenth-century Bengali saint Chaitanya represents the devotional strain within Hinduism. According to his biographies, he renounced the world in order to dote incessantly on his god, the Lord Krishna. The modern saint Ramana Maharshi, on the other hand, represents a more philosophical emphasis within the context of renunciation. Although Ramana did express devotion to the Lord Shiva from time to time, his life is primarily a dramatic illustration of the central theme in Hinduism of realizing one's essential identity with Brahman, the Absolute. His life is a modern example of a type of spirituality that has been practiced and honored in Hinduism since the time of the *Upanishads*. Taken together, Chaitanya and

Ramana, then, may be understood as typical of thousands of Hindus who over the centuries have renounced the world in quest of ultimate spiritual liberation. Chaitanya exemplifies the path of devotion, and Ramana, the path of knowledge.

Chaitanya

Devotional movements dominated Hinduism in the fifteenth and six-teenth centuries in North India. Several new movements were founded, older traditions were refashioned and revitalized, and a considerable amount of vernacular devotional literature was written. Rama and Krishna were the deities who dominated these movements. Earlier Hinduism con-sidered Rama and Krishna avatars of Lord Vishnu. In these medieval de-votional movements, however, Rama and Krishna were each affirmed by their respective devotees to be the supreme manifestation of divinity. The worship of Rama was most popular in the Hindi-speaking areas of North India, whereas the worship of Krishna was popular throughout the North, especially in Bengal. Devotion to both gods was extremely emotional and personal but differed quite significantly in accordance with their distinctive mythologies. Rama was the heavenly king who dwelt in celestial Ayodhya. His devotees approached him as subjects, taking as their model the obedi-ent, subservient Hanuman, the monkey ally of Rama in his battle against the demon Ravana. The mood of the devoted servant, therefore, dominated Rama devotion in these movements. Devotion to Krishna, on the other hand, was modeled on the cowherd women of the village of Vraja, partic-ularly Radha, and emphasized the emotions of ecstatic love. The aim of the Krishna devotee was to experience Radha's frenzied, all-consuming love for the beautiful Krishna. Thus, the mood of the lover dominated Krishna de-votion.

The most famous Krishna devotee of this period was Chaitanya (1486–1533). He was a native of Bengal and is usually said to be the founder of Bengal Vaishnavism.[23] The worship of Krishna, however, was well estab-lished in Bengal prior to Chaitanya, so it is more appropriate to think of him as the revitalizer of Krishna worship in Bengal and the person who was responsible for systematizing the theology of Krishna devotion there. Chai-tanya did not introduce Krishna devotion to Bengal; he appointed theolo-gians to articulate its underlying principles and in his life provided a model for all lovers of Lord Krishna. However, to this day in Bengal, and through-out India, Chaitanya's name is inextricably associated with Bengal Vaish-navism, and it is difficult to imagine what Krishna devotion in Bengal would have been like without him.

---

[23]Vaishnavas are worshipers of Vishnu or one of his avatars. Bengal Vaishnavas are worshipers of Krishna, who traditionally is understood to be an avatar of Vishnu.

FIGURE 2–2 Chaitanya. Art by Muralīdhara dāsa. (Courtesy of The Hare Krishna Movement.)

Unlike most other Hindu saints prior to modern times, a rich biographical literature is available on Chaitanya. None of these biographies is what we might consider an objective historical account of his life, however. All of them were written by devotees within the movement, and all take pains to illustrate the various ways in which Chaitanya either embodied aspects and attributes of Krishna himself or was completely overwhelmed by his identification with Radha, the Lord's beloved. The biographies, then, are more revealing of what an ideal devotee of Krishna should be like than of Chaitanya's distinctive personal characteristics. The central emphasis in several of the biographies is on illustrating an important Bengal Vaishnava doctrine, accepted sometime after Chaitanya's death, namely, that Chaitanya was an incarnation of both Radha and Krishna in one body. The *Chaitanya Charitamrita*, the most authoritative biography,[24] for example, begins with Krishna brooding in heaven about how desirable it would be to experience Radha's passionate love for him. Longing to feel her passion, Krishna decides to incarnate himself as Chaitanya and in the person of Chaitanya to fully experience Radha's love and longing for himself. For Bengal Vaishnavas, then, Chaitanya represents both Krishna and Radha in one person.

Chaitanya was born in 1486 in the city of Navadvip in Bengal. Many auspicious signs accompanied his birth, we are told, and the infant bore many favorable marks on his body. He was given the name Vishvambhar, which he changed to Krishna Chaitanya when he renounced the world in 1510. The biographies tell us that Chaitanya was characterized by extraordinary beauty as a child. He had an unusually fair complexion, was doted on by his parents, and delighted in misbehaving and playing pranks. Like Krishna, upon whom the biographies model Chaitanya's life, the child is said to have been fond of sweets and to have wandered from house to house stealing candy to satisfy his craving. We are also told that nothing could quiet the child except the repetition of the name of God, which would content and calm him immediately.

When Chaitanya was still young two events combined to sober him somewhat. His elder brother renounced the world to become a sannyasi (a wandering holy man), and his father died. His mother, Shachi, was distraught over these events and increasingly looked to her youngest son, Chaitanya, for comfort and support. Chaitanya is described as an excellent student and is said to have started his own school, which attracted hundreds of students, when he was only sixteen. In his school he taught primarily the traditional subjects of logic and grammar. Chaitanya also was married at about this time. Shortly after his marriage his young wife died, but he remarried soon afterward. Until about the year 1508, Chaitanya showed no indication that he would become Krishna's most renowned devotee in Bengal. He is portrayed by his biographers as a cultivated, citified teacher who on occasion mocked the worshipers of Krishna.

Around the year 1508 Chaitanya went to the city of Gaya in Bihar to perform funeral ceremonies for his departed father. While there he underwent a total change. He met a holy man, Ishvara Puri, who managed to turn Chaitanya's attention to Krishna. Upon his return to Navadvip, Chaitanya joined a group of Krishna devotees and immediately began to manifest those devotional characteristics that would typify him throughout his life. Hearing Krishna's name or singing with other devotees about Krishna's exploits, Chaitanya would fall into a swoon, tremble with emotion, and

---

[24]Krishnadasa Kaviraja, *Sri Sri Chaitanya Charitamrita*, 6 vols., 2d ed., trans. Nagendra Kumar Ray (Calcutta: Nagendra Kumar Ray, 1959).

weep. He found himself incapable of teaching grammar and logic and would spend hours telling his students about Krishna. He eventually gave up his teaching career and assumed the leadership of the Vaishnava community in Navadvip.

Popular worship of Krishna as practiced by the Vaishnavas was called *kirtan,* and it consisted primarily of singing songs in praise of Krishna or chanting his name repeatedly. This devotion was usually performed in small groups in private homes. Chaitanya, however, introduced the practice of public *kirtan,* in which he and his fellow devotees would parade around the streets of Navadvip singing and chanting in praise of their Lord. There was some opposition to these goings-on, which often lasted till late into the night, but the practice eventually became a normal part of Bengal Vaishnavism and continues to this day. As described in the biographies and as witnessed today, these group sessions were filled with great emotion and frenzy. Devotees danced, played musical instruments, and, identifying with the cowherd women, wept for their beloved Krishna. The *kirtans* sought to create the atmosphere of Vrindavana,[25] where devotees could meet their Lord in his favorite place and enjoy him intimately.

In order to refute criticisms of himself and his movement by outsiders who questioned his spirituality, Chaitanya decided in 1510 to renounce the world and become a sannyasi. His mother, wife, and most devotees opposed his decision, and Chaitanya's insistence upon going through with it underlines the extent to which genuine spirituality and renunciation of the world are linked in Hindu consciousness. By becoming a sannyasi, Chaitanya was able to stamp his movement with authority and to gain the respect and admiration of those who had formerly opposed or criticized him.

It is traditional for a sannyasi to leave his family and village after undergoing the rituals of renunciation. In conformity with this tradition, Chaitanya resolved to leave Navadvip. However, in deference to his mother, who was greatly distressed over his decision, he decided to make his new home at nearby Puri instead of far-off Vrindavana. Vrindavana was an important Krishna holy place, identified with the area of Krishna's past games, and Chaitanya would have preferred to reside there. Puri, another Vaishnava holy place, was much closer, however, and it was there that Chaitanya spent most of the rest of his life. His departure from Navadvip is described in the biographies as eliciting weeping and fainting on the part of his fellow devotees. That is, his departure is compared with Krishna's from Vrindavana. Like the cowherd women who wept when Krishna left them, Chaitanya's companions wept too, for indeed, the biographies say, Chaitanya

---

[25]Vrindavana is the place in Krishna mythology where Krishna sported with his devotees. It is identified with present-day Vrindavana in the State of Uttar Pradesh and since the sixteenth century has been an important Vaishnava pilgrimage center. For Krishna devotees, the highest heaven, where Krishna resides eternally, is also called Vrindavana and is an idealized version of his earthly home.

was Krishna, and whenever Krishna departs from a devotee that devotee is left in tears of sorrow and longing.

Chaitanya had not been living at Puri very long when he decided to make a journey to South India. Although his companions tried to dissuade him from making the long, dangerous trip, Chaitanya set out with one follower and for two years (1510–12) traveled throughout the South visiting holy places. Chaitanya's biographers describe his sojourn as a triumphant tour, a conquest of the quarters (north, south, east, and west), during which he converted to Krishna worship all those who saw him and refuted all opponents of his theology.

The *Chaitanya Charitamrita* describes a conversation that Chaitanya had with Ramananda Ray, a high government official, during his triumphant tour, and in many respects it summarizes concisely the central vision of Chaitanya and Bengal Vaishnavism. In their conversation, Chaitanya asks Ramananda to give his views on the ultimate meaning of the scriptures. Ramananda offers repeated statements concerning the essence of scriptures, but over and over Chaitanya says that the true essence lies beyond. Beginning with the view of the *Bhagavad Gita*, that Vishnu should be worshiped by devoting all actions to him alone, and moving toward a more emotional type of devotion as central to scripture, Chaitanya presses Ramananda further and further until Ramananda states that the highest spiritual path is to emulate Radha and the cowherd women in their love for Krishna. The statement by Ramananda that ends their conversation and finally satisfies Chaitanya says that to attain Krishna, the highest goal, one must adopt the attitude of Radha and the cowherd women, meditate on their dalliance with Krishna constantly, and never think of Krishna as having kingly attributes but only those of a lover.[26]

In a second conversation with Ramananda, Chaitanya asks Ramananda various questions, and his answers again summarize concisely the basic elements of Chaitanya's vision of divinity and human spiritual destiny.

Chaitanya:	What is knowledge?
Ramananda:	There is no knowledge except devotion to Krishna.
Chaitanya:	Who is the most illustrious among people?
Ramananda:	The person famous as a devotee of Krishna.
Chaitanya:	Which is the most valuable possession?
Ramananda:	Love for Radha and Krishna.
Chaitanya:	Which is the worst misery?
Ramananda:	Separation from Krishna's devotees.
Chaitanya:	Who is the freed soul?
Ramananda:	The one who has love for Krishna.

---

[26]Chaitanya's biography is summarized by A. K. Majumdar, *Caitanya, His Life and Doctrine* (Bombay: Bharatiya Vidya Bhavan, 1969). This conversation is found on pp. 178–83.

Chaitanya:	What song is natural to a person?
Ramananda:	Those which describe the secrets of Radha and Krishna's dalliance.
Chaitanya:	What should we constantly remind ourselves of?
Ramananda:	The name, qualities, and sports of Krishna.
Chaitanya:	What is the highest object of meditation?
Ramananda:	Radha and Krishna.
Chaitanya:	Which is the sweetest melody?
Ramananda:	Those which are tuned to the love songs of Radha and Krishna.[27]

When Chaitanya returned to Puri many people acclaimed him as a saint, and he soon became the center of a vigorous group of Krishna devotees, who worshiped the image of Krishna daily in the great Jagannatha temple in Puri. Chaitanya is said to have defeated in debate a famous monistic philosopher of the Shankara school and to have converted him to the worship of Krishna during this time. Such conquests and conversions occurred throughout his life, according to his pious biographers. The inner circle of devotees were renouncers like Chaitanya himself, some of whom had come with him from Bengal, and their routine form of piety was ecstatic devotion in the context of *kirtan*. Devotees from Bengal periodically would visit Chaitanya in Puri; these visits continued until his death and enabled Chaitanya's influence to increase in Bengal, where he achieved his greatest popularity. Also during his early years in Puri, Chaitanya encouraged some of his followers to preach the truth of Krishna worship throughout the countryside. This was undertaken with considerable success in Bengal and Orissa.

Chaitanya had an increasing desire to visit Vrindavana and its environs, the earthly place of Radha and Krishna's dalliance, and around 1514 he set out with a few followers on the long journey far to the west near Delhi. On the way he visited Varanasi, found the city dominated by monists, debated with pundits there, converted them to Krishna devotion, and then pressed toward Vrindavana. The biographies all stress Chaitanya's intoxicated state while making this pilgrimage. He constantly repeated the name of Krishna, and as he neared Vrindavana his emotional frenzy intensified. In Vrindavana he was overcome repeatedly by emotion at the sites of Radha and Krishna's play, and one biographer describes his blissful condition by saying that while he was there he danced rather than walked from place to place. On one occasion, while wandering along the banks of the Jumna River, he was so overcome by the memory of Krishna playing with Radha in the waters of the river that he leaped in and almost drowned. Every sight he saw triggered a memory within him of Radha and Krishna and sent him into fits of ecstasy.

---

[27]Paraphrased from ibid., pp. 183–84.

On his return trip to Puri, Chaitanya had an important meeting in Allahabad with the brothers Rupa and Sanatana Gosvami, devotees he had met earlier in Bengal. Chaitanya convinced them that they should renounce the world, retire to Vrindavana, establish Krishna temples there, and systematize the theology of Krishna worship as they had learned it from him. The two brothers agreed and, along with their nephew Jiva Gosvami, were primarily responsible for revitalizing Vrindavana as the center of Krishna devotion in India and composing the central theological treatises of Bengal Vaishnavism. In addition to their theological works, the brothers and Jiva also wrote many plays featuring Krishna's games with the cowherd women, and plays of this sort are still performed frequently in Vrindavana. Their importance is quite in keeping with the main objective of Krishna devotion, which is constantly to imagine the love play of Radha and Krishna until all else is emptied from the mind. The plays in this context are thus aids to meditation and devotion.

Chaitanya himself needed no such help in his devotion. Upon his return to Puri his ecstatic devotional swoons and outbursts became increasingly frequent. Any sight, no matter how apparently unlikely, might remind him of Krishna and trigger his devotional frenzy. The blue neck of a peacock might remind him of Krishna's complexion and send him into fits of joy.[28] A local hill might remind him of Mount Govardhana in Vrindavana, which Krishna is said to have raised as an umbrella to protect the inhabitants during a fierce rain storm. A pond, a river, or even the sea (Puri is located on the Bay of Bengal) might remind him of the Jumna River in Vrindavana. Indeed, Chaitanya saw Krishna everywhere, having completely emptied his mind of all other thoughts. Mentally he lived in Vrindavana, where he sported with Krishna constantly in the mood of Radha. Many descriptions of him during this period portray him as a lovesick girl, moody and downcast at some imagined slight on the part of her lover or grief stricken at his absence. Outwardly Chaitanya was an ascetic world renouncer. He ate the most meager meals, which he begged, avoided the very sight of women, and was reluctant to associate with anyone but other world renouncers and devotees of Krishna. Inside, though, he was the lovesick girl of Vrindavana, Radha, doting constantly on the beauty of her Lord Krishna, seeing him everywhere, and feeling miserable in his absence. So absorbed was Chaitanya in the mythical realm of Krishna that he was barely able to look after himself. His biographers say that he needed constant supervision to insure that he did not injure himself and that he neglected the routine actions of daily life, such as bathing and eating, or merely did them out of unconscious habit. In these last years Chaitanya had achieved the goal of all Krishna devotees: He dwelt almost constantly in the heavenly world of Krishna, his physical body alone remaining earthbound.

---

[28]Krishna's complexion is dark blue like the neck of a peacock.

Chaitanya died in 1533. During his life, and for some time after his death, his followers wrote devotional songs in his praise. A frequent theme of these songs is the intoxicating effect that he had on all those who saw him. Like Krishna, the very sight of Chaitanya was held to be redemptive by his followers. It is not primarily as a thinker, saint, or world renouncer that Chaitanya is celebrated in Bengal. He is celebrated because he revealed the beauty of Krishna and the beauty of devotion to Krishna. It is not surprising that subsequent generations of devotees concluded that Chaitanya had been an incarnation of Krishna himself, come to earth to taste the bliss of Radha's devotion for his own beauty.

Ramana Maharshi

For a great many Hindus the essence of their tradition is found in the *Upanishads*, which traditionally are called Vedanta (the end or goal of knowledge). In the *Upanishads* a central concern is the self-discovery of the ground and origin of reality. The *Upanishads* call this reality Brahman and identify one's essence or soul (Atman) with Brahman. The goal of one's spiritual pilgrimage, then, is defined as the realization of one's inner essence as divine and as indistinguishable from the underlying basis of all things.

The discovery of one's divine essence has continued to be the ultimate goal of Hindu spiritual seekers throughout the centuries, and the Hindu tradition has preserved many testimonies to the self-discovery of the Atman in the form of hymns of triumph.

> I am smaller than the minutest atom, likewise greater than the greatest. I am the whole, the diversified-multicolored-lovely-strange . . . universe. I am the Ancient One. I am . . . the Lord. I am the Being-of-God (*hiraṇmaya*: the golden germ out of which the universe unfolds). I am the very state of divine beatitude.
>
> Without hands or feet am I; of inconceivable power am I; without eyes I see; without ears I hear; I know all with all-pervading wisdom. By nature detached from all am I, and there is none who knows me. Pure spiritual essence am I, forever.[29]
>
> I am free from passion and similar taints. Suffering, a body, and other limiting peculiarities are not with me. I am the Self, the Only-lonely-one (*eka*), which is comparable to the infinite sky.[30]

There is no doubt about the centrality of the *Upanishads* as revered expressions of the highest truth prior to the eighth century. But it was the

---

[29]*Kaivalya Upanishad*, pp. 19–20; from Heinrich Zimmer, *Philosophies of India*, ed. Joseph Campbell, Bollingen Series XXVI (Princeton, N.J.: Princeton University Press, 1951), p. 447; copyright 1951 by Princeton University Press.

[30]*Avadhuta Gita* 1. 67; from ibid., pp. 449–50; copyright 1951 by Princeton University Press.

philosopher Shankara in the eighth century who systematized the basic principles of the *Upanishads* into a coherent and forceful philosophical system. To this day Shankara is considered unrivaled in his expression of the vision of the unity of Brahman and Atman as the underlying essence of reality. Shankara is also taken as a model for those seeking divine self-realization, and as such it would be appropriate to discuss him here as the best example of Upanishadic philosophy and the path leading to its realization. However, as Shankara and his philosophy will be dealt with in Part II, I have chosen as an example of this important strain in Hinduism the modern South Indian saint Ramana Maharshi. By discussing Ramana at this point I wish to underline the fact that traditional Upanishadic philosophy is still vital to Hinduism and represents for many Hindus today the central truth of their religion. Ramana's teachings and his path, furthermore, may be taken as representative of thousands of anonymous spiritual adepts over the centuries who have sought self-knowledge in Hinduism, and thus he may be understood as simply the latest and best known example of this still vital accent in the Hindu tradition.

The history of Hinduism during the period when Ramana lived (1879–1950) was dominated by two different but related phenomena: reform movements and the independence movement. Many Hindus, grappling with the task of renewing their self-identity after centuries of subjugation by the Muslims and later the British, and aware of criticisms of their tradition by Muslims and Christians, thought that Hinduism in the modern period was in need of reform. Many of the Hindus who became famous in this period, consequently, were people who in some way sought to accommodate Hindu thought and practice to Western religion. Ram Mohan Roy and Keshub Chandra Sen, leaders of the Brahmo Samaj, both became famous throughout India. Dayananda Saraswati, the founder of the Arya Samaj, also became famous for his attempts to reform Hinduism. Ramakrishna, perhaps the most famous modern Hindu saint, tried in his spiritual exercises to incorporate Western religions into his religious vision. His spiritual successor, Vivekananda, the founder of the Ramakrishna Mission, made a self-conscious attempt to defend Hinduism against Western criticisms. All these famous figures in one way or another were important in reasserting Hindu identity in relation to foreign influences.

Another group of illustrious Hindus during this period gained fame in the Indian independence movement. Such important figures as Bal Gangadhar Tilak and Mahatma Gandhi saw their political involvement as an integral part of their spiritual lives, and their lives represented important modern models for thousands of Hindus. In the history of Hinduism the nineteenth and twentieth centuries have been dramatic in maintaining and redefining Hindu self-identity for a vast number of Hindus.

In the life and teachings of Ramana Maharshi, however, one is almost totally unaware of these broader historical developments. Although Ra-

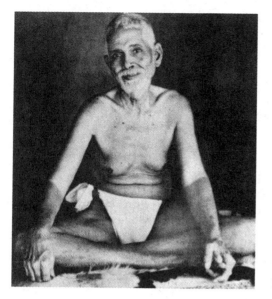

FIGURE 2–3   Ramana Maharshi. (Courtesy of The Mountain Path, S. India.)

mana lived in exciting times for Hindus, a time of reform and political struggle, he barely seemed aware of the historical developments taking place around him. His life and teachings have an air of timeless, classic structure. They seem as appropriate to twentieth-century Hinduism as they do to first-century Hinduism. Ramana is vivid testimony to the self-confidence of Hinduism in its ancient roots—testimony to the fact that Hinduism has persisted through much historical and cultural change in clinging to a timeless vision of human destiny, which declares that each individual is essentially divine and eternal and that renunciation of the world is the best way to realize this truth fully.

Ramana was born on December 30, 1879, the second son of Sundaram Aiyar and his wife, Alagammal, in the village of Tirucculi, about thirty miles south of the city of Madurai in South India. He was given the name Venkataraman, of which Ramana is an abbreviation. We are told that his birthday corresponded that year to the annual celebration of Lord Shiva as Nataraja, Lord of the Dance, and that the festival celebrated Shiva's victory over Andhaka, the blind demon who represents darkness. The day was a fitting one for the sage's birth, since he would triumph over the darkness of ignorance and individuality.

Ramana's family was middle class, his father being a pleader at the local court, and when Ramana was old enough he was enrolled in the local school. When he was twelve years old his father died, and his mother moved to Madurai to live with relatives. There Ramana was sent to Scott's Middle School and then to the American Mission School, where he learned English.

Ramana did not show much interest in school and seems to have been a rather poor student. However, he is remembered as having had a brilliant memory, being able to memorize long passages after reading or hearing them just once. He was much more interested in physical sports and seemed an unlikely candidate to renounce the world.

Around 1895 Ramana happened upon a copy of the *Periya Purana*, a twelfth-century biography of sixty-three Shiva saints of South India. He was drawn by the examples of the saints, and a desire to devote himself to the Lord and retire from the world began to develop within him. Then in 1896, when he was seventeen, he had a dramatic experience that resulted in his firm conviction to give up the world. Sitting at home one day, in fine health, he was suddenly overcome with the fear of death. Ramana anticipated what death would be like by lying down on the ground and stretching out his limbs and making them stiff. He held his breath and sought to take on the appearance of a corpse. Later in his life, relating this incident to his disciples, Ramana said that while in this deathlike attitude he had the following sequence of thoughts:

> Well, this body is now dead. It will be carried to the funeral pyre and there reduced to ashes. But do I die with the death of this body? Is the body I? It is silent and inert; but I feel the full force of my personality and even the voice of the "I" within me, apart from it. So I am the Spirit transcending the body. The body dies but the Spirit that transcends it cannot be touched by death. That means that I am the deathless Spirit.[31]

Ramana's imaginary death was simultaneously devastating and enlightening. After his experience he no longer had any taste for life in the world. His sense of ego, personality, and individuality had been destroyed. In "dying" Ramana had been reborn with a new identity grounded in the eternal, unqualified, and anonymous essence of reality, the Atman that is identical with Brahman. His imaginary death awakened him from the dream of individuality and allowed him to perceive his true, eternal identity.

Although Ramana was eager to abandon the worldly life, he knew his mother would oppose his decision. So he made plans to leave his family without telling them directly. Ramana had heard of the holy hill Arunachala, a dwelling place of world renouncers for centuries, about 120 miles southwest of Madras, and determined to flee there. He studied a map, calculated the cost of the trip by train, and under a pretext took five rupees from his family. Leaving behind a note, the youth set out for Arunachala, where he would spend the rest of his life. Like countless others before him in Hinduism, Ramana had become disenchanted with life in the world and the task of upholding the world order through dharma, and he set out to

---

[31]T. M. P. Mahadevan, *Ramana Maharshi, the Sage of Arunacala* (London: George Allen & Unwin, 1977), p. 17.

discover and experience directly redemptive knowledge that would release him once and for all from the endless round of birth and death.

Because of a miscalculation, Ramana found that he did not have enough money to reach Arunachala and was forced to sell his gold earrings. The earrings were worth about twenty rupees, and the person to whom he sold them offered him this figure. But Ramana only needed four rupees and would accept only that amount. The buyer gave Ramana his address and told him that he could redeem the earrings at any time. When Ramana left the man he tore up the address and in doing so symbolically renounced wealth. From then on he would lead the life of poverty, existing with as few possessions as possible, and would beg his daily food.

The next day, September 1, 1896, Ramana arrived at Arunachala and went directly to the main temple, where he felt great joy before the image of Shiva. When he was leaving the temple, someone recognized him as one who had renounced the world and asked if he wanted his head shaved, a traditional indication of world renunciation; he agreed. Later, he stood on the edge of a tank near the temple and threw away his few remaining coins; a packet of food given to him earlier by the man who had bought his earrings; his sacred thread, which indicated his high caste; and all his clothes except a single loincloth. Now Ramana's outward appearance was in harmony with his inward aversion to continued life in the world.

After spending his first few days at Arunachala in the main temple, Ramana soon sought a more secluded place. He discovered a neglected shrine under the main temple hall and sought solitude there in the dark chamber. In this place he meditated alone and rarely ventured outside. The walls and floor of the shrine were soon stained by the blood and pus that oozed from his many insect bites, but Ramana was indifferent to this affliction. He was completely immersed in the rapt realization of his eternal essence, the Atman, and ignored his body entirely. From time to time some young boys would taunt him and throw stones inside the shrine to pester him, but Ramana ignored them too. Another world renouncer, however, befriended Ramana and persuaded him to move to a more secluded shrine nearby, which Ramana did. He dwelt at this shrine for two months, and for most of this time he remained silent and motionless. He was looked after during this time by other residents of Arunachala, who sometimes had to feed him forcibly, as he was so rarely conscious of his physical surroundings and his bodily needs. He is described during this period as follows: "He sat on the floor for hours at a time without opening his eyes, and without being aware of what was happening around him. Ants and insects attacked him as before, without his noticing that he was being bitten. His hair became matted and his finger-nails grew long and curly."[32]

[32]Ibid., p. 27.

By this time Ramana had begun to attract disciples, who vied with one another in looking after him. Many visitors to the temple were also attracted to him and paid him honor. However, neither disciples nor devotees of the sage actually knew who he was, as until this time he had remained completely silent. One day one of his disciples asked if he might undertake worship of Ramana, as was appropriate to famous holy people. In Hinduism, from ancient times, those who have realized the Atman and thus have experienced their own essential divinity have been considered worthy of worship, so this request was not exceptional. Ramana, however, disapproved of the idea and wrote on a wall with a piece of charcoal that he did not wish this honor. Heretofore, his disciples had not known that he could read or write. When they discovered this, they entreated him to tell them who he was by writing his name and village on a piece of paper. The silent Ramana, however, did not respond in any way. Finally, one of the devotees threatened to fast until death if his master did not reveal his worldly identity. Reluctantly, Ramana wrote his name and the name of his birthplace and thus made known to his disciples, and eventually to the world, who he was.

When Ramana's fame began to spread, one of his relatives heard about him and journeyed to Arunachala to see if the sage was in fact his nephew. Upon recognizing him, he asked Ramana if he would agree to move back to Madurai, where he might live in a shrine attended by his relatives. Ramana did not respond to his uncle's request and did not even show any sign of recognizing him. Throughout his life, Ramana received all visitors—relatives, humble devotees, and various famous people—with the same equanimity, treating them all alike. Despite many offers to live in more accessible or sumptuous surroundings, Ramana steadfastly refused to leave the holy mountain of Arunachala.

Eventually, Ramana's mother found her way to Arunachala and begged him to return to the world. Ramana was observing a vow of silence at the time of her visit and refused to speak to her. He did write her a note, however, explaining that it was his destiny to abide at Arunachala until he died and that she should accept this without further protest. His mother left, disheartened, but years later she returned to join her son as a world renouncer herself.

From 1900 to 1916 Ramana dwelt in a cave attended by a faithful disciple. During most of this time he remained still and silent, conducting a wordless instruction to all those who sought him out. However, he did manage to compose, by means of gestures and writing, two short works that summarized his philosophy. At the request of a disciple and in response to questions put to him by disciples, he set forth an abbreviated rendition of Vedanta philosophy that emphasized the absolute nonduality of ultimate Reality grounded in Brahman. In these two works—*Self-Enquiry* and *Who Am I?*—Ramana teaches that one's ultimate destiny is to discover one's essential identity, which is the same as Brahman, and that this identity is best discovered by pursuing the question, "Who am I?" Like the *Upanishads* and Shankara before him, Ramana's vision of truth was grounded in the conviction that one's inner essence is eternal, unchanging, blissful, and divine and that all duality, individuality, and specificity observed in the world around us are ultimately only appearance grounded in the ignorant cravings of the ego, which is deluded into thinking it is complete unto itself. Realization of one's true identity results in peace, tranquility, indifference to the vicissitudes of life, and great joy. The ego dies away and the real "I," the Atman, is allowed to illuminate one's being entirely.

Although Ramana made no active attempts during his life at Arunachala to minister to the needs of others, many who came to see him credited him with solving their problems. A typical case is that of the woman Echammal, who had lost within a short time her husband and both children. Distraught and grieving, she made pilgrimages to many famous places, but her sorrow did not subside. Hearing of Ramana, she made her way to Arunachala in 1906. After climbing up to his cave, she sat in front of the sage for an hour saying nothing. The silent Ramana said nothing either, but by the time she rose to leave, Echammal's grief had vanished and she felt inner peace pervade her. In gratitude for his help, Echammal remained at Arunachala as Ramana's devotee. So it was with many others. Often without saying a word, with simply a glance or a gesture, Ramana seemed able to calm troubled petitioners and reveal to them their inmost identity. His presence alone, many devotees attest, was revealing and calming. A Westerner, Paul Brunton, described Ramana's silent presence on himself as follows:

> I cannot turn my gaze away from him. My initial bewilderment, my perplexity at being totally ignored, slowly fade away as this strange fascination begins to grip me more firmly. But it is not till the second hour of the uncommon scene that I become aware of a silent, resistless change which is taking place within my mind. One by one, the questions which I prepared in the train with such meticulous accuracy drop away. For it does not now seem to matter whether they are asked or not, and it does not matter whether I solve the problems which have hitherto troubled me. I know only that a steady river of quietness seems to be flowing near me, that a great peace is penetrating the inner reaches of my being, and that my thought-tortured brain is beginning to arrive at some rest.[33]

In 1916, following the death of her eldest son, Ramana's mother, Alagammal, came to Arunachala determined to remain there with her son for the rest of her life. Soon after her arrival Ramana moved out of his solitary cave and became the center of a small community of devotees on the eastern slope of the mountain. Eventually becoming known as the Dwelling of

---

[33]Arthur Osborne, *Ramana Maharshi and the Path of Self-Knowledge* (New York: Samuel Weiser, 1973), p. 54.

Ramana, it consisted of little more than a few simple huts and a kitchen that Ramana's mother directed. The location of the Dwelling was moved in 1922, six months after Alagammal's death, when Ramana, on one of his daily visits to her nearby grave, decided to remain there permanently. He lived at this site until his death in 1950.

Ramana's relations with his mother are unusual and revealing. In traditional Hinduism, world renouncers usually left their families and were never heard from again by their relatives. As we have seen, this was Ramana's intention also. His decision to leave the world involved his determination to leave his family as well. It was only by accident that he was found by his family and later approached by them to return home. This he refused to do. When his mother approached him for solace in her grief, however, Ramana did not spurn her; and during the years that she remained with him at Arunachala, he tended her when she was sick as any son would tend his mother. Ramana thus showed a strong strain of compassion that generally is not emphasized in biographies of Hindu world renouncers and revealed a warmth toward his fellow human beings that is appealing. He is described in other contexts, as well, as weeping with grief-stricken petitioners and in various ways manifesting empathy with the emotional turmoil of those who sought his help. Ramana himself, then, may well have transcended the distracting emotions that are engendered by an ego-centered way of living in the world—he may well have resided constantly in the silent, calm, inner realization of his eternal identity as Atman—but he was able to appreciate the feelings and troubles of others and helped them find peace.

In 1948 Ramana's health began to fail. A lump on his left elbow appeared and, despite the efforts of doctors, failed to heal. When one of the doctors suggested amputating the stricken arm, Ramana replied, "There is no need for alarm. The body is itself a disease. Let it have its natural end. Why mutilate it? A simple dressing on the affected part will do."[34] Throughout these last years Ramana appeared completely indifferent to his physical ailments. On the evening of his death, April 14, 1950, his devotees sat around his bed and sang hymns that Ramana had written in praise of the holy mountain, Arunachala. As they sang he died, a smile on his lips and his eyes filled with tears of bliss.

---

[34]Mahadevan, *Ramana Maharshi*, p. 76.

3

Dissent within the Hindu Religious Tradition

INTRODUCTION

The looseness with which orthodoxy (proper belief) is defined in Hinduism and Hinduism's traditional tolerance for different points of view have enabled the tradition to encompass a great variety of teachings without excessive friction. Partly because of Hinduism's lack of central authority, too, there have been very few divisive debates within the tradition that have led to irreparable splits. The Hindu attitude generally is that various beliefs and paths are appropriate to different people at different stages in their spiritual pilgrimages, which of course may include thousands of lives, given the doctrines of karma and samsara.

Hinduism is equally tolerant concerning orthopraxy, or proper religious practice. Again, certain types of rituals are understood to be appropriate to different spiritual types and different religious goals. Many rituals, for example, are prescribed only for the high castes and forbidden to the lower castes, which have their own, often quite different, rituals. In addition to this, the Hindu Law Books all agree that established practice and custom should usually be followed, and as religious and social custom has always varied widely in the many different cultural regions of India, a great variety of religious practices are tolerated. Generally, then, the situation in Hinduism is one of small groups, castes, subcastes, and regional traditions setting down clear guidelines for orthodoxy, and sometimes orthopraxy, and often strictly enforcing these guidelines, whereas in terms of the Hindu tradition as a whole, diversity in proper belief and practice is what is most characteristic.

Nevertheless, the Hindu tradition historically has drawn some limits that may not be transgressed without falling outside the orthodox fold and has affirmed some teachings and religious practices as proper for most, if not all, Hindus. Reverence for the *Vedas*, for example, is a prerequisite for any philosophical system or religious movement to be considered properly Hindu. This reverence may not be central to the philosophy in question and in fact may be merely tacit. To deny the sacredness of the *Vedas*, however, or to state that they are simply human products, is sufficient to remove a system from the Hindu fold. Traditionally, Hinduism divides all philosophies into orthodox and nonorthodox. Of the latter, all of which deny the sacredness of the *Vedas*, the most famous are the Buddhists and the Jains.

In many essential respects Buddhism and Jainism are very much like Hinduism. Both movements presuppose karma and samsara and define the ultimate spiritual goal in terms very similar to those used in Hinduism. In addition, spiritual techniques such as yoga are central to Buddhism and Jainism, as they are to Hinduism. Nevertheless, both religions are considered nonorthodox by Hindus primarily because they deny the authority of the *Vedas*, considering them mere human products.

Another guideline for orthodoxy in Hinduism is reverence for Brahmins and the implicit acceptance of the social hierarchy known as the caste system. Here again the Buddhists and Jains represent a dissenting view, declaring that Brahmins have no special religious status.

A quite different form of nonorthodox tradition was represented by the materialists, the Charvakas. They not only denied that the *Vedas* were sacred but denied that a spiritual reality impinged on the material world. Furthermore, they not only were atheistic but saw the human quest for some kind of imperishable spiritual goal as worthless. Needless to say, the materialists were castigated by Hindus, Buddhists, and Jains alike.

In a cultural sense Hinduism has also tended to consider foreigners outside the Hindu pale. Many restrictions traditionally have been placed on Brahmins that prohibit or discourage their traveling outside India, as to do so would mean contact with foreigners and foreign customs, which would be polluting. In a broad sense, then, orthodoxy for Hinduism historically has been defined as simply being Indian. The exception to this belief—besides the consciously dissenting groups such as the Buddhists, Jains, and more recently the Muslims and Christians—is the tribal peoples of India, who traditionally have lived in remote areas, where in semi-isolation they practice their own religions, which often differ markedly from Hinduism. With modern transportation and communication these tribes increasingly have become assimilated into the Hindu fold by adopting various Hindu teachings and practices. For centuries, though, they represented a sizable group of people in India who were considered non-Hindu.

Turning to the Hindu fold itself, we find many examples of protest against established doctrine and practice. Some of these movements appear more critical of certain cherished Hindu teachings or practices than the nonorthodox groups, but they either have considered themselves Hindu or have been considered so by other Hindus because of their refusal to deny the *Vedas* or their tacit conformity to other Hindu beliefs and practices. These movements generally may be characterized as being of two types: radical devotional movements (or radical individual devotees) and radical world-renouncing or Tantric groups that either cultivate antisocial behavior or indulge in antiestablishment criticism in their teachings and practice.

It is undoubtedly the case that the vast majority of Hindus have never practiced, or been allowed to practice, the rituals prescribed in the *Vedas*. These rituals, for the most part, are for upper-caste Hindus, and most Hindus do not belong to these castes. The religion of most Hindus today, and probably for centuries, consists of non-Vedic rituals of various kinds, pilgrimages, festivals, and devotion to local deities. Although high-caste Hindus have been prominent in the devotional movements, these movements frequently reflect disinterest in and sometimes dislike for established Vedic religious teachings and practice. Many famous devotees have come from low castes, many have been women (generally seen as spiritually inferior in the traditional Law Books), many have been illiterate, and many have had little respect for the traditional aspects of Hinduism that say they are spiritually inferior because they are socially inferior. Unfortunately we are not able to get a complete picture of the history of the devotional movements and the full extent to which they have protested established Hinduism, as many of these movements lacked literary representatives or lacked interest in preserving their traditions in written texts. We may surmise on the basis of the current situation in India, however, that a great many Hindus have devoted themselves to local deities, usually goddesses, and that their religious beliefs and practices have represented an indifference to Vedic Hinduism, if not a tacit protest against it. In the literary sources of the devotional movements that we do have, protest against established Hinduism is not uncommon. The clearest example of this protest is probably the Virashaiva movement, which will be discussed later.

Although asceticism and renunciation of society became an important aspect of orthodox Hinduism at a very early period, and although Hindus are generally tolerant of a great variety of religious behavior, there are some ascetic groups and movements that are often criticized by orthodox Hindus for their bizarre behavior and their apparent disregard for civilized custom. Several of these more radical groups are associated with the god Shiva, himself portrayed as an ascetic who lives on the fringes of society and indulges in odd, mad, or outrageous behavior. These groups often self-consciously act in a way that is offensive to those living within society.[1] The motivation for this behavior seems to be twofold. First, in so acting the practitioners model themselves on the divine Shiva and thereby seek to transcend the limitations of finite humanity. Second, by performing actions that are offensive to society, the practitioners separate themselves from society, thus reinforcing their vow to seek liberation apart from society. By attracting the scorn of society, they make society less and less attractive to themselves. Not surprisingly, much of the behavior of these groups represents an explicit or implicit criticism of established custom, belief, and practice. In undertaking the abolishment of their social role, the renouncers of society tend to leave behind their reverence for caste hierarchy, rules of ritual pollution, and other rituals, beliefs, and practices that are aimed at maintaining the stability of society generally. In some cases these groups mock the Brahmins as representatives of refined society and as the ritualists who seek to preserve the welfare of the world. Sacred texts are sometimes mocked as well and the most polluting practices advocated. Perhaps the clearest examples of this tendency are found in certain left-handed Tantric texts and in the central ritual of this movement, the ritual of the five forbidden things, which will be discussed later.

In recent times several figures in Hinduism have protested aspects of their traditional religion. Ram Mohan Roy was particularly critical of many ritual aspects of Hinduism, such as worship of images and the burning of widows (suttee). In an attempt to reform Hinduism he founded the Brahmo Samaj. He saw the essence of Hinduism as the worship of one Supreme Being, and he tried to strip Hinduism of many of its cultural trappings, which he held to be late degradations.

Mahatma Gandhi appreciated traditional Hinduism but was highly critical of certain aspects of the caste system. He was particularly pained by the treatment of the untouchables and tried throughout his life to change Hindu thinking concerning their traditional exclusion from much of Hindu society and religion.

B. R. Ambedkar, an untouchable himself, did not think Gandhi's program of persuasion would ultimately help the untouchables' plight very much; he therefore converted to Buddhism along with thousands of his followers, thus stepping outside the confines of caste Hinduism. All three figures, then, represent a modern unease with certain aspects of traditional Hinduism, primarily as it manifests itself in traditional caste hierarchy.

Despite its loose definition of orthodoxy and orthopraxy, the Hindu tradition has declared certain movements or philosophies heterodox, most notably the Buddhists, Jains, and Charvakas, each of which denies the sanctity of the *Vedas*. On the other hand, Hinduism has shown a remarkable

---

[1]For a discussion of some of these groups, see David N. Lorenzen, *The Kāpālikas and Kālāmukhas, Two Lost Śaivite Sects* (New Delhi: Thomson Press, 1972).

tolerance for movements that, while critical of many cherished views and practices, retain at least an implicit reverence for the *Vedas*. These radical Hindu groups may not actually practice Vedic rituals, or even be inspired by Vedic teachings, but insofar as they do not castigate the *Vedas* the tradition has considered them within the Hindu framework.

EXAMPLES OF DISSENTING MOVEMENTS

The Virashaivas

The Virashaiva movement was founded by Basavanna in the Kannada-speaking area of South India (present-day Mysore State) in the twelfth century. Virashaivas today number over four million and constitute nearly 20 percent of the population of Mysore State. Basavanna (1106–68) was a devotee of the god Shiva; the central religious fact of his life, and of the Virashaiva religion, is passionate devotion to Shiva as the Lord. As devotees of Shiva the Virashaivas are regarded as Hindus by the larger community, and over the centuries, although they came to form a separate caste, they generally have regarded themselves as within the Hindu fold. This is so despite the fact that Basavanna and the Virashaivas generally have been extremely critical of many facets of Hindu belief and practice.

The Virashaivas, inspired by Basavanna and other saints of the movement, represent a clear, articulate protest against the Hindu caste system, with its reverence for Brahmins and its hierarchical social structure. They are suspicious of many cherished Hindu beliefs and customs, deny the doctrines of karma and samsara, and mock the worship of images. Basavanna yearned for, and undoubtedly experienced, an unmediated vision of his Lord, and he held many traditional customs, beliefs, and rituals to be either obstacles to this experience or irrelevant to it. For Basavanna and the Virashaivas, devotion to the Lord is the only true measure of a person's worth. To love the Lord is to realize spiritual fulfillment. To ignore the Lord, to worship other deities, to put one's hope in rituals or formulas, even to put one's hope in good works, is to fail in the religious quest. In this emphasis upon passionate devotion, the Virashaivas are typical of many other devotional movements in Hinduism. However, the Virashaivas represent the most radical expression of the antiestablishment tendencies of these movements.

In their rejection of the caste system the Virashaivas allowed and even encouraged intercaste marriages. As the mixing of castes is particularly offensive to traditional Hindus, this practice sometimes resulted in persecution of the Virashaivas. The Virashaiva lack of respect for the caste system and for some aspects of traditional Brahmin religion is seen in many of Basavanna's poems. In the following poems he criticizes two features of

Brahmin traditional religion: the sacrifice of animals and the reverence for fire (Agni):

> *The sacrificial lamb brought for the festival*
> *ate up the green leaf brought for the decorations.*
>
> *Not knowing a thing about the kill,*
> *it wants only to fill its belly:*
> *born that day, to die that day.*
>
> *But tell me:*
> > *did the killers survive,*
> > *O lord of the meeting rivers?*[2]

> > *In a brahmin house*
> > *where they feed the fire*
> > *as a god*
> >
> > *when the fire goes wild*
> > *and burns the house*
> >
> > *they splash on it*
> > *the water of the gutter*
> > *and the dust of the street,*
> >
> > *beat their breasts*
> > *and call the crowd.*
> >
> > *These men then forget their worship*
> > *and scold their fire*
> > *O lord of the meeting rivers.*[3]

Another favorite target for Basavanna's scorn is the Hindu practice of worshiping images.

> > *How can I feel right*
> > > *about a god who eats up lacquer and melts,*
> > > *who wilts when he sees fire?*
> >
> > *How can I feel right*
> > > *about gods you sell in your need,*
> > > *and gods you bury for fear of thieves?*
> >
> > *The lord of the meeting rivers*
> > *self-born, one with himself,*
> >
> > *he alone is the true god.*[4]

Basavanna extended his critique of Hinduism to many popular practices, such as pilgrimage, astrology, and reverence for many objects. God

---

[2]A. K. Ramanujan, trans., *Speaking of Śiva* (Baltimore, Md.: Penguin Books, 1973), p. 76; reprinted by permission of Penguin Books Ltd. The epithet "lord of the meeting rivers" refers to Shiva, who dwells in a temple at the confluence of two rivers.

[3]Ibid., p. 85; reprinted by permission of Penguin Books Ltd.

[4]Ibid., p. 84; reprinted by permission of Penguin Books Ltd.

was everywhere for Basavanna, and to worship particular objects or to suppose one place was more sacred than another when the whole world was pervaded by Shiva was absurd.

> *They plunge*
> *whenever they see water.*
>
> *They circumambulate*
> *every tree they see.*
>
> *How can they know you*
> *O Lord*
> *who adore*
> *waters that run dry*
> *and trees that wither?*[5]

> *The pot is a god. The winnowing*
> *fan is a god. The stone in the*
> *street is a god. The comb is a*
> *god. The bowstring is also a*
> *god. The bushel is a god and the*
> *spouted cup is a god.*
>
> *Gods, gods, there are so many*
> *there's no place left*
> *for a foot.*
>
> *There is only*
> *one god. He is our Lord*
> *of the Meeting Rivers.*[6]

For the Virashaivas, devotion to Shiva was an end in itself, totally absorbing and imbued with its own intrinsic rewards. Allama Prabhu, a contemporary of Basavanna, even mocked good works as the basis for the religious life and declared in the following poem that the true devotee loves the Lord for his own sake and not out of desire for some heavenly reward.

> *Feed the poor*
> *tell the truth*
> *make water-places*
> *for the thirsty*
> *and build tanks for a town—*
> *you may then go to heaven*
> *after death, but you'll get nowhere*
> *near the truth of Our Lord.*
>
> *And the man who knows Our Lord,*
> *he gets no results.*[7]

---

[5]Ibid., p. 85; reprinted by permission of Penguin Books Ltd.
[6]Ibid., p. 84; reprinted by permission of Penguin Books Ltd.
[7]Ibid., p. 167; reprinted by permission of Penguin Books Ltd.

The Virashaiva saint Mahadeviyakka, also a contemporary of Basa-vanna, illustrates another theme of the radical bhakti cults. Her passionate love for God, often expressed in sexual terms, led to conflicts between her spiritual inclinations and the demands of the world. In Mahadeviyakka's case this tension is expressed in terms of the impossibility of serving two husbands, her earthly husband and her true husband, Shiva. In the follow-ing poem she speaks of cuckolding her earthly husband to be with Shiva.

> *I have Māyā for mother-in-law;*
> *the world for father-in-law;*
> *three brothers-in-law, like tigers;*
>
> *and the husband's thoughts*
> *are full of laughing women:*
> *   no god, this man.*
>
> *And I cannot cross the sister-in-law.*
>
> *But I will*
> *give this wench the slip*
> *and go cuckold my husband with Hara, my Lord.*
>
> *My mind is my maid:*
> *by her kindness, I join*
> *my Lord,*
> *   my utterly beautiful Lord*
> *   from the mountain-peaks,*
> *   my lord white as jasmine,*
> *and I will make Him*
> *my good husband.*[8]

Finally, the theme of making one's whole life an offering to the Lord by leading a life of devotion is often emphasized in Virashaiva poems and is contrasted with elaborate ritual, costly ceremonies, and lavish, material offerings to the gods. Many Virashaivas were from low castes, many were poor, and many were illiterate. For Basavanna this did not matter. Pure devotion, not splendid temples or costly rituals, was the path to knowing the Lord. The only offering to Shiva of any consequence was the offering of one's self. The theme is beautifully expressed in this poem.

> *The rich*
> *will make temples for Śiva.*
> *What shall I,*
> *a poor man,*
> *do?*
>
> *My legs are pillars,*
> *the body the shrine,*
> *the head a cupola*
> *of gold.*

[8]Ibid., p. 141; reprinted by permission of Penguin Books Ltd.

Listen, O lord of the meeting rivers,
things standing shall fall,
but the moving ever shall stay.[9]

Left-Handed Tantrism

Many Tantric rituals, texts, and practices reflect traditional Hindu themes. Sometimes the term *tantra* is used simply to refer to non-Vedic or post-Vedic rituals, and in this respect Tantrism expresses commonly accepted Hindu belief and practice. Such important Tantric themes as the use of mantras (mystic formulas) and yantras (mystic diagrams), the importance of a guru, the quest for liberation from karma and samsara, and the use of yogic techniques demonstrate that Tantrism is thoroughly Hindu and does not represent a rejection of Hinduism.

Within the Tantric tradition itself, however, a division is made between the right-handed and the left-handed paths, and in texts and rituals appropriate to the latter we find an implicit (sometimes explicit) criticism of certain Hindu ideas. The explanation of the left-handed critique of established Hinduism is probably threefold. First, it has been argued that Tantrism arose among village practitioners who were unlearned and probably from low castes. The ungrammatical Sanskrit of many Tantric texts and the sustained criticism of left-handed Tantrism by the Hindu establishment seem to support this view. Many Tantric adepts probably did not know, or were not permitted to perform, Brahminic rituals and probably had little respect for them. It is likely that the left-handed Tantric disregard for certain Hindu practices reflects an anti-Brahmin attitude.

Second, the emphasis in Tantrism generally is pragmatic and aims at the adept's direct realization of enlightenment by means of rituals. The quest generally is undertaken alone or with the help of a guru in an isolated location, and thus life in society generally is irrelevant to the success of the undertaking, at least in the left-handed path. In this respect left-handed Tantra shares with Hindu ascetic movements a certain disregard for social virtues and norms.

Third, the left-handed texts typically rank people according to spiritual accomplishment and describe the behavior appropriate to the various ranks. In the lowest ranks conformity to society and its customs is prescribed. In the highest rank, however, conformity to social norms is a matter of indifference. Adepts who have achieved this stage recognize the underlying unity of all reality and disregard the artificial distinctions made by the unenlightened. They treat dung and gold alike. They do not observe distinctions of caste. They have seen through the relativity of good and bad, clean and unclean, sacred and profane, and as such are no respecters of traditional practices and beliefs.

[9]Ibid., p. 88; reprinted by permission of Penguin Books Ltd.

The *Mahanirvana Tantra*, assuming the universality of Brahman and the underlying sanctity of all things, several times teaches the uselessness of traditional practices, such as pilgrimage, funeral ceremonies for ancestors, and worship of the Hindu gods.[10] As Brahman cannot be polluted, the text says, adepts may eat anything they wish, at any time and in the company of any person, regardless of caste. The text also makes a point of saying that a Brahmin who is not versed in proper Tantric doctrine is lower than the lowest caste person but that a Chandala, a very low-caste Hindu, who knows and practices proper Tantric doctrine surpasses a Brahmin.

Implicit in these passages is a critique of ascribed religious status and of the logic underlying popular Hinduism, according to which one gains merit by performing traditional practices, such as Vedic rituals and pilgrimages.

Other Tantric texts are more explicit in their negative attitude toward establishment religion or society's values, and some passages from left-handed Tantric texts seem to take delight in shocking the reader by describing particularly forbidden scenes as religiously desirable. In the *Kalivilasa Tantra*, for example, we read, "Having drunk and drunk again, having fallen to the ground, rising and drinking again man is liberated."[11] The *Kaulavali Nirnaya Tantra* describes the Tantric adept in his ritual setting as follows:

> On the left is the woman skilled in the art of dalliance and on the right, the drinking cup, in the front is hog's flesh cooked hot with chillies [Hindus consider hog's flesh particularly polluting]. On the shoulder is the well-tuned vina [a stringed instrument] with its melodious music. Kuladharma [Tantric practices] which contains the teachings of the great Guru [Shiva] is deep in meaning and difficult of attainment even by Yogis.[12]

In a commentary on the *Mahanirvana Tantra* we read, "Inserting his organ into the mother's womb, pressing his sister's breasts, placing his foot upon his *guru*'s head, he will be reborn no more."[13]

Tantric texts make use of a kind of code language in which terms may have multiple meanings, and it is possible, even likely, that passages of this sort have a meaning different from the literal one. Nevertheless, that such passages were, and are, considered outrageous by traditional Hindus is obvious, and that such passages go hand in hand with an antinomian tendency in left-handed Tantrism is also clear.

[10]Arthur Avalon, trans., *Tantra of the Great Liberation (Mahānirvāna Tantra)* (New York: Dover Publications, 1972), pp. 36, 51, 53, 56.

[11]Arthur Avalon, ed., *Tantrik Texts*, Vol. VI: *Kālivilāsa Tantra*, ed. Pārvatī Charana Tarkatīrtha (London: Luzac & Co., 1917), p. 6.

[12]Arthur Avalon, ed., *Tantrik Texts*, Vol. XIV: *Kaulāvalinirnaya Tantra* (Calcutta: Agamanusandhāna Samiti, Sanskrit Press Depository, 1928), p. 23.

[13]Quoted in Agehananda Bharati, *The Tantric Tradition* (London: Rider & Co., 1965), p. 171.

The central ritual act in left-handed Tantra is that of the five forbidden things, the *pancha tattva* ritual. In the eyes of traditional Hinduism this ritual is highly offensive, as it involves partaking of particularly polluting things: wine, fish, parched grain (probably a drug of some kind), meat, and illicit sexual intercourse. In the eyes of many Hindus this ritual is seen as an excuse for libertinism under the guise of religion and has been the subject of scorn and satire. In the tenth-century drama *Karpuramanjari*, by Rajashekhara, for example, a Tantric adept is made to say in a slightly drunken voice,

> *As for black-book and spell—they may all go to hell!*
> *My teacher's excused me from practice and trance.*
> *With drink and with women we fare mightly well,*
> *As on—to salvation—we merrily dance!*
>
> *A fiery young wench to the altar I've led.*
> *Good meat I consume, and I guzzle strong drink;*
> *And it all comes as alms,—with a pelt for me bed.*
> *What better religion could anyone think?*
>
> *Gods Vishnu and Brahm and the others may preach*
> *Of salvation by trance, holy rites, and the Vedies.*
> *'Twas Uma's fond lover [Shiva] alone that could teach*
> *Us salvation plus brandy plus fun with the ladies.*[14]

According to the logic of left-handed Tantrism, however, this ritual makes sense; although some may have exploited it as a means to carnal indulgence, Tantric texts are clear that the ritual is not intended as such and that undertaking it properly is extremely difficult. The rationale for the ritual is based on the idea that everything in the world is pervaded by Brahman and that until this underlying unity is perceived by adepts they will remain bound by ignorance. The *pancha tattva* ritual is a dramatic, radical attempt to shock adepts into realizing this truth. By ritually partaking of five forbidden things, by affirming their underlying sanctity, they dissolve all their notions, prejudices, and habits concerning what is holy and what is profane, what is polluting and what is not, and so on. They break a host of artificial, contrived barriers that cause them to perceive the world as fragmented and compartmentalized. In the language of the left-handed texts the adepts save themselves by means of those things that cause the downfall of others. Thus they are considered heroes, and the texts are clear that only those of heroic nature should undertake this ritual, as it is highly dangerous to all others.

The left-handed Tantra, then, represents a clear critique of those aspects of Hinduism that emphasize conformity to social norms and custom

---

[14]I. 22–24; quoted in Ernest Payne, *The Śāktas* (London: Oxford University Press, 1933), p. 30.

as spiritually meritorious. For the left-handed Tantrics the ultimate truth concerning the sanctity of all things makes a mockery of a religion based on a world divided into sacred and profane, pure and polluting, high and low. Ultimately the adepts realize that, as they themselves are Brahman, or identical with the underlying reality of the world, nothing may pollute or degrade them.

4

Hinduism and the Arts

INTRODUCTION: ART AS REVELATION

Indian culture is so saturated by Hinduism (and other native Indian religions) that nearly all Indian art may be considered religious in one way or
another. Nearly every work of art in traditional India, and to a great extent
even today, deals with an explicitly religious theme. From the refined art
of royal courts to the rustic work of the folk traditions, religious images and
motifs dominate the landscape. From the grandest South Indian temple to
the crudest, earthen image of a local village goddess, art in India has always
tended to express religious themes.

Furthermore, the creation of art in traditional India was seen as a
religious endeavor. In texts on sculpture, architecture, painting, poetry,
drama, and music, art is said to involve spiritual techniques or rituals on
the part of the artist. It is therefore no exaggeration to say that until very
recently religion and art were hardly distinguishable from one another in
India. The arts almost always expressed religious themes, and the artistic
process itself was understood to involve a kind of yogic discipline that enabled the artists to perceive directly the divine images or events they sought
to depict.

Indian art is as rich and complex as the religions it expresses, so it is
difficult to summarize neatly what it teaches us about Hinduism. Nevertheless, a few general observations may be made about how the Indian artistic
tradition reveals central Hindu ideas.

According to Hindu aesthetic theory a central aim of art is embellish-ment. The aim of art, and of the artist, is not to imitate or accurately depict nature but to depict nature as it should be, as it might exist ideally. Indian aesthetic texts describe in elaborate detail the ideal ways of depicting var-ious aspects of nature, and deviation from these norms is considered poor art. For Hindu artists the task is to render a subject in its paradigmatic form, its idealized form, which is without imperfections and without par-ticularity. In this sense, Hindu art is not realistic but idealistic and puts a premium on the ability of artists to perceive and then express in their art highly elaborated, embellished versions of idealized subjects.

Underlying this emphasis upon embellishment is the Hindu insis-tence upon *loka-samgraha*, maintaining the world, as a crucial dimension in the spiritual quest. In a variety of ways, the Hindu tradition states that hu-man destiny is to refine and perfect oneself and one's world, to make the world habitable and civilized. There is nothing desirable about unrefined nature, either in its human or nonhuman aspects. Insofar as possible, peo-ple are destined to create and maintain a world that is as sophisticated and refined as possible and that in many respects finds its fullest expression in divine or mythic models. The function of much of Hindu art is to express a world that has been perfected by civilized people or a world that faithfully reflects a divine model.

Perhaps the clearest example of this tendency is found in classical Sanskrit poetry. Although beauty and perfection were measured in a variety of ways in Sanskrit poetry, one criterion for high quality was elaboration. The poetry avoids brief, direct, matter-of-fact statements and often makes use of obscure words and subtle and sophisticated allusions. It is immedi-ately apparent to anyone reading such poetry that it evokes an extremely rarified atmosphere. Certain unrefined aspects of nature, such as jungles and mountains, may be the subject of a poem, but their description invar-iably will be accomplished in the most elaborate and embellished way. In both content and style Sanskrit poetry strives to transcend the ordinary limitations of the world by describing ideal types in highly perfected lan-guage.

Another example of Indian art as an expression of the aim to perfect nature is found in temple architecture. In many cultures, the circle is looked upon as an image of wholeness. It is seen as a natural shape, having no sharp or artificial lines to it, and as such is a symbol of unrefined nature. Hindu architecture rejects the circle as a model precisely because of its naturalness, and the square is taken as the fundamental form from which all else must proceed. The square, that is, conveys an elaboration of the natural, a refinement of it, an ordering and perfection of space. Because the Hindu temple, at least in part, seeks to be an embodiment in miniature of a perfect, divine world, the square is regarded as basic to its overall form. A temple when completed may have sweeping curvilinear lines and a fluid grace, but it will be based on a square or rectangle that has been imposed on or carved out of unrefined, raw space. Temple architecture strives to imitate the supernatural, not the natural. "The square is the essential and perfect form of Indian architecture. . . . The circle and curve belong to life in its growth and movement. The square is the mark of order, of finality to the expanding life, its form; and of perfection beyond life and death."[1]

Another characteristic of Hindu art is the centrality of epic and myth. The deeds of the heroes in the *Ramayana* and *Mahabharata* and the activities of the gods and goddesses in the mythological texts dominate sculpture, poetry, drama, dancing, and painting to such an extent that it is difficult to make sense of Hindu art without considerable knowledge of these all-important narratives. For hundreds of years these legends and stories have provided an inexhaustible treasury from which Hindu artists have drawn, and to this day these heroic and divine deeds are featured prominently in such modern media as films and comic books.

A study of the ways in which these heroes and their exploits are depicted in Indian art can be informative concerning important emphases in the Hindu vision of reality. Although the written stories and myths themselves are often revealing, an effective rendering of the same event in sculpture or painting can convey an eloquent, wordless instruction. The way in which an artist renders the great dancing Shiva may tell as much not only about this particular god but also about the Hindu vision of the cosmic processes and human destiny within that cosmos. Hindu art, that is, can emphasize central truths to an observer immediately and dramatically.

One of the most popular subjects is the creation of the world by the god Vishnu while he lies sleeping on his serpent couch in the primordial waters. The texts on which the art is based depict the mythological period just prior to the creation of the world or the moment of the creation itself. In many texts creation takes place when a cosmic lotus emerges from Vishnu's navel. When the lotus blossoms, the god Brahma appears from inside the lotus and carries on the creative process by fashioning a multitude of worlds, of which our world is simply one. The creation of the worlds by Vishnu and his agent Brahma, furthermore, is an endless and cyclical process. Periodically and regularly Vishnu destroys the worlds by inhaling them back into himself and renourishing them. In this context of periodic and endless creation and destruction of universes, our world is an insignificant speck among countless other specks that are effortlessly and spontaneously created and destroyed by Vishnu. Within this mind-boggling cosmic process, the eternal dance of bubbling universes, human destiny begins to be understood as complete liberation from the great wheel of time. That is, our physical world is shown to be insignificant, an ephemeral bubble in the eternal rhythms of the divine.

[1]Stella Kramrisch, *The Hindu Temple*, vol. I (Delhi: Motilal Banarsidass, 1976), p. 22.

Artwork of this scene conveys beautifully and economically the idea that this earth, which we often think of as so solid and eternal, is ultimately only the fleeting dream of a great god. In most renditions Vishnu is massive. His eyes are closed, and he is relaxed and serene. He represents the monumental substance of uncircumscribed space and time compared to which this world of ours is infinitely small and transient. The scene conveys to us immediately the truth affirmed in the Hindu moksha tradition that the world is not special. It is the spontaneous, incidental (perhaps even accidental) creation of Vishnu, his dream, as it were, from which our final spiritual destiny is to wake up.

As in other religious traditions, art in Hinduism presents an ongoing, often vivid and dramatic, presentation of and commentary on central religious truths. The overall effect of Hindu art, then, is to convey in the economy of an image, gesture, or poetic phrase the often subtle, complex, and sublime truths of Hindu visionaries through the ages.

Another important function of Hindu art is concretization of divine models, the presentation in tangible form of ideal worlds to which Hindus strive to journey. Hindu art tries to present heaven on earth or to create a temporary atmosphere, as in drama, in which the connoisseur may be transported beyond the limitations of the finite world and mortal existence. Although this tendency appears in temple architecture, images of the divine, and other aspects of Hindu art, it is perhaps clearest in Hindu dance-drama and poetics and in the aesthetic texts that provide the theoretical basis of these arts.

In Hindu dance-drama the aim of the actors is to imitate perfectly gestures that are described in the *Natya Shastra*, a book on dance that traditionally is held to have been revealed by the god Brahma. Each gesture described in this book is believed to be patterned on the gestures of the gods. Each emotional mood is to be expressed with the appropriate eye movement, finger gestures, posture of the body, and so on. To accompany these outer gestures the dancer-actors also are instructed to identify themselves mentally and emotionally with the characters they are portraying, usually divine or legendary beings. The actors' aim, then, is to become the characters they are imitating as fully as possible and thus to present these characters directly to the audience in visible form. In their endeavor to do this the actors strive to achieve the state of the "other mind," in which they transcend their own individuality and particularity and become the eternal models they seek to portray.

The physical and mental discipline of the actor-dancer is rigorous and is perfected only after years of study under a master. Insofar as the final aim of these practitioners is to identify fully with the models they portray on stage, their discipline is sometimes compared to the spiritual exercises of yoga.

Acting, in the true sense of the term as understood in India, is not mere im-personation, however clever or illusionistic the effect. The actor is compared to a *yogī*, meaning thereby that he is one who treads the path of *yoga* (union) or mental concentration, whereby the subject and the object, the worshipper and the worshipped, the actor and the acted become one.[2]

The rigorous mental discipline needed to identify fully with the object to be expressed in art is also central in the fashioning of images. The artists, like the actors, are instructed to meditate upon the descriptions of the deity contained in texts and manuals until they have fully and directly perceived the deity in their minds. Then they are to depict faithfully this mental im-age in their art.

The artistic creation, particularly in dance-drama, aims at enabling the connoisseur, or the audience generally, to experience *rasa*, which is a kind of aesthetic, transpersonal bliss. The dance-drama, effectively per-formed, seeks to transport the audience out of this world and into an ideal-ized, divine world. Although the aesthetic experience is only temporary, thus differing from ultimate spiritual emancipation, it is often compared to the spiritual experience of the mystic.

> This blissful condition reproduced in the reader [or audience] by the ideal-ised creation of poetry [or dance-drama] is given as almost equivalent to the philosophical *ānanda* [divine bliss]. In explaining that it affords escape from the natural world by replacing it with an imaginative world, Sanskrit theorists rightly emphasize, that, even from the reader's [or audience's] point of view, the function of art is that of the deliverer.[3]

To the extent that Hindu art seeks to express divinity or to enable the one who appreciates it to transcend human limitations, we can say that Hindu art aims at revelation. The artist, ideally, seeks first to identify fully with the divine image, character, or scene to be depicted and then to re-produce it so faithfully that the one who perceives it is enabled to glimpse the divine. In this way Hindu art seeks to re-create heaven on earth by making the divine immediately perceptible.

ILLUSTRATIONS OF HINDU ART

Two Hindu Temples

Hindu temple architecture illustrates clearly the theme in Hindu art of imitating divine models. Hindu books on architecture assume as funda-mental that all temples must be founded upon a complex pattern of squares

---

[2]K. Bharatha Iyer, *Kathakali: The Sacred Dance-Drama of Malabar* (London: Luzac & Co., 1955), p. 26.

[3]Sushil Kumar De, *Sanskrit Poetics as a Study of Aesthetic* (Berkeley: University of California Press, 1963), p. 69.

that represents the spatial distribution of the gods of the Hindu pantheon. The ground plan of the temple therefore reflects the eternal order of divine space. The temple structure also may aim at imitating the divine palace or the favorite dwelling place of the particular god enshrined, for example, Shiva's dwelling place on Mount Kailasa in the Himalayas. The Hindu temple is the earthly dwelling place of a deity and is supposed to conform, even if only in a stylized way, to the deity's heavenly abode.

Some temples also emphasize the human form, a microcosm of the larger cosmic order, as a model for architecture. Throughout the Hindu tradition, humans are believed to consist of sheaths or layers. The outer sheaths are physical, and the inmost essence is spiritual, indeed the Atman itself, which is identical with Brahman. When a Hindu temple is patterned on this model, the outer courts, arranged concentrically around the center, represent the outer, physical sheaths of the human being, whereas the innermost sanctum of the temple, which houses the image or symbol of the god, is identified with the Atman. In a variety of ways, then, the Hindu temple marks off a sacred space and within that space seeks to express divine order. As examples of these tendencies it is helpful to look at two quite different temples: the Kandariya Mahadeva temple, dedicated to Shiva, as representative of North Indian architecture; and the Shri Ranganatha temple, dedicated to Vishnu, as representative of South Indian temple style.

FIGURE 4-1   The Kandariya temple. (Courtesy of Air India.)

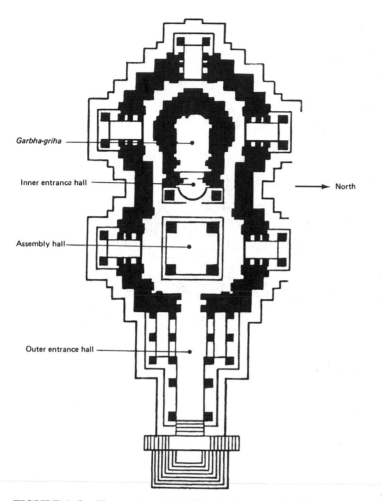

Garbha-griha

Inner entrance hall

North

Assembly hall

Outer entrance hall

FIGURE 4–2   Floor plan of the Kandariya temple. (From Eliky Zannas and Jeannine Auboyer, *Khajuraho* ['s-Gravenhage, The Netherlands: Mouton & Co., 1960].)

   The Kandariya temple is one of about eighty temples at Khajuraho, located in central India in the State of Madhya Pradesh. Along with most other temples at this site, the Kandariya temple to Shiva was built under the auspices of the Chandella kings sometime in the eleventh century C.E. In overall plan and in many specific details this temple is a beautiful example of North Indian temple architecture and may be taken as representative of most North Indian temples in its religious symbolism.

   The Kandariya temple consists of the following basic elements: the inmost sanctuary, the *garbha-griha*, or "womb room," which contains the symbol of Shiva in the form of a lingam, a stylized phallus; a soaring tower rising above the enclosed sanctuary, called a *shikhara*; an entrance hall ad-

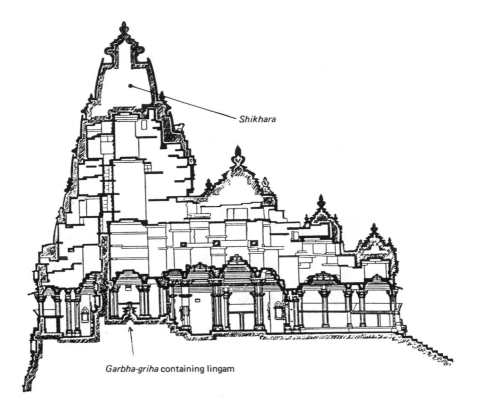

Shikhara

Garbha-griha containing lingam

FIGURE 4–3 Cross section of the Kandariya temple at Khajuraho. (From Eliky Zannas and Jeannine Auboyer, *Khajuraho* ['s-Gravenhage, The Netherlands: Mouton & Co., 1960].)

joining the *garbha-griha* in which the officiating priest prepares the necessary articles for worship of the image; an assembly hall where devotees and pilgrims gather to watch the worship or have a view of the image inside; and an outer entrance hall. Viewed from outside the temple, the roofs of the three halls rise in ascending heights toward the *shikhara*. The temple rests on a raised foundation that is large enough to accommodate a walkway around the temple on which devotees may circumambulate the entire structure. The temple faces east and is entered from that direction by means of a wide staircase. Both inside and out the temple is adorned with statues, many of them deities, which are among the most beautiful examples of Indian sculpture. Each statue is about two and one-half to three feet in height, and there are over 850 such statues. The entire structure is built of stone.[4]

[4]For a description and discussion of the Kandariya temple and the Khajuraho temple complex as a whole, see Eliky Zannas and Jeannine Auboyer, *Khajuraho* ('s-Gravenhage, The Netherlands: Mouton & Co., 1960).

The success, both artistic and religious, of the Kandariya temple resides in its visual impact upon the observer or devotee. When approaching the temple from any direction, but particularly from the east, one's first impression is of soaring, vertical lines in the form of stepped peaks (the roofs of the three halls), which ascend in carefully modified degrees to draw one's eyes ever upward to the *shikhara* itself, which is composed of subsidiary *shikharas*, all soaring upward toward the topmost peak, which is crowned with an elaborate dome. The fact that the temple proper is built on a high platform and that the devotee must ascend a long flight of steps to approach the temple further emphasizes the structure's heavenward thrust. The viewer's gaze is drawn increasingly upward and is meant to continue upward, beyond the top of the temple, to the transcendent, heavenly abode of Shiva.

In overall design and impact the Kandariya temple is modeled on a cosmic mountain, either on mythical Mount Mandara (which according to Hindu mythological geography stands at the center of the world and connects the cosmic regions—heaven, earth, and the underworlds) or on Shiva's own mountain, Mount Kailasa (which itself is sometimes said to be the *axis mundi*, or center pillar of the world). The soaring temple, then, represents a spiritual axis, intersecting all planes and dimensions of existence, at which the devotee may have access to sacred power. The regularity and refinement of detail and line of the temple, of course, do not remind the viewer of any mountain that he or she has ever seen. But then this is no ordinary mountain but an idealized, embellished mountain, the perfect mountain transcending the imperfections of nature. The idealized mountain both is, and points upward to, a realm of perfection toward which the devotee strives.

The devotee's circumambulation of and entrance into the temple illustrate other aspects of its success artistically and religiously. The vertical thrust of the *shikhara* is increased as the devotee, circumambulating the temple, finds it necessary to look nearly straight up at it. The main *shikhara* is over one hundred feet above the platform, and to see its top one must throw one's head far back and look up at the sky. Circumambulating the temple, one is also preoccupied with the many fine sculptured figures, several representing Shiva alone or with his consort in various attitudes. In several niches, arranged in tiers, most of the Hindu pantheon is depicted, along with attendants: musicians, servants, dancers, and so on.

Many of these images are shown in explicitly erotic poses, and though a variety of interpretations of this eroticism have been suggested, two meanings seem obvious. First, the gods in their paradises are known to dally with their consorts or with heavenly nymphs, and many heavenly abodes are described as pleasure groves. The erotic scenes are suggestive in a physical way of the blissful nature of these abodes. Second, the erotic couples suggest fertility and abundance, the fact that from this cosmic and spiritual center radiate all life, vigor, and energy. This assumption is aptly conveyed in the sexual attraction of males and females.

Entering the temple proper, the devotee is confronted with other figures of divine beings, and as one progresses from the entrance in the east toward the *garbha-griha* and the central image of Shiva under the *shikhara* at the western end of the temple, one has the sensation of going deeper and deeper into the cosmic mountain. The light becomes weaker and weaker, the images become fewer and fewer, until the devotee is confronted by the single image of the god enclosed in a dark room with unadorned walls. *Kandariya*, an epithet of Shiva, means "lord of the cave." The Kandariya Mahadeva temple, then, is the abode of the Great God (Mahadeva) who is Lord of the Cave. At the center of the cosmic mountain, representing the center and the distillation of the universe, in a cave underlying and supporting the mountain, resides Shiva, the essence of reality. Having left the outer world behind, having journeyed into the dark recesses of the temple, the devotee or pilgrim glimpses the god, and in so doing glimpses the essence of himself or herself as well. Deep within the temple the devotee also remembers the soaring *shikhara* directly above the image and is reminded of the god's, and his or her own, transcendent, heavenly, vertical identity, which he or she seeks to experience and behold. The Kandariya temple, so experienced by a devotee, is a dramatic example of art and religion in intricate and pleasing union.

The Shri Ranganatha temple, dedicated to Vishnu and located on an island in the Kaveri River near Madras, is a good example of the South Indian temple architectural tradition and in overall conception and plan has a different impact upon the devotee or the observer. Built, rebuilt, and expanded by various dynasties over the centuries, this vast temple complex is ancient, perhaps going back as far as the fifth century, although temple legend says that it arose from the primordial waters at the very beginning of creation at the center of the world.

The present-day Shri Ranganatha temple covers an area of 156 acres and includes seven rectangular walls (*prakaras*) arranged concentrically to enclose the central temple that houses the *garbha-griha* with its image of Vishnu. The main entrance faces south (there being gates in each southern wall), and each gate (there being more than one gate in each encircling wall) is flanked by and covered with soaring *gopuras*, pyramidal structures adorned with images of deities. Outside the western gate there is a large lotus tank, where the image of the god is taken on certain ceremonial occasions. Inside the corridors formed by the encircling *prakaras* there is a veritable city, which includes offices of the temple establishment, many subsidiary temples and shrines, and shops that cater to the needs of the large temple community and to pilgrims and devotees. The precincts of the temple proper and the surrounding island consist of an independent munici-

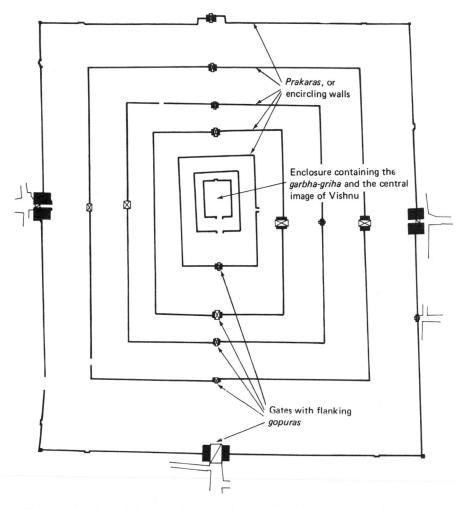

Prakaras, or
encircling walls

Enclosure containing the
garbha-griha and the central
image of Vishnu

Gates with flanking
gopuras

FIGURE 4–4 Plan of the Shri Ranganatha temple with its seven enclosures. (From Jeannine Auboyer, *Srī Ranganāthaswāmi: A Temple of Vishnu in Srīrangam* [Paris: SHC/ WS/129, 1969]. Diagram reproduced by permission of UNESCO.)

pality that in the 1961 census numbered 42,000 people, almost all of them directly connected with the temple in some way.[5]

Approaching the temple from a distance one is impressed first by the cluster of tall *gopuras* and the immense façade of the outermost encircling wall. The central temple cannot be seen from outside. Its size and height

[5]For a detailed description of the Ranganatha temple, see Jeannine Auboyer, *Srī Ranganāthaswāmi: A Temple of Vishnu in Srīrangam* (Paris: SHC/WS/129, 1969).

are diminutive compared to the immense *gopuras* towering over the gateways. To glimpse the central temple it is necessary to thread one's way through the encircling enclosures or climb to the roof of one of the inner enclosures. This is no accident. Unlike the Kandariya temple at Khajuraho, the Shri Ranganatha temple is meant to be glimpsed only after one has passed through the labyrinth of alleyways leading to the main shrine. The central shrine, the center of the world and of reality, Vishnu himself, is to be found only by those who specially and specifically seek him out. The inner courtyards are open only to Hindus, off-limits to the merely curious, and the experience of the devotee is one of descent rather than the ascent of the Kandariya temple.

The seven concentric enclosing walls represent the sheaths of a human being. The outermost wall represents the merely physical, transient sheath. The innermost wall, housing Vishnu himself, represents the human's eternal, unchanging soul, the Atman. Progressing ever inward, ever more deeply inside one's nature—ever downward, as it were—the devotee penetrates the various enclosures, each marked with its guardian deities, finally reaching the source, the naval of the earth, the center of existence, Lord Vishnu himself, with whom the devotee is essentially identified, from whom the devotee has emerged, and with whom he or she seeks ultimate union. The outer courts are open to all and reflect the hubbub of the world. Tourist shops, bustling throngs of people distracted with worldly concerns, and a generally busy atmosphere suggest that one is still within the normal, everyday world. As one enters more deeply into the temple complex, fewer and fewer such distractions are in evidence. The innermost court, almost entirely covered by a roof, is dimly lit and gives the impression of being far from the bustle of the distracting world. In the dim, quiet womb room of the temple, lit only with flickering oil lamps, resides a huge image of Vishnu reclining on the cosmic serpent, Shesha, who floats on the waters of pre-creation. The image is blackened and polished and gleams from the annual anointments of special oil. Above the central shrine rises a low, domed roof completely covered with gold leaf. In the presence of the deity, within the dark heart of the huge temple complex, the devotee has the feeling that he or she has penetrated to the center of the earth, the vital, fecund midpoint from which all began and from which all vigor and universes emanate in the form of the sleeping god's creative, ceaseless dreams.

The Kandariya temple to Shiva and the Ranganatha temple to Vishnu, then, seek to create similar religious experiences in the devotee: the discovery and direct experience of the divine in its transcendent form. Both temples draw the devotee out of the normal world and into the divine world. They do so in different ways, however. The cosmic mountain of the Kandariya temple does so by means of a vertical, heavenward thrust. The Ranganatha temple does so by drawing one deep within its maze of enclosures to the navel-like center of things.

Kangra Paintings of Radha and Krishna

In the Hindu devotional tradition the god Krishna is one of the most beloved and popular throughout India. The devotional tradition shows particular partiality to Krishna's youth, when he lived in the humble town of Vraja and loved the women of the village in the nearby groves of Vrindavana. It is as a beautiful, youthful lover that Lord Krishna is most widely worshiped by his devotees. The stories of Krishna's love for the cowherd women of Vraja appear as early as the fifth century, the most popular account being found in the tenth-century *Bhagavata Purana*, which probably was written in South India. Radha, Krishna's favorite among the cowherd women, appears in a few scattered references before the twelfth century, but it is in Jayadeva's beautiful Sanskrit poem, the *Gita Govinda*, that she assumes a position of preeminence in Krishna mythology. Jayadeva, a native of Bengal, devoted his entire poem to Radha's love for Krishna, and in the course of the poem he explores the nuances of the various aspects of the relationship. By the fifteenth century Radha had become firmly established as Krishna's favorite and in Krishna devotional movements had become the model of the ideal devotee, especially in Bengal among the followers of Chaitanya.

Although Jayadeva's poem is a beautiful work of art and devotion in itself, it was adorned in the eighteenth century by Manaku,[6] an artist of the Kangra school of painting in Northwest India. Manaku, under royal patronage, illustrated a copy of Jayadeva's poem with a series of paintings of Radha and Krishna that are among the finest in the Indian artistic tradition. The illustrated *Gita Govinda*, dated 1730, is the end product of a long devotional tradition that probably started in South India, gained its most refined poetic expression and famous devotees in Bengal and Orissa in East India, and became most beautifully expressed pictorially in Northwest India.

The State of Kangra in the foothills of the Himalayas in the Punjab was dominated by a series of rulers in the eighteenth century who attracted and patronized painters from many parts of North India. The atmosphere of their paintings is courtly. Many are refined scenes of city life, and much of the local atmosphere of palace life finds its way into the paintings. A central and favorite theme of the rulers and the painters is Radha and Krishna's love, which is depicted against the background of royal life. Although many early descriptions of Krishna and Radha portrayed a rustic setting for their love, the Kangra paintings, with their delicate and refined detail, perfectly capture the grace of Jayadeva's lines and emphasize the

---

[6]Most of Manaku's illustrations and a good portion of the text of the *Gita Govinda* are found in M. S. Randhawa, *Kangra Paintings of the Gita Govinda* (New Delhi: National Museum, 1963).

FIGURE 4–5 Cowherd women (*gopis*) in the groves of Vrindavana. A painting by Manaku illustrating the *Gita Govinda*. (From M. S. Randhawa, *Kangra Paintings of the Gita Govinda* [New Delhi: National Museum, 1963].)

centrality that Krishna and Radha had come to have in the aesthetic tradition of the time as the ideal lovers. Manaku's paintings adorning the *Gita Govinda* express both a warm devotional mood and an appreciation for artistic models of the love relationship found in various aesthetic works. The end result is a captivating rendition of one of Hinduism's central divine visions and another illustration of how art in the Hindu tradition has successfully expressed a transcendent model toward which its devotees yearn.

One of the dominant appeals of Krishna mythology is the ideal environment in which God encounters his devotees, symbolized by the women of Vraja, particularly Radha. The environment is the cowherd village of Vraja and the idyllic bowers of Vrindavana. Vraja is far removed from the concerns of city life, and the groves of the nearby forest of Vrindavana are isolated from the everyday world with its binding social roles and responsibilities. The affair between Radha and Krishna is illicit, as she is a married woman; the environment is outside the world of dharma and thus is both dangerous and exciting. Outside the normal world, in the secret groves of the forest, Radha and Krishna dally in a world of their own, an idealized world where the only rules are suggested by the love relationship itself. There is risk involved in stepping out of ordinary life to meet God, but the treasures to be found in doing so are beautifully described in countless

FIGURE 4–6 Radha and Krishna. A painting by Manaku illustrating the *Gita Govinda*. (From M. S. Randhawa, *Kangra Paintings of the Gita Govinda* [New Delhi: National Museum, 1963].)

Krishna texts that extol the extraordinary beauty and lushness of Vrinda-vana.

Manaku's paintings, most of which are set against the background of Vrindavana, are fitting adornments to Jayadeva's luscious descriptions. The groves in which Radha and Krishna dally are filled with humming bees, love-maddened birds calling to their mates, and entwining creepers, all of which heighten the erotic mood. The vegetation in the paintings is volup-tuous and delicately drawn. Trees, shrubs, and vines are covered with blos-soms. In Vrindavana it is always spring, the ideal season for lovers, and vegetative life exudes vigor and color.[7] In Manaku's paintings the natural setting of Vrindavana reflects and seems to participate in the joyous love of Radha and Krishna.

Another central appeal of Krishna mythology is the approachability of the divine in the form of the youthful Krishna. Although Krishna is ac-knowledged to be the supreme Lord of the universe by his devotees, he is always approachable in Vrindavana. In the woods he beckons his devotees (symbolized by Radha and the other cowherd women) with the irresistible call of his flute, and when they respond to his call he makes love to them,

---

[7]See ibid., Pl. III, p. 78.

FIGURE 4-7 Radha and Krishna. A painting by Manaku illustrating the *Gita Govinda*. (From M. S. Randhawa, *Kangra Paintings of the Gita Govinda* [New Delhi: National Museum, 1963].)

relating to them in the most intimate ways. Radha and Krishna's love affair in the groves of Vrindavana expresses the love of humans for God, and God for them, and emphasizes its sublime, exciting, tender aspects. It is an affair that involves both God and his devotees totally. The approachability of God in the form of the lovely Krishna is beautifully captured in several of Manaku's paintings that show Radha and Krishna embracing tenderly.[8] The two lovers, Radha and Krishna, devotee and God, are shown as equal partners in a warm, intimate relationship.

The Radha-Krishna model of the divine-human relationship reminds Westerners of the Garden of Eden before the Fall when God dwelt with humankind in intimacy. In Hinduism, Vrindavana represents an eternal paradise, the highest heaven for Krishna devotees, whose ultimate goal is to revel with Krishna there in eternal dalliance. In this cult the earthly passions of love are refined, idealized, and endlessly embellished so that they may become the vehicles through which humans transcend their earthly limitations. The poem and the paintings lure one into Krishna's beautiful world and invite the devotee to remain there always as an eternal lover of the Lord.

[8]See ibid., Pls. VII and XVIII.

PART *II*

AN ANALYSIS OF THE
HINDU TRADITION

5

Central Hindu Beliefs

INTRODUCTION

As we have already indicated in a variety of contexts, the central beliefs of the Hindu religious tradition cluster around two concepts, dharma and moksha. These concepts impose different demands upon human destiny. At the heart of the Hindu tradition lies a twofold, and to some extent paradoxical, assertion: To fulfill one's human destiny (1) it is necessary to uphold, preserve, perpetuate, and refine the physical world generally, and human society specifically (dharma); and (2) it is necessary to find ultimate release from the world (moksha), which is often accomplished by renouncing society.

In a variety of ways and formulas the Hindu tradition has sought to harmonize these two demands or to show how the two are somehow essentially related. But the distinctiveness of Hinduism lies not so much in these formulas as in the awareness of generations of Hindus that the two demands, dharma and moksha, imbue human existence with a lively tension. Over the centuries, the Hindu tradition has been able to affirm with uncompromising force the truth that a human being is both a social animal governed by physical needs who must live with other humans and a uniquely spiritual and solitary animal who at some point yearns to transcend all physical and social limitations. The dharma tradition emphasizes the former aspect of being human, and the moksha tradition emphasizes the latter.

Karma and Samsara

The tension between dharma and moksha in Hinduism is played out against the background of two important concepts: karma and samsara. Karma is the moral law of cause and effect, according to which one reaps what one sows. Samsara refers to the idea of rebirth, or the endless round of births, according to which one is reborn over and over. Taken together, these two concepts create a mood or ambience that is characteristic of Hindu spirituality.

The term *karma* literally means "works" or "deeds" and in the earliest Hindu scriptures usually refers to ritual actions. However, the concept of karma as it has existed for centuries in Hinduism concerns the idea that all actions, particularly moral actions, have predictable effects. In the most general sense, the idea of karma teaches that each person is ultimately responsible for every action he or she performs. Every action has its moral consequences. According to the idea of karma, the present condition, character, and peculiar circumstances of a person are the result of his or her past deeds. A person is what he or she has done. One shapes one's present condition according to all of one's previous thoughts, actions, inclinations, and emotions. In a very specific sense, the idea of karma teaches that each wrinkle in the skin, every idiosyncrasy of one's character, and each facet of one's social and psychic makeup has been determined by past actions. Similarly, every action one performs in the present will influence the nature of who one will be in the future.

Samsara is the idea that one's present life is only the most recent in a long chain of lives extending far into the past. In the past, according to this idea, each individual has lived countless lives, all of which have some bearing on one's present life. One's cosmic biography may include not only many lives in human form (both male and female) but also lives in nonhuman form. There are many stories in Hindu literature of individuals being punished for sins by being reborn as lowly animals, while other stories tell of individuals reaping rewards for extraordinary merit by being reborn as heavenly beings or minor deities. According to the idea of samsara, then, each individual existence is only a brief scene in a long drama that spans hundreds, or perhaps thousands, of lives and includes human as well as nonhuman existences.

In Hindu thought the different species of existence (plant, animal, human, demonic, and divine), just like the different human castes, are ranked in hierarchical order. Both the species to which a being belongs and the caste to which a human belongs are indicators of where one is in the spiritual hierarchy. The circumstances into which one is born, the species or the caste, are determined by one's previous lives and all the karma that has accrued over one's long career. That is, the particular life form into which one is born is determined by one's past karma. Each being has determined its place in the cosmic scheme of existence according to its past actions. One's present spiritual predilection or potential (*adhikara*) is not something that is based on chance or fate; it is something one has earned in terms of one's past lives. The Brahmin, who is considered the most spiritually inclined and mature human, has acquired this caste because of all his or her past actions in former lives. A person born into a low or marginal caste, similarly, is believed to have earned this birth through his or her actions in past lives.

In the context of Hindu religion, karma and samsara, taken together, provide a particularly effective rationale for both the apparent inequalities of the caste system and the apparent moral anomalies in individual lives. The Brahmin's privileged status or a low-caste person's harsh life is understood to be the result not of chance but of actions in past lives. And what may appear to be the undeserved suffering of a righteous person may be explained as the result of karma in a previous life. One's present life, and the stresses, strains, and joys accompanying it, are understood to be the "fall out" of one's past actions, both in this life and in former lives. The workings of karma are understood to be completely just, and as such one's individual place in society is entirely appropriate to one's spiritual potential. Because this is so, one should not strive to perform the dharma of another caste but should remain content to perform the dharma of one's own caste, lowly though it may be.

While the concepts of karma and samsara are considered entirely just and fair, and while they may appear attractive in terms of explaining what might be seen as undeserved suffering or unmerited blessing by setting the individual in a broader context of countless earlier lives, the general attitude toward karma and samsara from within the moksha stream of the Hindu tradition is negative. That is, from the point of view of one who seeks moksha, karma and samsara bind one to a limited, ignorance-dominated, ego-centered existence. *Moksha*, literally "release," means, in most contexts, release from karma and samsara. Moksha implies the transcendence of embodied individual existence, the end of rebirth.

From the perspective of dharma, then, karma and samsara are important ideas that underlie, explain, and give rational coherence to apparent inequities in the Hindu social system. From the perspective of moksha, however, karma and samsara are viewed as limiting conditions from which one strives for release.

Dharma: The Temporal Perspective

The dharma tradition is firmly rooted in Vedic literature. With the exception of the *Upanishads*, Vedic religion was concerned primarily with insuring the continued fertility and well-being of the world. Primarily by means of rituals, Vedic religion continually and periodically sought to rein-

vigorate the cosmic order by nourishing those gods and powers who sustained the world. Vedic religion focused primarily on human existence in
the world, and when it concerned itself with life after death it described an
afterlife that was a continuation of earthly life in most respects. Health,
wealth, children (particularly sons), and a long life were the chief concerns
of Vedic religion, and it was a male's principal religious duty to insure these
blessings by performing appropriate sacred rituals. Vedic rituals aimed at
maintaining an overarching cosmic order, which when functioning properly insured a long, robust life full of blessings.

Although Vedic rituals continued to form an important part of high-
caste, especially Brahmin, religion well after the Vedic period and continue
to be performed by many Hindus today, by the time of the *Bhagavad Gita*
(ca. 200 B.C.E.), all human actions, not just specific rituals, were believed to
contribute to the maintenance of cosmic and social order. In the *Gita* the
term *dharma* is used to refer both to the orderliness of human society and
to each person's duty to uphold that order through every action. The term
loka-samgraha, support of the world, as used in the *Gita* came to capture what
lies at the heart of the dharma tradition. Each person, no matter how low
born, no matter how menial a social task he or she may inherit according
to caste birth, has a fundamental obligation to perform his or her ascribed
social function for the welfare of society as a whole. Although Vedic rituals
continue to play an important part in cosmic stability, the *Gita* generalizes
support of the world to include every action, no matter how apparently
insignificant. Every action, according to the *Gita*, is a ritual having cosmic
consequences if properly understood and undertaken.

In less creative ways, perhaps, but in much greater detail, the Hindu
scriptures on dharma known as the Law Books stress the importance in
Hinduism of maintaining cosmic and social order. A basic assumption of
the Law Books is that individual well-being and prosperity can occur only
when society and the cosmos as a whole are well ordered. A person's first
obligation is to others, to social groups such as family, caste, region, and
kingdom. Another underlying assumption of these works is that disorder
of various kinds is a constant threat to human existence. A human is called
upon to strive steadfastly to create and maintain a habitable world within
which one may not only survive but prosper and to some extent even transcend one's physical limitations by creating an ideal environment on earth.
All the Law Books advise rulers to use punishment liberally to maintain an
orderly world, and they teach that without firm controls human society
would return to the law of the fishes, in which the strong destroy the weak.

The nature of the ideal social order in Hinduism touches upon other
important aspects of Hindu belief and enables one to appreciate the essentially Hindu nature of the dharma tradition's emphasis on supporting the
world. In all Hindu writings concerned with dharma, the ideal human society is described as fundamentally hierarchical and characterized by ranked

and carefully circumscribed social groups, called castes, into which one is born. Most castes are characterized by particular social functions. Each caste has a traditional occupation, such as agriculture, business, or building, and each serves and upholds society by dutifully performing this occupation. At the top of the system are the Brahmins, whose traditional occupation is to undertake Vedic rituals that maintain the cosmic order as a whole. As envisioned in the Law Books, Hindu society is a vast organism with many interdependent parts, the primary aim of which is to support the Brahmins, who in turn maintain cosmic order, which benefits all castes.

Underlying the caste system are two central presuppositions. First, it is assumed that rank and hierarchy are intrinsic to human relations. Rank, furthermore, is ascribed by birth and not achieved by merit, except perhaps within one's own caste. The relative rank of a caste is also determined by the nature of its social role. Some occupations, for example, are considered highly polluting, whereas others are thought to be pure. Any occupation that involves contact with bodily dirt is believed to be highly polluting; therefore barbers, launderers, and those who collect human waste are generally ranked at the very bottom of the caste system. Each caste, however, no matter how low, is necessary to the smooth functioning of the social system as a whole and is thus recognized as being an intrinsic part of society. Hierarchy in social relations is also extended to family relations. Husbands and wives, elder and younger brothers, and so on are all ranked in the Hindu tradition in such a way that life in society involves a whole series of hierarchical relations for every individual. The end result of this system is that each individual is carefully placed in a social situation in which he or she is the recipient of a variety of obligations from those beneath and in turn is obliged to serve those above in prescribed ways. Social mobility is almost entirely excluded, and the aim of social life—indeed, the aim of dharma generally—is to learn and fulfill a given, ascribed social role that is necessary to the orderly functioning of society.

Given the assumptions of hierarchy and rank, one may wonder what the social system offers the lowest castes. The answer is, at least in this lifetime, not very much. However, a second presupposition of the social system tends to soften the burden for low-caste Hindus. This is the assumption that people are continually reborn according to their actions in the past. Karma, the moral law of cause and effect by which one reaps what one has sown, and samsara, rebirth, combine to teach that the particular caste into which one is born is determined by one's past actions and that the caste that one will be born into in the future is being determined by how one acts in the present. Brahmins have earned their high birth by faithfully serving society in the past, undoubtedly in a variety of roles and castes, whereas low-caste Hindus have earned their present rank by poorly serving society in the past, perhaps even as Brahmins. Thus for the individual, social mobility may only take place over lifetimes.

In general, then, the dharma tradition focuses upon the maintenance of the caste system, the purpose of which is to maintain social and cosmic stability through the performance of Vedic rituals by Brahmins. The centrality of the dharma tradition, and of the caste system, is affirmed and illustrated in many ways in Hindu mythology, and Hindu mythology to a great extent is only intelligible when this is recognized. That is, in many respects Hindu mythology legitimizes the ideal social system of the Hindu Law Books.

The oldest and probably best-known myth that affirms the dharma tradition concerns the sacrifice of the giant Purusha, which is first mentioned in the *Rig Veda* (X. 90). The cosmos and human society were instituted, so this myth goes, when the gods assembled to sacrifice a giant man. From his body the world was created: The sun came from his eyes, the moon from his mind, the sky from his head, the earth from his feet, and so on. The Brahmins, furthermore, were created from his head; the warriors came from his arms; the merchants, from his stomach; and the Shudras, or serfs, from his feet. The caste system is thus divinely instituted according to this hymn.

In a less formal way, the mythology of the god Vishnu also underlines the centrality of dharma in Hinduism. Vishnu is said to be the universal king, whose primary function is to create and uphold the world. When the world is periodically threatened by demons, who are the eternal enemies of the gods, Vishnu embodies himself in an appropriate form and restores cosmic balance.

Other deities concern themselves with cosmic stability, too. Shiva, although usually portrayed as a lone, meditating figure who engages in antisocial behavior and lives in wild places, is involved in the world of dharma when he marries the goddess Parvati for the welfare of the world. Many goddesses are typified by their eternal wakefulness vis-à-vis the cosmic order, and one of the most famous of them, Durga, is a great battle queen who periodically defeats demons who have threatened the positions of the gods. In much the same way as Vishnu, she assumes appropriate forms when called upon to rescue the world.

In the dharma tradition, then, the social order is believed to be divinely sustained. Humans, for their part, are responsible for observing the rules of dharma, which results in the Brahmins performing their rituals, which nourish the gods, whose task it is to maintain the world by protecting it from demons. Every person has a part to play, and each part is held to be necessary in some way to the ultimate end, the preservation and perfection of a habitable world for humanity.

Moksha: The Eternal Perspective

Counterbalancing one's social obligations, or dharma, is one's eternal destiny, moksha, release or liberation from all limitations and restrictions. In the moksha tradition of Hinduism, society and the world itself are of only contingent reality. This is made clear in a variety of beliefs and symbols but perhaps is most vivid in the Hindu concepts of cyclical time and infinite space. Hinduism presupposes a quite different view of time from that of the Western religions, in which time is linear and has a definite beginning and end. In Hinduism time has neither beginning nor end and spins itself out in cycles of varying lengths.

According to Hindu belief, this world (and every other world, of which there are an infinite number just like this one) passes through four periods of time in its sojourn from creation to destruction. These periods are called *yugas*, and the names of the yugas come from throws of the dice, implying, perhaps, that life is a giant dice game. The first age is the krita yuga, which lasts 1,728,000 years. The second is the treta yuga, which lasts 1,296,000 years and is followed by the dvapara yuga of 864,000 years. The fourth and final age is the kali yuga, the age we are now in, and it will last 432,000 years. Each yuga diminishes in length of time because each represents an increasing decline in virtue. The mythical cow that represents dharma stands on four legs during the krita yuga, three during the treta yuga, two in the dvapara yuga, and only one in the bleak kali age, in which morality and virtue are at an ebb. Each cycle of four yugas is known as a *mahayuga* (a great age) and comprises 4,320,000 years. One thousand mahayugas, or 4,320,000,000 years, is said to be equal to *one day* in the life of the creator god, Brahma. This period of time is known as a *kalpa*. After each mahayuga there is a minor dissolution of the world, and for a mahayuga of time there is a return to cosmic nondifferentiation, or rest. At the end of each kalpa there is a major dissolution that lasts for a kalpa of time. But even this immense cycle, in which the world is created and dissolved a thousand times over, seems insignificant when we learn that there is an even greater cycle, which revolves around the lifetime of Brahma. Brahma is said to live for one hundred Brahma years of Brahma days and Brahma nights (that is, $4,320,000,000 \times 2 \times 365 \times 100$), or for 315,360,000,000,000 human years. At the end of his lifetime all things totally dissolve, including Brahma himself, and for a Brahma century nothing exists but primeval substance. At the end of this eternity the great cycle begins again and continues endlessly.

From this perspective of eternity, individual biographies, social roles, the mechanisms of the dharmic order that govern life in society, society itself, and history seem insignificant and even superfluous. The life one leads today is only a scene in an endless drama of lives, for, given the beliefs in karma and samsara, each individual is continuously recycled to play endless social roles forever. Many of the gods, even Brahma himself, are said to be trapped in these cycles as well, for the gods (except for the great gods such as Vishnu, Shiva, and the Great Goddess) are none other than reincarnations of superrighteous individuals from the past who eventually will fall from their high positions. Heavens and hells also exist during periods when the world exists, but these are mere way stations where excesses of very good and very bad karma are worn off. These realms are subject to continuous recycling, too, and do not represent the final spiritual goal. Like the worlds, they continually come and go.

On the endless merry-go-round of life after life after life, endlessly adrift in a sea of bubbling universes that ever come and go, each individual is trapped by the remorseless laws of karma and samsara, bound by his or her deeds to live as a limited and ignorant being forever. Moksha is the end of this cycle and represents a person's ultimate spiritual goal in Hinduism. The term itself means "release" and involves primarily release from karma and samsara. It also involves release from all embodied limitations, such as ignorance and suffering. Moksha is the end of births and usually is characterized as an anonymous, impersonal, blissful state.

Of the various schools of Hindu philosophy, most of which are sympathetic to moksha, the schools of Yoga and Advaita Vedanta most clearly articulate the vision of humankind's ultimate destiny as liberation from rebirth. The practice of yoga is ancient in India and is employed as a religious technique in nearly all Hindu philosophical schools and cults. Classical yoga, as defined in the *Yoga Sutras*, aims at stopping the constant, inward mental chatter of the mind and the mind's tendency to be perpetually distracted by the senses. Yoga recognizes that the bodily organism is naturally oriented to the outside world and is distracted every moment by the data that the senses continually receive from it. One's natural condition, therefore, is to be attentive to the world of matter and inattentive to the inner world of spirit. Yogic techniques aim at reorienting individuals so that they may glimpse their inner, eternal nature and thus enjoy immortal calm—what yoga calls *samadhi*, a trancelike state that completely transcends individuality, ego, and finite material existence. Yogic techniques, basically, aim to reverse the tendencies of the senses or, perhaps better, to sabotage or annihilate the senses so that an adept may peer inward instead of outward. The technique of meditating on one spot for hours or even days, for example, is a way of starving the senses and denying them their natural tendency to gather in as much of the material world as they can. The yogi seeks, through various techniques, to master every bodily function so that the body no longer works "by itself," as it were, but is controlled by the yogi. As long as the body and its senses are in control, final calm will be impossible; thus yoga aims at taming the body by controlling it with the mind, which itself is then annihilated.

In yogic technique this process is described as "going against the stream," that is, reversing the natural processes of material nature, which in yoga is called *prakriti*. Prakriti left to itself always evolves into increasingly grosser and specific forms of matter. It spins itself out instinctively until it forms concrete organisms whose primary aim is to satisfy their senses and reproduce themselves. Sensual gratification and multiplication are the natural ends toward which prakriti evolves, and the yogi's task is to reverse this process by the devolution of prakriti in himself or herself. Samadhi, which represents the triumph over prakriti, is a state in which the yogi is at last able to discover his or her inner spiritual essence, which is called *purusha* in yoga. The purusha is without individual characteristics, is completely free from the influences of prakriti, and is immortal and unchanging. Having identified with this inner, hidden essence, the yogi is reborn no more and enjoys eternal bliss.

The appropriate environment to undertake the successful yogic quest is outside society, and throughout the history of Hinduism, world renouncers are typically described as performing yogic exercises. Some of these exercises aim specifically at mortifying the physical body, and the practice of austerities is extremely common in descriptions of those in pursuit of moksha, or ultimate liberation. The assumption is that within society actions are usually aimed, either directly or indirectly, at satisfying material or bodily needs, whereas outside society one is free to renounce these needs and gain bodily mastery. For yoga, and for the moksha tradition generally, life in the world is either distracting to the spiritual quest or inimical to it.

In yoga philosophy the world is fundamentally dualistic. On the one hand there is material nature, prakriti, and on the other hand there is purusha, pure spirit. The yogi's task is to isolate the latter from the former. Advaita Vedanta denies any such duality, but in spirit and ultimate intention it is similar to yoga in trying to bring its practitioners to final release from the round of karma and samsara. In Advaita Vedanta, which was formulated most thoroughly and brilliantly by Shankara (788–820) in his commentaries on earlier writings such as the *Upanishads*, there is only one reality, Brahman. Brahman is unchanging, eternal, conscious, blissful, and unqualified by time, space, or any other delimiting attribute. Essentially, in Shankara's philosophy, individuals are not ultimately real. All individuals are really Brahman and as such transcend their individuality and particularity. Underlying all manifestations of being is Brahman, and to realize that one's inner soul, the Atman, is nothing but Brahman is to lose all consciousness of being an individual and to die to the whole game of ego-centered life with its desire-motivated actions that bind one eternally to rebirth. To become fully conscious of one's real identity is to slough off previous false identities and to rest content in actionless, desireless bliss and redemptive knowledge.

For Shankara, and for other moksha philosophies as well, false identity and the appearance of multiplicity—indeed, the whole phantasmagoria of biographical existence—are the result of maya, a central concept in both Hindu philosophy and popular literature. Maya is what prevents humans from seeing things as they really are. For Shankara maya is the process of superimposing false ideas on the one reality, Brahman. Maya represents our tendency to fill up our world with ego-centered, prejudicial, and ultimately false concepts that prevent us from realizing the underlying unity of existence. We thus become completely enmeshed in our own individuality, which prevents us from knowing our eternal identity. In popular literature maya is often spoken of as arising from the creative powers of the gods. It is described as bewitching and dazzling and as having the same effect as it does in Advaita Vedanta; that is, it prevents us from knowing who we really are. Maya, then, prevents us from being able to perceive ourselves from the perspective of eternity and enables us to remain content with the limitations of finite existence. In this sense, maya is a kind of drug that prevents us from becoming sick or dizzy in our endless rounds of birth and rebirth and keeps us firmly bound to the world of appearance and desire-motivated actions.

Hindu mythology presents the truths of the moksha tradition in a variety of ways and provides several stunning divine portraits that aim at awakening people to their eternal destiny, which is to renounce the world and seek liberation. The two most dramatic illustrations among the Hindu pantheon are the ascetic god Shiva and the bloodthirsty goddess Kali. For centuries Shiva has provided a divine model for world renunciation in Hinduism. He typically is described as dwelling on his sacred mountain in the Himalayas in deep yogic trance; when the Hindu god of lust, Kama, tries to distract him from his meditation, Shiva burns him to ashes. Shiva is characterized by antisocial behavior. He is fond of hallucinogens; haunts inaccessible places such as forests, mountains, and caves; dances with an entourage of goblins and ghouls in cremation grounds; carries a human skull; and wanders the cosmic regions naked. In his role as world renouncer he clearly stands outside the orderly confines of dharma and is a reminder of one's ultimate desire for moksha.

The goddess Kali reminds Hindus of their eternal destiny, too, but in a somewhat different way. She is described as black, fierce, fanged, and fond of blood. She has disheveled hair, wears a garland of severed human heads and a girdle of severed arms, and dwells in cremation grounds, where she seats herself on a human corpse. In appearance and habit Kali reminds us of certain inevitables from which the order of dharma is incapable of protecting us: death, especially untimely death; old age; sickness; and suffering generally. She reveals to us the truth that life is inherently painful and that life feeds on death. No matter how comfortable and secure we may think ourselves unexpected and tragic events can turn the world topsy-turvy. By revealing the inherent painfulness of physical, individual existence and the fragility of the dharmic order, Kali wakes us up to our eternal destiny, which transcends all limitations of life in the world.

Reconciliations

The Hindu tradition has sought to reconcile the tension between dharma and moksha in several ways, and many of these formulas have become central in defining Hinduism itself. In many Hindu scriptures the

FIGURE 5–1 A world renouncer dressed in a garment made of strips of castoff clothing. (From Richard Lannoy, *India, People and Places* [New York: Vanguard Press, 1955].)

ideal life is described as having four stages, or ashramas;[1] theoretically a high-caste male Hindu is supposed to pass through these stages in his sojourn from birth to death. (Expectations for women are discussed in Chapter 7.) The first two stages, those of the student and the householder, involve obligations to society. The individual is supposed to study the sacred scriptures and learn sacred rites that uphold the world and to marry, procreate, and serve society by means of his caste dharma. The last two stages, those of the forest dweller and the wandering world renouncer, on the other hand, aim at enabling him to realize his eternal destiny, moksha. Entering the third stage of life, a man leaves his family, gives up his social roles, and retires to the forest with his wife to meditate. In the fourth stage he leaves his spouse, wanders the world begging his food, and seeks to subdue desire completely and rid himself of all false identities.

Another important formula that tries to harmonize the dharma and moksha tendencies in Hinduism is the common affirmation that there are

[1]The four stages are (1) brahmacharya, the stage of the student; (2) grihastha, the stage of the householder; (3) vanaprastha, the stage of the forest dweller; and (4) sannyasa, the stage of the wandering mendicant.

various paths, appropriate to different individuals, all of which lead to the same goal of liberation. The most frequent list of such paths describes three routes to liberation: the path of works, the path of knowledge, and the path of devotion. Although the path of knowledge usually is pursued outside society, in a monastery or in isolated meditation, the paths of works and devotion are often said to be appropriate to life in the world, that is, appropriate to the realm of dharmic order. The key to finding liberation while remaining in the world for both paths is the ability to act without desire for fruits, to act without regard for worldly ends. The *Bhagavad Gita* best articulates this logic; it describes devotion as a technique for undertaking desireless action. If one undertakes every action as an offering to God, if one acts in every action for God instead of oneself, the binding effects of karma will not take place and moksha will be achieved.

Various myths or descriptions of deities also seek to illustrate the interdependence of dharma and moksha, or at least the necessity for both points of view. Perhaps the most striking example is seen in the complex mythology of Shiva. As mentioned previously, Shiva is typically portrayed as the model of the aloof, isolated, meditating world renouncer who behaves in disruptive ways. On the other hand, the most common symbol of Shiva is the lingam, the phallus, and Shiva is affirmed to be the underlying vigor that sustains the world. In many myths Shiva is described as being persuaded by the other gods to involve himself in the maintenance of the world. In general, the mythology portrays him as alternating between two poles, the ascetic pole, in which he remains aloof from the world, and the erotic or social pole, in which he willingly or unwillingly involves himself in the process of creation and world maintenance. In Hindu mythology Shiva is both world renouncer and family man and represents the possibility of living out both obligations of dharma and moksha.[2]

It is doubtful if very many Hindus in any given generation successfully combine their double obligations to dharma and moksha. In each generation it seems clear that the vast majority find themselves involved primarily in the world of social roles and obligations. For them, Hinduism is primarily the day-to-day task of insuring cosmic stability, especially as this task manifests itself in immediate personal concerns. It is also true, however, that nearly every Hindu is aware of the teachings of the tradition concerning moksha and that most hope to realize ultimate liberation, if not in this life, then in some future life. It is also the case that there are always some Hindus who are striving heroically to make this life their last, who have renounced the world in hope of moksha, and who provide vivid living witness to this Hindu teaching. The ability to encompass and cherish both points of view, the temporal and the eternal, without surrendering entirely

---

[2]For an excellent treatment of Shiva's double role, see Wendy O'Flaherty, *Asceticism and Eroticism in the Mythology of Śiva* (London: Oxford University Press, 1973).

to one or the other, characterizes the distinctive genius of the Hindu tradition.

REPRESENTATIVE THINKERS

Shankara

Hinduism traditionally recognizes six schools of philosophy as *astika*,
or orthodox. These schools differ markedly from one another on a variety
of issues, and to this day they continue to debate with one another over
important philosophical and religious issues. Although no one particular
school has been unanimously declared triumphant over the others, many
students of the Hindu tradition and many Hindus over the centuries have
affirmed the school of Advaita Vedanta as best expressing the genius of
Hindu philosophical thought. *Advaita* means the absence of duality, and
vedanta means the end or essence of knowledge and also refers to the *Upanishads*. The school of Advaita Vedanta, then, teaches that the essence of
knowledge (which is found in the *Upanishads*) is that ultimate reality is non-
dual in nature.

The most brilliant and systematic exponent of Advaita Vedanta was
Shankara (788–820), a South Indian Brahmin. Although he died at the age
of only 32, he had an eventful life, and his writings have had more impact
upon Hindu philosophy than anyone else's. A considerable amount of legendary material is available on Shankara in Sanskrit, and stories about him
are found in oral traditions throughout India to this day.

Shankara was born in a small village in Kerala, in Southwest India, to
a childless couple who had petitioned Shiva to grant them a son. Shankara's
various biographies say that he was an embodiment of Lord Shiva himself,
who came among humans to teach them the truth. Shankara is described
as being a particularly precocious child, mastering the *Vedas* at a very young
age. He is also described as showing little interest in worldly life and as
desiring to renounce the world even as a child. His father died when Shankara was about eight years old, and as he was an only child, his mother
opposed his wish to give up the world and become a sannyasi, or wandering
mendicant. Shankara obtained his mother's permission, however, in a curious incident that is told in most of his biographies. While bathing in a
river, he was seized by an alligator. In his predicament, he shouted to his
mother for her permission to enter the stage of the sannyasi, and thinking
her son near death his mother agreed. The alligator subsequently freed the
boy, and with his mother's permission Shankara soon afterward left the
world in search of liberation.

Shankara went north and succeeded in finding a guru, Govinda Bha-
gavatpada, who lived in a cave. Govinda initiated Shankara as a sannyasi

and then instructed him in Vedanta. Govinda soon recognized the brilliance of his new student and advised him to go to Varanasi, the spiritual center of Hinduism, to compose his philosophy in the form of commentaries on the *Upanishads* and teach this philosophy to all. Shankara did as he was advised and, having settled in Varanasi, began to write his commentaries and to attract disciples.

Sometime during his initial stay in Varanasi, news of his mother's death reached him. Although he had renounced the world, including his family, Shankara returned to his village and supervised the funeral rituals for his mother. His final tie to the world now severed, he returned to Varanasi and continued to write his commentaries on the *Upanishads*, the *Bhagavad Gita*, and the *Brahma Sutras*. The *Brahma Sutras* are short, often obscure sayings on Brahman and were collected several generations before Shankara. His commentary on them, *Brahma Sutra Bhashya*, is probably his most famous and systematic work and taken by itself is a succinct rendition of his entire philosophy.

At the height of his career, Shankara's biographies tell us, he decided to undertake a tour of the entire Indian subcontinent. This tour, which took Shankara to every corner of India, is called a *dig-vijaya*, a conquest of the quarters, and its purpose for Shankara seems to have been twofold: (1) to defeat philosophical rivals and convince them of the truth of his own system and (2) to set up monasteries throughout India where world renouncers might study his philosophy and undertake the appropriate spiritual exercises to realize the truth of nonduality in their own lives. Many of the monasteries founded by Shankara survive to this day and are able to trace the spiritual lineages of their presiding teachers all the way back to Shankara's disciples.

Of the debates Shankara took part in, the one with Mandana, an advocate of the Purva Mimamsa school, is perhaps the most interesting, because it underlines the ancient tension in Hinduism between the path of works and rituals and the path of knowledge. Purva Mimamsa takes its inspiration from the ritual sections of Vedic literature and emphasizes the centrality of performing these rituals for both cosmic stability and individual spiritual and physical prosperity. This school is primarily a defense of the dharma tradition in Hinduism because it stresses the welfare of the world. Shankara, on the other hand, saw little use in rituals or in actions generally, and (following the *Upanishads*) he stressed the acquisition of redemptive knowledge. For Shankara, all rituals are based on the assumption that an outside power may be invoked to bring about a general improvement in one's spiritual condition or to bring about the circumstances in which one might find liberation. This assumption is false, he argued, inasmuch as moksha involves self-knowledge, which demands an essentially inward orientation and quest. Redemptive power does not reside outside a person but within, and to undertake rituals that aim at mastering the outside world for one's own benefit, or even the benefit of the world, is useless and misleading. In fact, Shankara argued, there is no essential relationship between self-realization and any action whatsoever. Even yogic techniques do not guarantee the acquisition of this knowledge, although they may be helpful in setting the stage, as it were. Final awakening to the truth about one's eternal identity necessitates overcoming false identities, and there is no set of rituals, even mental rituals, that is guaranteed to result in this triumph. To a great extent, the dawning of knowledge and fading away of ignorance is an inexplicable, mysterious event in one's spiritual sojourn; Shankara affirmed this by saying that although many religious actions are permissible and helpful in maintaining worldly order, ego-centered actions are always grounded in a false notion of one's identity and therefore have no essential connection with discovering the truth. For Shankara the acquisition of redemptive knowledge was a basic fact, but he failed to discern any cause-and-effect relationship between achieving this knowledge and traditional pious actions. Since all actions are grounded in false notions of individuality, and since redemptive truth is that one's true identity is anonymous, transcending any notion of individuality, Shankara asserted that truth could not be found by undertaking actions.

Shankara is also said to have debated with heterodox schools, such as the Buddhists and Jains, on his triumphant tour and is remembered in the Hindu tradition as having converted vast areas of South India back to Hinduism. Although the legends about his success may be exaggerated, Shankara's thought did come to represent for the Hindu tradition the most cogent philosophical refutation of Buddhism and Jainism.

Shankara's death is shrouded in mystery—there are many different traditions concerning his last days. Some say that he was cursed by an opponent and became sick and died. Others say that he went to the Himalayas when he realized that his death was near, entered a cave, fell into a trance, and passed away. Still others say that he died peacefully in Varanasi. Whatever the circumstances, from Shankara's own point of view they would have made little difference, as death for him would have represented the final release from samsara. Having worn out his last body, he would have understood his death as his final emancipation from a long nightmare of ignorance as an embodied creature.

Shankara's main concern in his philosophy was to reconcile two contrasting facts: (1) the fact that the truth as declared in scripture (the *Upanishads*, *Bhagavad Gita*, and *Brahma Sutras* primarily) and as experienced by those who had gained liberation, undoubtedly including himself, is that ultimate reality is one and indivisible, unchanging, and eternal; and (2) the fact that most people view the world as multifaceted, diverse, changing, divided into innumerable opposites, and populated with individual persons and entities. His basic task was to assert and philosophically defend the absolute unity of ultimate reality and to explain how false notions of reality arise and persist for most people.

For Shankara the truth is that there is only Brahman. Brahman is without qualities (*nirguna*). It is not an object that may be circumscribed by the mind or senses, but rather it completely transcends any physical or mental picture of it. Brahman is not a personal god, and though devotion to such a god with qualities (*saguna*) is not necessarily harmful, it is based on a false notion of Brahman. Brahman is eternal, unchanging, and inactive because it is entirely full and complete and thus has no need to act. Though it is often described as possessing being (*sat*), consciousness (*cit*), and bliss (*ananda*), Brahman is actually the ground of being itself, the ground of consciousness itself, and the very fullness of bliss itself. Brahman is not a being, no matter how perfect.

This Brahman is none other than Atman, the eternal, unchanging Self, or soul, underlying all individuals. Like Brahman, the Atman is *nirguna* and thus completely devoid of individuality and particularity. It is unchanging and eternal. It does not act and is often described as the passive, eternal witness of all actions prompted by people's false notions of themselves as individuals. Atman is the ground upon which individuality is based, or the ground upon which it is possible for individuality to arise, but in its essential nature is completely aloof and isolated from all notions of personality and ego.

Moksha comes about when, and only when, the identity of Atman and Brahman is fully realized by a person. Moksha comes about when a person makes the startling discovery that he or she is the eternal, unqualified, unchanging Brahman itself. Release and liberation result, as we might say in the language of the Western religious traditions, when a person can declare as a result of discovering his or her true identity, "I am God." Of course Brahman is imagined quite differently from Western ideas of a personal god, but the radical nature of the self-discovery that wakes a person up to liberating knowledge in Advaita Vedanta is suggested in this statement. For Shankara, humanity is essentially divine, and all other notions that compromise this essential truth are false and binding and involve a masquerade. Until people wake up to their divine nature, they playact, assuming a variety of roles that obscure who they really are. Infatuated by false notions of who one is, a person is continually destined to transmigrate, playing one role after another in life after life.

In contrast to the ultimate truth, namely, that Brahman is all and that Atman is identical with Brahman, is the way in which most people view the world. They see the phenomenal world, the world of objects perceived by the mind and senses, which is characterized by diversity and change, as real and understand their individuality to be unique and self-sufficient. They see the world as characterized by plurality and as composed of a number of knowing subjects and known or knowable objects. This way of looking at reality is rooted in the notion of ego. An underlying assumption is that the ego acts, wills, and enjoys a world of form and diversity and in turn is acted upon by that world in different ways.

Although Shankara attributes conditional reality to the phenomenal world (the world of things, emotions, desires, and individuals), he argues that this world is not ultimately real because everything about it is subject to change. Its existence necessitates an unchanging substratum (which is the unchanging Brahman). The phenomenal world, the world as most of us perceive it, is a false idea of ultimate reality, and it arises because of maya, a central concept in Shankara's philosophy.

Maya may be understood from two points of view in Shankara: (1) as something arising from the individual, or from a subject, and (2) as something impinging upon that subject. From the first point of view, maya is essentially the process of superimposing false notions on what is real. Shankara often uses two examples of this process: mistaking shell for silver and mistaking a rope for a snake. The "silver" and the "snake" do not really exist; they are false notions superimposed on something else, and as such they are illusions that mask the true nature of reality. Similarly, individuals superimpose false notions on Brahman, the substratum of the world, indeed the only reality. Because of maya, reality appears to be something it is not, and this false appearance completely vanishes when the real nature of things is discerned; that is, the "silver" and the "snake" disappear when the shell and the rope are perceived. The most disastrous false notion superimposed on Brahman, or on things as they really are, is the notion of separate, individual egos that are self-sufficient and independent of their base and source. Spiritual progress for Shankara is the process, gradual or sudden, in which this notion of ego is dispelled, in which the "snake" of biographical independence is subdued and vanquished.

Maya also may be understood as something that impinges upon a person from the outside, as it were (there being in actuality no inside or outside from the point of view of Brahman). In this sense, maya is spoken of by Shankara as something that veils the true nature of something else and that causes a series of inward reactions. To return to the example of the rope/snake: Having superimposed a "snake" on the rope, the individual then reacts to it with alarm and fear and proceeds to undertake a series of actions—running away, grabbing a stick for self-defense, and so on. That is, he acts as if maya were something impinging upon him from "outside," when in reality, of course, the "snake" is only a figment of his imagination. It is similar with the false notion of individuality and ego: Having falsely arrived at this notion of selfhood and having superimposed it on the world, the individual sees the world as centered in the ego and thus becomes thoroughly ego-centered. That is, the world appears to be oriented toward the ego, and everything that happens is viewed in a highly selective way so that the idea that the ego is the most important thing in the world is continually reinforced.

A contemporary example of how maya works, and how maya warps the true nature of reality, is the New Yorker's map of the United States. In this map of reality Manhattan is drawn in great detail and is shown as much larger than it really is geographically. The four other New York City boroughs are also shown in great detail. Places that New Yorkers frequently travel to or vacation in also figure prominently in this map. Miami, for example, is clearly indicated in large letters, as are Los Angeles and Palm Springs. However, the rest of the United States is drawn inaccurately. Various states, especially Midwestern and Western states, are misplaced, misspelled, or entirely left out. Most states are represented as much smaller than they actually are, and the names of cities often replace the names of states, as when Massachusetts is called Boston and Illinois is called Chicago. New Yorkers, the implication is, know nothing and care nothing about Massachusetts apart from Boston.

And so it is with every individual. Everyone has a map of reality, which always places that individual squarely at the center and thus quite effectively warps and distorts the true nature of reality. This maya map, furthermore, is perfectly real to its creator and to a great extent governs his or her life. The map both reflects and reinforces one's false notion of who one is and what the world around one is all about.

The way out of the wonderland of maya for Shankara is through the realization of ultimate truth. Knowledge of Brahman-Atman occurs simultaneously with the dropping away of false knowledge. Although this may seem to be a gradual process, the simultaneous awakening to truth and dying of ignorance are usually said to be instantaneous in Shankara's philosophy.

Shankara provides guidelines that are believed to be helpful in bringing about this stunning awakening. First, he recommends renunciation of the world. Life in the world is too distracting for those seeking to wake up to their true identity. Becoming a sannyasi, ever wandering, begging food, without family or home, helps obliterate false maps of reality. To dispel ignorance (false maps) it is helpful to physically change one's familiar environment and habits. The best cure for a New York-centered view of the world might well be exile to a part of the Amazonian jungle where nobody has ever heard of New York. Second, Shankara encourages yogic exercises to annihilate one's identification with the physical world and one's instinctive tendencies to orient oneself outward toward the magic show of the world. Third, he recommends meditation on sacred scriptures, especially the *Upanishads*. Basically, these exercises help place one in circumstances conducive to the discovery of Brahman within.

For people who are overwhelmed by the knowledge of their basic nature as Brahman, moksha is at hand. Such a person is called a *jivanmukta*, one who is liberated while still alive. To others jivanmuktas may still act and look like normal, unawakened individuals, but essentially they are not. They have died to the world of individuality, are inwardly empty of all but Brahman, and are completely unaffected by the whirligig of the world of maya. And to that world of maya they will never return. They are released. Or rather, perhaps, they have realized that all along they have been inwardly and essentially free but simply did not know it. They have, as it were, waked up from a long and bad dream and now know that their recently discovered nature has always been their real nature.

Gandhi

In thinking about how the essential beliefs of Hinduism are expressed in everyday life, it is helpful to look at the life of Mohandas Karamchand Gandhi (1869–1948). Gandhi's life and thought are also instructive in showing the extent to which many central Hindu ideas have persisted into the twentieth century. In many respects Gandhi was a sophisticated modern man. He was a discerning student of modern politics and economics and was educated in England in Western law. Nevertheless, his distinctive power and appeal to both Indians and Westerners is classically Hindu. A review of his life and teachings illustrates the centrality of both the dharma tradition in Hinduism, the importance Hinduism has always placed on one's obligation to society, and the moksha tradition, which teaches that one must never completely lose sight of one's ultimate destiny, which is to transcend the world. In the life of Gandhi we find a stunning example of someone who successfully served both ends and in the process enriched the meanings of both dharma and moksha for the Hindu tradition.

Gandhi was born in Kathiawar in western India to parents who belonged to a merchant caste. His forefathers had served the hereditary rulers of the area in the past, and his family still maintained considerable interest in politics. Gandhi said that his mother was a deeply religious woman who often fasted in order to exercise self-restraint, and probably to a great extent her early influence aroused his fierce spiritual tendencies, which persisted throughout his life. After being married at the age of thirteen (a common practice in late nineteenth-century India) to Kasturbai and graduating from high school, Gandhi left for England to study law. He matriculated at London University in 1890 and returned to India in 1891.

Gandhi practiced law in Bombay for two years, during which he was both unsuccessful and unhappy. In 1893, however, he accepted an invitation from a client to represent him in South Africa. It was there that Gandhi developed his basic political, economic, and religious philosophies and undertook the first of his campaigns, on behalf of the Indian community, that would gain him his initial fame and reputation. Soon after his arrival in South Africa, Gandhi had an experience that deeply offended him and galvanized his intention to help his fellow Indians in the racially divided country. On his way by train to Pretoria to undertake his case, Gandhi was asked to give up his seat and leave the first-class compartment when a white man entered his car at Maritzburg. Gandhi refused to leave, protesting that he had purchased a first-class ticket, and subsequently he was forced from the train by a policeman. It was night, and in Maritzburg at that time of year it was quite cold. Gandhi spent the whole night in the station, shivering and hungry, and later in his career recalled this incident as crucial in awakening him to the plight of his people, both in South Africa and in India itself, which was ruled by the British.

In 1894, after winning his client's case and helping the Indian community organize itself to gain basic civil rights, Gandhi prepared to return to India. Just as he was about to depart, however, news of new racial laws proposed by the South African government was released, and the leaders of the Indian community persuaded Gandhi to remain in South Africa to help resist the laws. Gandhi quickly founded the Natal Indian Congress Party and began a weekly paper, *Indian Opinion*, to advocate the Indian cause. As leader of the new party, Gandhi's basic strategy was nonviolent resistance and noncompliance to laws that abridged Indian civil rights. Initially Gandhi referred to his strategy as passive resistance but soon replaced this phrase with the Indian term *satyagraha*, which literally means "seizing the truth." Satyagraha came to characterize all Gandhi's later campaigns and was a powerful blend of fearlessness, truthfulness, and nonviolent resistance to laws that Gandhi thought oppressed his fellow Indians. These campaigns often involved breaking the law, and throughout his career Gandhi and his followers periodically were thrown into jail. During the Indian independence movement itself, the simple prison garb required of all prisoners became the official uniform of Indian Congress Party leaders and to this day is still worn by many government officials there. Prison clothing was regarded as an outward symbol of one's willingness to suffer in a righteous cause for the welfare of India and her people.

Gandhi proved to be an effective organizer and spokesman for the South African Indian community and eventually succeeded in having many of the racist laws repealed. In the process of this campaign, which lasted eight years, more than two thousand men and women risked imprisonment by marching in protest against the laws, and Gandhi himself was jailed several times.

In 1904 Gandhi founded his Phoenix Settlement, a kind of communal home, and in 1910 he established his Tolstoi Farm. Throughout this period of his life he continued to direct the South African community's resistance to government harassment, but the most interesting developments in Gandhi's career during these years involved important changes in his personal life-style. Over the years in South Africa Gandhi had come more and more to appreciate a self-sufficient life-style and to identify with the vast majority of humanity, and Indians, who lived in poverty. He first experimented with self-sufficiency when South African barbers refused to cut his hair. Though he made a mess of it at first, he was soon quite adept at this task. Similarly, Gandhi undertook to do his own laundry and soon began to appreciate the

FIGURE 5–2   Mahatma Gandhi bows his head in acknowledgment of the cheers of his followers outside his residence in Bombay following his release from Yeravada jail. UPI Photo

independence such simple manual labor gave him over his environment and the insights it gave him into the lives of the poor.

Gandhi's emphasis at the Phoenix Settlement and the Tolstoi Farm on self-sufficiency meant that every member of the community followed his example and learned to do a variety of simple manual chores that in the Hindu caste system were often relegated to low castes. Gandhi even insisted upon cleaning his own latrine, the lowest and most polluting task in the hierarchical Hindu caste system, and throughout his career he insisted that all those who lived in his communities do the same. During these years Gandhi came to emphasize the cleansing power of manual work and the philosophy that any set of actions, no matter how lowly, if done with a spirit of service to one's fellow humans, can be redeeming. Gandhi's emphasis on self-sufficiency, which he experimented with and developed in South Africa, eventually resulted in his campaign of wearing only native-spun cloth (*khadi*) when he returned to India and became involved in the independence movement. His emphasis on the importance of manual labor also resulted eventually, and in conjunction with the *khadi* campaign, in his learning how to use a spinning wheel and his daily use of it throughout much of his life.

Gandhi's turn toward a more simple, self-sufficient style of living also resulted in his adopting poverty as a way of life. During his South African years, he and his family continually reduced their material possessions. By 1914, the year he left South Africa for the last time, Gandhi had little to his name except a few clothes and books, and Kasturbai had gradually given away all her jewelry and fine clothes. In 1921, at the height of his *khadi* campaign in India, Gandhi finally adopted the "uniform" in which he was to become most widely recognized. Declaring that the poor could not even afford to buy clothes, he threw away all his clothes except his loincloth and sandals. For the rest of his life these were the only clothes he owned, and it was in this simple attire, more appropriate to a world renouncer than to a famous political leader, that Gandhi met heads of state and conducted the campaign to liberate India from Britain.

In addition to self-sufficiency and poverty, Gandhi experimented with another style of life that was to characterize his own particular path of satyagraha. After much thought and after consultation with his wife, Gandhi in 1906 took a vow of complete celibacy, which he maintained until the end of his life in 1948. It had become Gandhi's conviction that all his actions, insofar as possible, should be selfless ones directed at the welfare of all. In his experiments with truth, all of which were aimed at this goal of acting selflessly, he found that he could not reconcile sexual indulgence with acting only for others.

One further Gandhian experiment with truth while in South Africa came to typify him throughout his life. Even as a child Gandhi was interested in various diets and even secretly experimented with eating meat, which was anathema to his strictly vegetarian family. In London he foreswore meat and tried different vegetarian diets. In South Africa these experiments continued until Gandhi finally discovered that fruits and nuts constituted the most nourishing diet. Underlying Gandhi's vegetarian diet were two assumptions. First, the doctrine of ahimsa, noninjury, forbade killing animals, so for Gandhi meat became forbidden, since noninjury increasingly dominated his vision of acting truthfully. Second, his emphasis on simplicity and avoidance of bodily indulgences led him to prefer those foods that needed little preparation and were easily obtainable.

In all these experiments Gandhi increasingly resembled a world renouncer in outward appearance and habit, and indeed he was explicit in saying that ultimate liberation was his goal. In his autobiography he wrote, "What I want to achieve—what I have been striving and pining to achieve these thirty years—is self-realization, to see God face to face, to attain Moksha. I live and move and have my being in pursuit of this goal."[3]

Although Gandhi may have looked like a world renouncer, although he may have acquired the habits of one in pursuit of moksha outside soci-

---

[3]Mohandas K. Gandhi, *An Autobiography or the Story of My Experiments with Truth* (Boston: Beacon Press, 1957), p. xxi.

ety—namely, simplicity, poverty, chastity, and a simple and meager diet—he increasingly and continually involved himself in society until his dying day. Gandhi left South Africa in 1914 for the last time and entered the stage of his life that made him world famous.

During his years in South Africa Gandhi had made several trips back to India to publicize the plight of Indians there; thus when he returned to India permanently he was already known and admired by many of the leaders of the Indian Congress Party, which was trying to gain India's independence from Britain. It was not long before Gandhi was actively involved in this campaign and became its leader. It was at about this time that the poet Rabindranath Tagore gave Gandhi the title Mahatma (one having a great soul), and though Gandhi himself disliked the epithet, he is best known to history by this name.

Gandhi soon established a community in Ahmedabad in western India in order to train volunteers in satyagraha. As in his earlier settlements in South Africa, life was simple and manual labor encouraged. All members took vows of fearlessness, truthfulness, ahimsa (nonviolence), and celibacy and like Gandhi were encouraged to exercise self-control in all actions. Members were allowed to wear only homespun native cloth symbolizing self-reliance, and they worked for the removal of untouchability. Over the years Gandhi had become deeply grieved over the plight of the untouchable castes in India. Members of these castes usually undertook highly polluting kinds of work, such as laundering or refuse disposal, and were avoided by almost all other Hindus. Economically and socially they were extremely deprived; birth into such a caste meant a life on the fringes of society with no hope for traditional social advantages like education. From this period in his life, around 1915, until his death, Gandhi made the abolition of untouchability one of his major social issues. It was Gandhi who named these people Harijans, that is, those born of God. He involved untouchables in his communities (sometimes to the distress of his followers), made it his habit to stay with them when traveling and meeting with officials (thus forcing the officials to have social contact with them), and conducted several all-India campaigns aimed at bringing about a fundamental change in their situation. Although untouchability still exists in India, Gandhi's efforts (along with those of others) resulted in many constitutional guarantees for the Harijans when India became independent.

Gandhi was soon able to apply the tactics he had learned in South Africa to the Indian situation. His first campaign was undertaken in Bihar in 1917 to combat laws forcing peasants there to plant indigo for European businessmen. The situation was severely exploitative of the peasants, and Gandhi, using typical tactics, was soon successful in having it remedied. As in his South African campaigns, his approach was to discover the facts of the situation, to protest if it seemed unfair, and always to remain nonviolent. In Bihar he began by interviewing peasants for days on end to gather all the facts. Then he made his findings known to the local authorities and protested the circumstances. When they ordered him to leave the district as a troublemaker, he refused to go. He was then summoned to court, where he simply pleaded guilty to disobeying the authorities. At this point the governor of the state intervened, appointing a committee to investigate the case with Gandhi as one of its members; the situation was eventually changed because of the committee's recommendations. In this campaign, as in all others, Gandhi firmly believed that openness and good will toward one's opponents would win out eventually if one supported a just cause. He always let those who were opposing him know exactly what he was doing and what he hoped to achieve.

Gandhi's campaigns in India were many and were aimed at various grievances. Eventually, however, all campaigns took on the overall aim of gaining independence for India. Perhaps his most famous and successful single campaign was the civil disobedience against the salt tax in 1930. This protest was against a tax that imposed penalties on very poor people, those who collected natural salt at the seashore, and that made the collection of salt a government monopoly. Gandhi's idea was simple. He proposed to march to the sea and then to encourage people to collect their own salt. He set out from Ahmedabad with 78 followers and began his famous walk to the sea 240 miles away. At Dandi, Gandhi and thousands of followers who had joined his procession along the way picked up salt and thus symbolically broke the law. Gandhi was arrested and jailed, and as people everywhere followed his example, there were also mass arrests.

Perhaps the most dramatic example of the courage, intensity, and dedication Gandhi instilled in his followers (called *satyagrahis*) is seen in the "raid" on the Dharasana Saltworks that occurred during this campaign. Gandhi himself was in jail, so the leadership of this "raid" was in the hands of Sarojini Naidu, a poet and particularly impressive follower of Gandhi. The plan of the satyagrahis was simply to enter the saltworks and help themselves to salt. Gandhi, as was his custom, had warned the government of his intentions, and the authorities had enclosed the factory with barbed-wire fences and brought in armed police to keep the marchers out. It was May 21 when Gandhi's "troops" arrived at Dharasana, and before the day was over the temperature would reach 116 degrees Fahrenheit and hundreds of satyagrahis would lie seriously injured; several would be dead. There were about twenty-five hundred satyagrahis, led by a select group who waded across the ditches surrounding the factory and made the initial approach to the barbed-wire fences. This group was followed by additional waves of satyagrahis. All the participants had been trained to make no effort at resistance, and when they refused to retreat at the order of the authorities, a dreadful scene took place. An American journalist from the United Press, Webb Miller, was at Dharasana that day and described what happened:

> Suddenly, at a word of command, scores of native policemen rushed upon the advancing marchers and rained blows on their heads with their steel-shod

lathis. Not one of the marchers even raised an arm to fend off the blows. They went down like ten-pins. From where I stood I heard the sickening whack of the clubs on unprotected skulls. The waiting crowd of marchers groaned and sucked in their breath in sympathetic pain at every blow. Those struck down fell sprawling, unconscious or writhing with fractured skulls or broken shoulders. . . . The survivors, without breaking ranks, silently and doggedly marched on until struck down. Although everyone knew that within a few minutes he would be beaten down, perhaps killed, I could detect no signs of wavering or fear. They marched silently, with heads up, without the encouragement of music or cheering or any possibility that they might escape serious injury or death. The police rushed out and methodically and mechanically beat down the second column. There was no fight, no struggle; the marchers simply walked forward till struck down.[4]

Gandhi's campaign against the salt tax did more than change an unfair law. It dramatically illustrated to the world, and to Indians themselves, that Britain was not the equal of India in this struggle. As one author has put it, "The British beat the Indians with batons and rifle butts. The Indians neither cringed nor complained nor retreated. That made England powerless and India invincible."[5] This moral victory, in which the Indian cause was shown to the whole world to be just (and the British cause unjust), was Gandhi's doing. In his own life he had often shown how moral justice can overcome brute force. At Dharasana his followers demonstrated that they could muster the courage and self-control of their leader in the face of vicious violence and without the use of violence themselves triumph over their opponents by means of satyagraha.

Gandhi's life from 1930 until his death was dominated by political negotiations with the British over Indian independence and by his untiring efforts to promote self-sufficient cottage industry in India and to abolish untouchability. Round-table meetings began shortly after the salt-tax campaign and were aimed at negotiating the terms and date of Indian independence; it soon became clear that a major issue concerned the status of the Muslim minority in an independent India. The Muslim League, and its chief spokesman, M. A. Jinnah, were concerned about the fate of Muslims at the hands of a Hindu majority and pressed for the creation of two independent nations, India and Pakistan. This position was strenuously opposed by Congress Party leaders, especially by Gandhi himself, but eventually the Muslims won.

The Hindu-Muslim issue eventually generated considerable hostility between the two communities, and in the months just preceding and following independence in August 1947, terrible riots spread throughout many parts of India in which both sides murdered each other by the tens of thou-

---

[4]Louis Fischer, *The Life of Mahatma Gandhi* (New York: Harper & Row, 1950), pp. 273–74.
[5]Ibid., p. 275.

sands. Gandhi, shocked by the violence, went to the worst trouble spots and tried to restore calm. He walked the fear-stricken countryside of Bengal to urge both sides to resist violence, and he went to live in a Muslim village in savagely torn Bihar to try to instill courage in his Muslim compeers. In the end, Gandhi confessed that he could take no joy at all in India's independence because of the bloodshed that accompanied it and the division of India that had resulted. Throughout this traumatic period, however, Gandhi, persisting in the courage that had characterized his entire life, stood by the persecuted time and again at great personal risk. In fact, it was a disgruntled conservative Hindu who would finally murder Gandhi because of his efforts to reconcile the Hindu and Muslim communities.

For several long periods during these last eighteen years of his life, Gandhi withdrew from Indian politics. Dissatisfied with certain policies of the Congress Party, he accused it at one point of adopting nonviolence simply as a tactic instead of as a basic principle; he sought to bring about his own policies through direct involvement at the village level. Having helped found the All-India Village Industries Association and having begun a regular newspaper, the *Harijan*, to advocate the abolition of untouchability, Gandhi moved to the village of Wardha in central India and there made his headquarters for social change. Convinced that long-term economic and social changes would not be brought about by political independence alone, he sought to institute these changes at the grass-roots level.

In January 1948, Gandhi fasted in protest over the continued violence between Muslims and Hindus. For five days he ate nothing, ending his fast only when the Muslim and Hindu leaders signed an agreement to uphold nonviolence. He was still recovering from the effects of his fast on January 30 when on his way to a daily prayer meeting he was shot dead by a Hindu fanatic.

The Hindu scripture that Gandhi cherished above all others was the *Bhagavad Gita*, and his ability to combine the twin responsibilities of dharma and moksha represented a living expression of the *Gita's* teaching concerning disciplined action. In the *Gita* Krishna teaches that true renunciation is not the physical abandonment of the world and of society but rather the surrender of ego-centered actions. To act not for oneself but for society as a whole, or for God, is to act without incurring the binding effects of karma. Through selfless action in society, the *Gita* teaches, the ego is controlled and eventually subdued, and the true self, the Atman, may shine forth. For Gandhi, truth and God, which he firmly equated, could be found only in the world in the midst of humanity. He thought that to abandon the world in search of individual salvation was both useless and selfish. Service to others, he said, was the best way of realizing God and achieving liberation.

Man's ultimate aim is the realization of God, and all his activities, political, social and religious, have to be guided by the ultimate aim of the vision of

God. The immediate service of all human beings becomes a necessary part of the endeavor simply because the only way to find God is to see Him in His creation and be one with it. This can only be done by service of all.... If I could persuade myself that I should find Him in a Himalayan cave I would proceed there immediately. But I know that I cannot find Him apart from humanity.[6]

[6]Krishna Kripalani, ed., *All Men Are Brothers: Life and Thoughts of Mahatma Gandhi as Told in His Own Words* (Paris: UNESCO, 1958), p. 63.

6

Worship in the Hindu Tradition

INTRODUCTION

In the *Bhagavad Gita* Krishna tells Arjuna that to find liberation he should consider each of his actions a sacrifice to the Lord. The goal of the spiritual quest, Krishna says, is to make of one's whole life a continuous act of worship and in doing so to transcend one's attachment to ego and individuality and wake up to one's eternal identity as Brahman. In Hinduism, as in other religious traditions, the ideal religious person is one who expresses piety in every action. In this sense, it is somewhat artificial to point to specific ceremonies, rituals, festivals, or practices and call them worship. The implication is that worship is something that takes place only at special times or in special places, which is misleading in the case of many Hindus. Nevertheless, most Hindus do acknowledge that some ceremonies, rituals, and practices are particularly sacred, powerful, or spiritually fulfilling. Such acts are greatly varied and numerous in the Hindu tradition.

Vedic literature describes a host of rituals for a variety of occasions and purposes. Most of them center around a sacrificial fire and are called *yajna*. They are performed at temporary altars, established specifically for the ritual; they do not involve images of deities; many of them require several specially trained Brahmin priests; and most of them are restricted to the twice-born castes. In general, *yajna* is of two types: public, in the sense of being performed for the general welfare of the world or a kingdom, and domestic, in the sense of being designed for the good of a household. The public rituals naturally benefit the sponsor of the ritual, usually a king, and the household rituals may benefit the world as well as the householder, so the two types of rituals are not always clearly distinguishable in terms of intention. The most important difference is that the public rituals are more complex, lengthy, and costly than the domestic rituals. The great horse sacrifice and the *rajasuya* ceremony for the consecration of a king (described later in this chapter) are grand affairs and may be undertaken only by powerful and wealthy individuals. The *agnihotra* ritual, on the other hand, is supposed to be performed daily by every twice-born household and as actually performed is a quite simple and brief rite.

In general, most *yajna* rites are intended to establish, maintain, or reinvigorate cosmic order and human welfare. Their aim is not to achieve moksha but to nourish various gods and powers so that they will continue to uphold and nourish the world in return. Many of these rituals are quite explicit in requesting long life, many children (particularly sons), many cattle, political power, and plentiful crops. The underlying vision of the *yajna* rituals is of a world pervaded by cosmic powers that are nourished through sacrifices. By performing *yajna*, either public or domestic, humans participate in the ongoing process of creation and re-creation of their world. The ritual fire is the central focus of these rites and represents the means of access between humans and the gods. Offerings of different kinds, both plant and animal, are sacrificed to the fire and thereby transmitted to the sphere of the gods. The sacrificial fire itself is a great Vedic god, Agni, who is described as a holy priest, the intermediary between humans and gods, and the divine spark in all living things. In a sense, to nourish Agni in *yajna* is to nourish Agni himself, the other gods, and all living things.

Another common type of ritual is puja. Puja rituals are not found in Vedic literature and represent a later type of worship in the Hindu tradition. Nevertheless, puja is much more common in Hinduism today, and has been for centuries. It is less restrictive than *yajna* in being more widely available to those not of the twice-born castes. Like the term *yajna*, *puja* refers to a great variety of rituals and ceremonies, from the most lavish and complex to the very simple. Unlike *yajna*, though, puja usually involves the image of a god or goddess, frequently takes place at a temple or some permanent sacred place, and does not necessarily or even typically involve offerings into a sacred fire. In general, puja represents an act of devotion by a devotee to a god or goddess. Temple puja basically involves three actions. First, the devotee presents offerings to the deity, either at a large public temple or at a local or domestic shrine. The offerings, accompanied by appropriate praise, may include flowers, incense, or food, all of which are believed to please the deity. The god also may be served through symbolic bathing, entertainment, or other acts of service, for example, the very common ritual of waving lights before an image. Second, and sometimes simultaneously with these acts of service, the devotee takes darshan of the deity, which means that he or she is given a view or glimpse of the deity's image. This is an extremely special affair in large, famous temples housing renowned images, but much less so in daily puja performed in one's own home. Third, the devotee takes *prasad*, which refers to the offerings made to the deity that are later distributed to the worshipers. *Prasad* is usually food, which is eaten by the devotee, although flowers are also commonly used. *Prasad* also means grace, and by accepting *prasad* the devotee ritually accepts the blessing of the deity.

The logic of puja is in some ways the logic of *yajna*. The devotee pleases the god by his or her service and in return accepts, or perhaps expects, the god's blessing. However, in *yajna* a person is more of an equal to the gods in terms of maintaining cosmic order. Without the *yajna* rituals the gods would weaken and the world run down. Thus the gods are as dependent on humans as humans are on the gods. In puja, however, the relationship is not one of equals. The deity who is worshiped is not dependent upon the devotee's offering, but the devotee is dependent upon the deity. Puja represents the devotion of an inferior to a superior.

Another series of rituals described in Vedic texts that are popular to this day are the life-cycle rituals, the samskaras. *Samskara* means "refinement," and these rituals aim at perfecting each individual so that he or she may achieve full civilized humanity. The samskaras circumscribe the entire life cycle, extending from prenatal ceremonies to postmortem rituals, and are too numerous to describe in detail. As in other cultures, the most important ones cluster around birth, puberty, marriage, and death, crucial events in the human life cycle that mark significant transitions for the individuals and families involved. Although marriage ceremonies are the most elaborate and in many ways the most important of the life-cycle rituals in Hinduism, the sacred-thread and funeral ceremonies are probably the most distinctively Hindu.

The sacred-thread ceremony for high-caste males, although strictly speaking not a puberty ceremony because it usually does not coincide with puberty, does mark the transition from childhood to adulthood by qualifying the initiate to participate in sacred lore and ritual. At the end of the ritual, or as a result of it, the initiate is entitled to study the *Vedas* and thus is qualified to learn Vedic rituals and to establish his own domestic altar when the time comes to marry and begin a household. The high point of the ritual is the bestowal of the sacred thread itself, worn only by the upper castes. It is as a direct result of this ritual that the initiate becomes "twice born," since the sacred-thread ceremony represents for the initiate a second birth. He has died to the profane world of childhood and is reborn to a world of sacred responsibility. So it is that the three highest castes are referred to as "twice born," they alone being privileged to undergo this ceremony and wear the distinguishing sacred thread.

Ceremonies performed at death are collectively called *shraddha*. Some texts say that these ceremonies should last for a year, but in practice they last twelve days or less. Immediately after death the corpse is cremated, the funeral pyre being lit by the eldest son. The remaining ceremonies are meant to nourish the deceased on their long journey to the world of the dead, the kingdom of Yama, where they join their ancestors, and to create new bodies for them. The ceremonies consist of offering small rice cakes, which represent both nourishment for the dead and a new body. The shraddha rituals are very ancient, going back to early Vedic texts, and there is hardly any mention in them of the ideas of karma and samsara. The emphasis in the shraddha ceremonies, despite the Hindu idea of reincarnation, is to insure the safe journey of the dead to the realm of their ancestors, where they are continually nourished by the shraddhas of their descendants in years to come. Basically the ritual represents a transition and transformation whereby the person who has just died passes from the state of the living to the state of an ancestor deserving of worship.[1]

Another group of Hindu rituals focuses on pilgrimage. The underlying assumption of pilgrimage is that the world is dotted with places possessed of sacred power, which may be appropriated by a devotee who goes to that place and performs suitable rituals. Another assumption is that to leave one's familiar surroundings and undertake a journey, often a long and perilous one, earns religious merit. In the most general terms a pilgrimage represents a person's journey from the world of the profane or ordinary to the world of the sacred and as such is often marked by the characteristics of a rite of passage in which the participant undergoes a three-stage process of separation, threshold, and incorporation.[2] Before the actual journey, the pilgrims undergo rituals that separate them from their normal world. They may shave their heads and put on special clothes to indicate that they are entering a new state, to show by a change of external appearance that they are "dying" to an old way of life. The second stage involves the actual journey itself, in which the pilgrims enter a threshold state between states of being. On the journey itself they are neither the person they were nor the person they will become. The very reality of traveling conveys the "neither here nor there" nature of this stage in the pilgrimage process. The thresholders have died, as it were, to their normal state of being but have not yet been reborn to a new state of being. At the

---

[1]For a description and discussion of Hindu funeral ceremonies, see David M. Knipe, "*Sapiṇḍikaraṇa:* The Hindu Rite of Entry into Heaven," in Frank E. Reynolds and Earle H. Waugh, eds., *Religious Encounters with Death: Insights from the History and Anthropology of Religions* (University Park: Pennsylvania State University Press, 1977), pp. 111–24.

[2]For a discussion of the structure of pilgrimage, see Victor Turner, "Pilgrimages as Social Processes," *Dramas, Fields, and Metaphors* (Ithaca, N.Y.: Cornell University Press, 1974), pp. 166–230.

pilgrimage center the pilgrims enter the third stage of incorporation, in which in one way or another they appropriate the power of the place and become renewed, refreshed, or "reborn" as sacred beings, or beings who have come in close contact with sacred power.

There are thousands of sacred places of pilgrimage all over the Indian subcontinent. In general these places are of two types: those that seem to be naturally sacred, such as mountains, rivers, or other geographical locales that are in some sense unusual or awesome; and those that have become sacred because of their association with particular human or divine events. The two types are often blurred, as when a "naturally" sacred place, such as a mountain, becomes associated with certain saints or myths, or when a city or a temple within a city becomes associated with the cosmic mountain at the center of the world. Historically it is clear that the two dimensions of a sacred place come to reinforce each other. A naturally sacred place will tend to attract saints, who will take up residence there and make the place even more sacred by their presence. Temples then may be built where none existed formerly, and eventually the "natural place" may become a large city that itself may become the focus of the pilgrimage.

The importance of pilgrimage in Hinduism and the very number of locations underline the important idea that India itself is a holy place, the center of the world, and that for a Hindu it is important actually to live in this environment in order to partake of sacred power. To be a Hindu is to live in India.

The kinds of rituals that a pilgrim undertakes at a pilgrimage center will vary according to the nature of the site, and sometimes according to the pilgrim's social status. At almost all sites there will be priest-guides to instruct the pilgrim in the proper rites, which sometimes will be the same for all pilgrims. At a large, complex site such as Varanasi, however, the twice born will undertake rituals that few low-caste people ever do or can afford to do. In Varanasi the former usually will perform rituals to their ancestors, whereas low-caste pilgrims generally visit the shrines of local saints or the temples of deities favored by them or their social groups. Although most pilgrims to Varanasi will perform a ritual in honor of the Ganges, which flows through the city, in other respects the pilgrimage generally will differ markedly from caste to caste.

In the case of a remote site, such as the headwaters of the Ganges in the Himalayas, the pilgrimage primarily involves reaching the place and having darshan of the site, which itself is held to be a sacred experience. At other sites the time of year or the proper astrological moment is crucial for experiencing the full sacredness of the place. Many sites have an annual celebration, whereas others tend to attract great numbers of pilgrims only at special times. The most famous example of the latter is the Kumbha Mela held in Allahabad. The festival is held only once every twelve years, when certain astrological factors are in harmony. At these times millions of pilgrims descend on the city, whereas in ordinary times it attracts only a trickle of pilgrims. To sum up, Hinduism affirms that certain places and certain times are particularly sacred, and pilgrimage rituals aim to involve the pilgrim directly in those times and places.

Yoga rituals are also typical of Hinduism and lend it a distinctive character. Rarely communal, these rituals are often undertaken in solitude by those who have renounced the world. Many Hindus who remain in society, however, also practice yoga rituals, which are acknowledged to achieve certain physical as well as spiritual ends. In classical yoga texts it is clear that the aim of yoga is to gain release from the realm of birth and death and from the material world in general. Yoga allows the aspirant to gain control over his or her physiological system and to triumph over it. However, in mastering one's physical body one also may achieve various supernormal powers, and there are many examples of people undertaking yoga to achieve worldly ends, such as longevity, wealth, and power.

Most yoga rituals, aimed at gaining mastery over the body and mind, consist of physical and mental exercises. The goal is to overcome the normal involuntary functions of the body. As long as the body works by itself, as it were, the aspirant remains controlled by it, enmeshed in it. Such exercises as breath control aim at making the practitioner conscious of, and master over, the respiratory process so that it ceases to be random and wasteful. Although yoga intends to overcome the body, the necessity of first controlling the body is asserted. The aim of yoga is not the culture of the body but the eventual destruction of it.

Hinduism also has a group of rituals appropriate to renouncing the world and living as a mendicant. According to Hinduism high-caste males should pass through four stages of life: student, householder, forest dweller, and wandering mendicant (sannyasi). Passing from the stage of a householder to the third or fourth stages represents a dramatic shift in life-style, which is marked by various rituals. In the first two stages Hindus have been responsible primarily for engendering and sustaining their families and upholding society. Moving to the forest or becoming a sannyasi, they now seek their own release from the world that they formerly sought to uphold. They renounce, or die to, one way of life and enter a new way of life, and this shift is marked by appropriate rituals.

Entering the fourth stage of life, the Hindu gives away all his possessions, then performs his own funeral ceremonies. After these rituals are finished, the sannyasi-to-be shaves his head, clips his nails, and takes a bath to purify himself. After performing his household rites for the last time, he burns all his ritual instruments to signify the end of his former mode of life, which centered around the household and the household sacrificial fire. The sannyasi-to-be is then instructed to "deposit the fire within himself" and to bid farewell to his family with the words, "To me belongs no one, nor do I belong to anyone."[3] Having ritually died to the world, he should now meditate on the vileness of the human body and the transitory nature of all things, wander naked or with only a single cloth to cover him, live in uninhabited places or in a cremation ground, and seek to achieve a state of mind that transcends the world.

In general and in summary, then, Hinduism is marked by a great number of rituals appropriate to a variety of circumstances, castes, and regions. These rituals also have different goals. Many of them, including most Vedic rituals, aim at upholding and nourishing the world and society. Many others, particularly yoga rituals and those surrounding the last two stages of life, aim at the achievement of moksha, final release from the world and the endless chain of rebirth.

EXAMPLES OF WORSHIP IN HINDUISM

The *Rajasuya* Ceremony

The *rajasuya* ceremony is illustrative of Vedic ritual as a whole. The many rituals that make up the *rajasuya* are often variations of shorter Vedic rituals, the themes that dominate the ceremony are typically Vedic, and the overall intention of the ceremony, namely, the re-creation and reinvigoration of the cosmic order, is representative of other Vedic rituals. Although the *rajasuya* ceremony is far more elaborate and lengthy than most other Vedic rituals and therefore was designed primarily for rulers or kings, it provides a typical view of Vedic religion and ritual.[4]

Although the ritual sometimes is described as a royal coronation ceremony, the term *rajasuya* itself means "king-engendering." Probably the ceremony was performed on a recurring basis, with a ruler or king as the central figure, and was concerned primarily with the reinvigoration of the cosmic order. The intimate connection between kings and the proper functioning of cosmic rhythms is clear in Vedic religion, as it was in other religions. The *rajasuya*, though it may have served the purpose of inaugurating a new king, seems to have had as its primary aim insuring the continuance of the cosmic rhythm of birth and rebirth symbolized by the birth, growth, death (harvest), and rebirth of vegetation.

In its complete form the *rajasuya* ceremony may have lasted nearly two years, although some authorities abbreviated the length of time required to perform it. The ceremony actually consists of a series of smaller rituals and

---

[3]Pandurang Vaman Kane, *History of Dharmaśāstra* (Poona: Bhandarkar Oriental Research Institute, 1941), vol. 2, pt. 2, pp. 958–59.

[4]The *rajasuya* rituals are described and interpreted by Johannes C. Heesterman, *The Ancient Royal Indian Consecration* ('s-Gravenhage, The Netherlands: Mouton, 1957). I have followed Heesterman in my description and interpretation of this ceremony.

may be divided into three main parts. The first involves preparatory rites that extend over a year. In these rituals the sacrificer—the ruler or king—is purified, and the identification of the sacrificer with the cosmos as a whole is begun. The second part includes the rituals of the *rajasuya* proper and lasts about ten days, the last of the year. These are the most interesting and dramatic rituals and symbolize the birth, or rebirth, of the king and, through his birth, the reinvigoration of the cosmic order. The unction of the king takes place at this point in the ceremony. The third part includes a variety of rituals that may extend over an entire year and reinforces the themes of unction by symbolizing the king's rebirth and the extension of his power throughout the world.

The preparatory rites begin with a soma sacrifice. Soma is an invigorating drink cherished by the gods. This sacrifice is followed by offerings to the goddesses Nirriti and Anumati, including a first-fruits offering. These rites last two weeks. The rest of the year is punctuated by a series of three rituals performed at four-month intervals. Each of them is to some extent a whole unto itself, and the same themes are repeated in the different components of the *rajasuya*.

The soma sacrifice inaugurating the *rajasuya* begins with a one-day *diksha* ritual. This is a consecration ritual to purify the sacrificer (in this case the ruler) so that he may take part in subsequent sacred rites. The priests are Brahmins and considered in a more or less permanent state of sacredness. In the *diksha* ritual the ruler is restricted to a small hut and must observe certain food taboos and refrain from sexual intercourse. His nails and hair are cut, and he is instructed not to speak and to stay awake all night if possible. When the sacrificer is allowed to speak he is instructed to stammer and keep his fingers closed in his hand. Throughout the *diksha* he sits on an antelope skin, which is particularly sacred in Vedic rituals as a symbol of the cosmos. The sacrificer is restricted to milk for nourishment. The general symbolism of the *diksha* is clear. The sacrificer becomes consecrated by a process of rebirth. The hut and the antelope skin represent the womb and the amnion, respectively, of an embryo. The sacrificer drinks only milk, appropriate to an infant, and when he speaks he stammers like an infant. In effect, the ruler dies to a profane state of being and is reborn into a pure, sacred state of being that qualifies him to participate in the coming rituals.

The soma sacrifice is itself an elaborate ritual with several optional subsidiary rites. Basically the sacrifice consists of offering soma[5] to various gods in the morning, at midday, and in the evening. Soma is the beverage that invigorates the gods and through them the cosmic order. It is also known as the king of plants, and in the context of the *rajasuya* ceremonies,

---

[5]Soma recently has been identified with a hallucinogenic mushroom. See chap. 2, fn. 2.

the soma sacrifice probably is intended to reinvigorate vegetation and the crops. For the *rajasuya* ceremonies, an extra offering is included in the soma sacrifice, a sixteen-part offering. In Vedic numerology sixteen is an auspicious number that is thought to encompass all reality. The great god Indra of Vedic mythology, although the youngest of the gods, gained supremacy by means of this rite, and so in this context the king gains supremacy by performing the same rite.

The offerings to Anumati and Nirriti and the offering of first fruits come next. The actual offerings consist of baked rice cakes on potsherds with an accompanying offering of clarified butter into one of the three sacrificial fires. Anumati is a goddess of good fortune, whereas Nirriti is a goddess of misfortune. At an obvious level this ritual aims to appease Nirriti so that she will keep away from the sacred proceedings and to attract Anumati so that she will be present. However, the offerings also suggest a symbolic birth, the rebirth of the sacrificer, the ruler. This aspect is suggested by the use of a black garment, associated with Nirriti, which is thrown away by the sacrificer. From other Vedic rituals we know that this garment is identified with the afterbirth of the cosmic god, Prajapati. Anumati, on the other hand, is associated in many Vedic texts with the goddess Aditi, who is identified with the unlimited sky. The offerings to these two goddesses, Nirriti and Anumati, then, represent the birth—the emergence from the womb—of the ruler.

The offering of first fruits consists of twelve cakes on twelve potsherds and a firstborn calf. Also, the sacrificer gives away the garment he wore while undergoing *diksha*. The symbolism here seems clear and is twofold. The twelve cakes represent the twelve months, and the aim of the rite is to appropriate the full year, which in Vedic religion is a potent cosmological entity. The cakes themselves are a mixture of new and old grain, representing the continuity of the vitality of the crops. Giving away the sacrificer's *diksha* garment suggests again his release from the embryo and his rebirth. The rebirth of the ruler, then, is in sympathetic harmony with the ongoing process of rebirth as seen in the annual cycle of vegetation. An underlying assumption of these rituals seems to be that human fertility and human growth generally interact with similar natural rhythms in such a way that the two reinforce each other.

The remainder of the year prior to the second stage of the *rajasuya* is punctuated by the three sacrifices, which are spaced at four-month intervals. The first of these is the all-gods sacrifice, in which offerings are made to all the deities. Trees with budding branches are used for the sacrificial fire, and a stew is made from plants that are just beginning to grow. This is a spring rite, and one of its aims is to promote growth.

The second rite involves making images of sheep from grain; the sacrificer covers them with wool and marks them as male or female. These images are offered to various gods, and the remainder are eaten by the sacrificer. As with the first sacrifice, the aim here seems to be to promote growth, in this case the increase of the flocks. By eating part of the offering himself, the sacrificer also partakes of the sacrificial potency.

The third ritual features offerings to the ancestors and to Rudra, a god considered inauspicious in Vedic religion. Like the sacrifice to Nirriti, the purpose here seems to be to keep Rudra away from the sacred proceedings by appeasing him with offerings. After this ritual the preparatory rites of the first stage are complete, and the stage is set for the second, and central, part of the *rajasuya* ceremony.

The opening rite is a sacrifice to Indra of the plow. It is much like earlier sacrifices, but the connection between the plow and fertility is noteworthy. It is likely that this rite involves the connection seen in many cultures between plowing and sexual intercourse and that it aims at insuring the continuity of fertility in the crops.

The next rite also is primarily a sacrifice to Indra and alludes to his victory over the demon of chaos, Vritra. Through his victory Indra allowed the creative powers of the universe to flow, and in this ritual the victory is commemorated and to some extent reiterated.

The next rite, which takes place at night, consists of spreading apart the central sacrificial fire to the four quarters (north, south, east, and west) and then gathering them together. In essence, the rite reflects a dominant myth of Vedic sacrificial literature and seeks to identify the sacrificer, the ruler, with the hero of the myth. It tells of the cosmic deity Prajapati (often identified with the god Agni), who practiced austerities through which he accumulated immense vigor and heat. At a certain point Prajapati fell apart, his energy pervading the entire cosmos, giving it strength and life. Much of Vedic ritual aims at gathering together this dispersed energy in order to reinvigorate Prajapati, who again practices austerities and again disperses his energy back into the world. The myth expresses the Vedic view of the world, which centers on the cyclically recurring rhythms that are reflected in the seasons. Vedic ritual is humanity's part in the process, as it were, in which people help restore the cosmic powers by distilling Prajapati's power in various ceremonies and then offering it back to him. At this point in the *rajasuya*, the spreading out of the fires represents Prajapati's collapse and the subsequent creation of the world; the gathering together of the fires to the central altar represents his reconstitution. In different ways in this rite the sacrificer is identified with Prajapati, the source of all creative might.

The next ritual is a sacrifice to various deities, all of whom are associated with fertility or birth. Four goddesses and one god are given offerings, and the aim of increasing or insuring fertility is clear. The next two rites also are concerned with promoting growth, and the sacrificer again is identified with Prajapati in various ways. The rites as a whole in this part of the *rajasuya* seek to relate the king to Prajapati and to put the king at the center of the cosmic rhythms that underlie the world.

In the next ritual the ruler makes offerings in the houses of his principal subordinates. The theme of the king impregnating the houses of his subordinates with his accumulated vigor is clear. The king is called Prajapati, and his act is likened to the god impregnating the cosmos with his power. Indra's conquest of Vritra is mentioned, too, and it may be that this ritual is meant to reiterate the cosmic event in which Indra released invigorating powers. In any case the ritual aims to bring about a marriagelike bond between the king and his ministers. By symbolically traversing his realm, the king appropriates that realm and demonstrates his power over it.

The next rite is another offering to the gods that repeats one of the themes of the *diksha* ceremony, namely, reducing the sacrificer to embryonic form. This theme is appropriate at this point in the overall ceremony, as the next ritual is the unction proper, in which the king is believed to be reborn. In general terms a threefold process is discernable in the rites of the second stage of the *rajasuya:* insemination (spreading the fires and visiting the houses of the king's subordinates); embryonic growth (the rite now being discussed, which repeats *diksha* themes); and birth, the unction ceremony.

The unction ceremony begins with a soma sacrifice, including a preliminary *diksha* rite, which lasts five days and is followed by gathering and preparing of the unction fluid. Seventeen kinds of water are collected and poured into four cups. These waters come from a variety of sources, and the ritual formulas that are pronounced over them make it clear that an attempt is being made to distill all the auspicious qualities of the cosmos into the unction fluid. The waters are identified with the god Varuna, the child of the cosmic waters, and in turn the ruler is identified with Varuna. The gathering of the waters and the pouring out of the waters on the king are said to represent Varuna's, and by association the sacrificer's, birth (or rebirth). There is also the attempt to mix together male and female qualities in the various kinds of waters, and thus this rite again emphasizes the aim of insuring growth and fertility. The theme of mixing fiery and watery substances is also emphasized, and the king himself is believed to be engendered in that mixing. Another theme is the combination of Brahminic and ruling powers in the king, who thus becomes a powerful and potent union of priestly and warrior power.

Prior to the actual pouring, there are further preparatory rites in which the king is clothed in special garments, purified by ointment, equipped with bow and arrows, and made to raise his arms. The accompanying formulas make it clear that the king again is identified with various gods, particularly Indra when he is given the bow and arrows, and increasingly is becoming an embodiment of sacred, cosmic power. When he raises his arms he is called the sacred pillar and thus is identified with the axis of the world, which connects the three-part Vedic world of sky, midspace, and earth. The ruler then undergoes a rite in which he walks toward the five directions (the four quarters and the zenith). He thus is said to appropriate the universe and the world of the gods.

Just before the unction itself the king steps onto a tiger skin and, as he stands there, kicks away objects of various metals. This rite represents the victory of certain gods such as Indra over demons like Namuchi, and also the king's emergence from his embryo. The tiger is associated with kingly might, symbolizing that the king has become, as it were, a tiger among men, or a superior man.

While the king stands on the tiger skin facing east, the unction fluid is poured over him by four priests situated at the four quarters. The priests are all Brahmins, but they are associated with different segments of the population; thus in a symbolic sense the ruler is anointed by all of his people. The *rajasuya* ritual declares at certain points that the king is the embryo of the people, and it is appropriate that the people as a whole are represented here at the high point of the ceremony as giving birth to the king by pouring the potent unction fluid over him. As the fluid is poured, certain powerful gods are identified with the king. This part of the ceremony concludes with the king taking three steps in imitation of the god Vishnu's three strides that encompass the entire universe. By doing this the king again appropriates the universe and demonstrates his power over it.

In essence, the unction rite of the *rajasuya*, the central rite of the entire series of rituals, represents the birth of a ruler with a new body. In the preparation of the unction fluid a new, potent essence is prepared and identified with the ruler, and pouring the fluid over him represents his rebirth in a form embodying this sacred essence.

An interesting series of rituals follows the unction, including a chariot race and a dice game. Both rites aim at demonstrating the superior power of the "newborn" ruler. Another series of rites extends for as long as a year after the unction and reiterates the themes of fertility and reinvigoration of the cosmos by the king, who is now the distilled essence of cosmic power and who has control over the cosmic rhythms.

In conclusion, the *rajasuya* reflects the Vedic view of the world, in which the rhythms of birth, growth, death, and rebirth are central. The rituals that make up the *rajasuya* aim in one way or another to harness these rhythms for the welfare of the world and the welfare of the king and his realm. Unlike certain aspects of the later Hindu world view, Vedic believers saw the world as essentially good. They saw themselves as partners with the gods in maintaining and enriching the world and sought through their rituals to enjoy its blessings in full. In the *rajasuya* ceremony, the full and abundant blessings of the world are to be realized by insuring the potency and power of the king, the representative and ruler of all the people. To this end the rituals of the *rajasuya* aim at distilling the powers of the universe in the person of the king and bringing about his rebirth in a new cosmic body.

Common Worship of the Goddess

The *rajasuya* ceremony, although intended for the welfare of the entire cosmos, was designed only for rulers and kings. A variety of ritual specialists were necessary, and the investment of time and wealth was considerable. In contrast are many rituals in Hinduism that are designed for ordinary individuals. These rituals require little paraphernalia and no particular liturgical training, and participants may be from any caste. As representative of this simpler, more common form of worship in Hinduism we shall look at *samanya puja*, common worship, as described in the fourteenth-century *Kalika Purana*, a text devoted to the worship of the Great Goddess.[6] In general form and in most details, the description of common worship in the *Kalika Purana* is applicable to other deities as well. It is even possible that the author described this ritual as it was performed for other deities and merely substituted the Goddess as the principal deity.

The overall aim of common worship as described in the *Kalika Purana* is the identification of the adept with the Goddess. In this respect, common worship is not dissimilar from the *rajasuya*, in which the ruler becomes identified with various deities and with cosmic power in general. However, common worship does not aim at the invigoration of the cosmic processes and the general welfare of the world. It is undertaken by an individual both by and for himself or herself and in this respect reflects the concern in later Hinduism with individual release (moksha) from the round of birth and rebirth (samsara), although the adept may very well undertake the ritual for a specific worldly purpose.

No priests are necessary for common worship, the adept acting as his or her own liturgist. No sacred fires are required, and the ritual may be performed virtually anywhere. The *Kalika Purana* suggests a solitary place, such as a mountain top or a cave, but says that the ritual may be performed in the adept's own house as well. The use of an image is optional, a mental image serving just as well as a physical one. The text also adds that the ritual will be even more potent if conducted at a holy place, particularly one sacred to the Goddess.

The materials needed for the ritual are minimal. As stated above, an image is not necessary; the adept only needs some flowers, a bit of food, and a jar of water, all of which will be offered to the Goddess. The ritual may be performed at any time, apparently by a person from any caste, and by men or women.

Although common worship is nowhere described in Vedic literature, and although it clearly belongs to a later period in Hindu religious history, some themes and presuppositions are similar to the Vedic ritual world. In

---

[6]*Samanya puja* to the Goddess is described in K. R. Van Kooij, *Worship of the Goddess according to the Kālikāpurāna* (Leiden, The Netherlands: E. J. Brill, 1972). I have followed Van Kooij's description and interpretation of this ritual.

common worship, as in Vedic ritual, a correspondence is assumed between the macrocosm, the universe as a whole, and the microcosm, the individual person; both types of ritual, *yajna* and puja, seek to articulate and manipulate this correspondence in such a way that the worshiper becomes identified ritually with the essence of cosmic power. The use of mantras is also common to both. (A mantra is a ritual formula believed to have sacred power.) In Vedic rituals these formulas are almost always taken from the Vedic *Samhitas*, collections of hymns to the gods. In the puja rituals, Vedic mantras are sometimes used, but non-Vedic ones are more common. Non-Vedic mantras often consist simply of a series of syllables, such as *om hum phat*, that do not form actual words. Another common feature of both Vedic and later puja rituals is the theme of rebirth. In the *Kalika Purana* version of common worship, the adept, like the ruler in the *rajasuya* ceremony, undergoes a symbolic rebirth during the course of the ritual.

Although common worship as described in the *Kalika Purana* consists of an unbroken series of actions, for practical purposes the ritual may be said to have four parts: (1) acts of preparation, (2) meditation, (3) worship of the Goddess proper, and (4) concluding rites. The text does not say how long the ritual takes, but we can imagine that it would not take much more than an hour or two to complete and might be undertaken in abbreviated form in a much shorter time. In the following description of the rite, which is performed by both males and females, let us imagine that the practitioner is a male as shown in Figure 6–1.

The rites of preparation have two main aims, the purification of the adept and the delimitation of a sacred space within which the worship of the Goddess may take place. First, the adept bathes. The text recommends a sacred bathing place but adds that any water is suitable. The adept is also instructed to sip water, which symbolizes inner purification. By way of further purification the adept is advised to ask the Goddess to dismiss all evil from his mind. With the exclamation *hum phat* the adept looks with an angry expression in all directions and at himself, and thus expels from himself all sins and evil.

Having purified himself, the adept approaches the spot chosen for worship. The spot itself should be free from impurities, and the adept should sprinkle it with water while pronouncing the appropriate mantra. Upon entering the sacred spot the adept should carefully examine the items to be offered to insure that they, too, are free from impurities. Flowers, for example, should be free from insects. The items to be offered also are purified with water and mantras. The adept is advised to further purify the place by expelling invisible demons by uttering the mantra *om hum sah*. Now the adept draws a schematic diagram (*mandala*) on the ground with his finger. He is instructed to start in the north and proceed to the west in a counterclockwise direction. This sequence is the reverse of the auspicious clockwise direction and may suggest the theme of death and dissolution

FIGURE 6-1 An adept performing common worship. (Courtesy of Air India.)

that is central in the next part of the ritual. After drawing the mandala with one continuous motion, the adept is told to perform a rite called fencing the quarters. He does this to further mark off the place of worship and to protect it from undesirable influences, especially evil spirits.

The adept now turns his attention to a jar of water. While saying mantras he picks up the jar and places it within the sacred area. With hand gestures (mudras) and mantras he then transforms the water into nectar suitable for offering to the Goddess. The water in the jar is now believed to be as sacred as, or identical with, Ganges water. The preparatory rites close with mantras to insure the stability and purity of the earth and the spot where the adept will seat himself during the remainder of the ritual.

The second part of common worship involves a series of acts that are primarily mental. This extended meditation continues one of the central aims of the preparatory part of the ritual by further purifying the adept. The mental purification, however, is considerably more thorough than the foregoing rites, as it aims at the symbolic death and dissolution of the adept, the overriding motif of this meditation. The text explains the necessity of this part of the ritual by saying that the body is composed of impure elements—mucus, feces, urine, and so on—and as such is unfit to be an instrument of worship. The mental death of the adept is followed by the mental re-creation of the world with the Goddess in its center and the identification of the adept with the re-created world and particularly with the Goddess herself. This part of the ritual, then, is meant to destroy the adept's impure self and body and re-create a new body that is fit to worship the Goddess because it is identified with the Goddess herself.

After assuming the correct posture and breath control, the adept takes a flower in his hands and begins a ritual that releases his life force, his jiva, from his body and then symbolically destroys the body itself. Mentally the adept imagines his jiva passing through various stages connected with certain elements: fire, wind, water, and sound. Finally, identifying his jiva with space, the adept imagines his life force leaving his body through an aperture at the top of his skull. This aperture is opened with the exclamation of the mantra *om hum phat* at the very moment the jiva is released, which signals the death of the adept. The aperture is said to be the exit of the jiva at actual death, and it is clear that the adept is mentally destroying himself in this part of common worship.

The adept then proceeds with the second stage of the ritual by destroying his physical body (or "corpse"). The destruction of his body, a microcosm of the macrocosm, also represents the destruction of the cosmos and takes place in four stages. First, the adept imagines his body dissolving; then he imagines it burning (as at actual death rituals); then he imagines the ashes blowing away; and finally he imagines a shower of pure nectar. These four stages are accompanied by the uttering of single syllables (*bijas*, or "seeds") that stand for the four elemental substances of matter (wind, fire, earth, and water). In effect, the adept has destroyed the cosmos and himself by reducing them to their elemental constituents. His ultimate purification is now complete, and he is ready to be reborn.

The adept next begins to re-create the cosmos mentally by pronouncing the seed syllable (*bija*) of the Goddess, which sets the whole creative process in motion. Then he visualizes the various parts of the cosmos and finally the Goddess herself seated on a throne in the center of the cosmos. The adept now identifies himself with the Goddess by placing the flower in his hands on top of his head and pronouncing the words: "This is me." The adept's deification is further reinforced by means of mudras and mantras that identify parts of the cosmos with parts of his body. The adept now has provided himself with a new, divine body (actually identified with the Goddess herself) and is prepared to undertake the worship of the Goddess proper.

The adept begins his worship of the Goddess by performing inward worship of her. That is, he mentally pays homage to the Goddess who resides within himself. By doing so, the adept is made aware of his own divinity, the divine power of the Goddess in himself. He visualizes her along with her attendants residing in his heart in much the same way that he will when he performs outer worship of her.

The worshiper now leads the Goddess from his heart into the mandala by exhaling through the right nostril onto a flower he holds in his hands and pronouncing the syllable *yam.* The Goddess now resides in the flower and is placed in the center of the mandala. The Goddess also may be trans-ferred from the adept's heart to the mandala with mudras, by which the adept catches her in his hands and places her in the mandala.

The Goddess is now praised with mantras, some of which are Vedic. She is treated as an honored guest, and the adept serves her with actions similar to nearly all puja rites. She is offered the water-become-nectar from the jar for bathing and may be offered a variety of articles, physically or mentally, by the adept, whose aim now is to serve the Goddess in all ways pleasing to her. The relationship of the adept to the Goddess at this point, and in nearly all puja rites, is one of inferior to superior. The adept's role is that of an attentive servant toward his mistress.

In large temple pujas the attendance upon the deity may be main-tained throughout the day every day by a staff of priests and may include elaborate rites and costly gifts. In many temples the daily routine includes waking the deity with the sounds of bells, waving lights before him, bathing him, drying him, fanning him, feeding him, and even putting him to bed. In common worship the acts of attendance are simpler, and the physical offerings include little more than specially prepared water and flowers. The emphasis in common worship, as opposed to temple puja, is on visualizing the acts of service mentally rather than performing them outwardly with costly paraphernalia. The *Kalika Purana* says the adept should visualize the Goddess with her ornaments, her typical setting or seat, her animal vehicle (*vahana*), and all her attendant deities. The adept, that is, "fills up" the man-dala with a detailed mental image of the Goddess in her heavenly court and worships her.

The adept also is instructed in the *Kalika Purana* to pronounce re-peatedly and continuously the Goddess's special mantra. He is to do so with or without the help of a rosary while meditating on the essential identity of the mantra he is reciting, his guru who has given him the mantra, and himself. We see here again an underlying theme of common worship, namely, the realization of the union of worshiper and worshiped, adept and Goddess. While the adept pronounces the mantra, he imagines the Goddess residing in his heart and in other spiritual centers of his body.

Outward worship of the Goddess in the mandala closes with a final offering that usually consists of rice or some other grain. In more elaborate puja to the Goddess this offering may be an animal. An entire chapter in the *Kalika Purana* suggests offerings appropriate to the Goddess and the rewards that may be expected from them. The adept now dismisses the

Goddess by circumambulating the flower that represents her and mentally visualizing her return to her normal abode: heaven, the adept's heart, or some particular holy place. If the Goddess is visualized as returning to the worshiper's heart, the adept smells the flower that has represented the Goddess and then places it on his head.

Having completed the worship proper, the adept now concludes the rite by erasing the mandala and disposing of the remains of the offerings. He rubs away the mandala with his fingertips while saying the appropriate mantra and then rubs the dust of his fingers on his forehead. This probably symbolizes the interiorization of the mandala and the cosmos that it represents. To dispose of the remains of his offerings, the adept draws a small mandala and worships the power remaining in these articles, which are thought to retain sacredness. Fierce goddesses are associated with these leftovers and must be propitiated before the ceremony can be complete. The remains themselves may be discarded after being worshiped by leaving them in water or at the foot of a tree. A prayer to the sun is optional as a final rite and is said to make right any mistakes the adept has made during worship.

In essence, common worship is a ritual through which the worshiper is deified. Ritually undertaking one's own death and dissolution, one re-creates the world and oneself. In this act of re-creation the Goddess (or whichever deity is being worshiped) is identified with the worshiper. The two are declared to be essentially one. In this sense common worship is worship of one's own inner sacred essence as well as worship of a superior divine being.

The *Kalika Purana* states that this ritual enables one to have every wish fulfilled and that after living a long and fruitful life one will dwell with the Goddess in her heaven for a long time before being reborn. It is probably also the case, although the text does not state this explicitly, that the adept may achieve moksha by means of this ritual.

7

Sacred Female Imagery and Women's Religious Experience in Hinduism

GODDESSES

A remarkable feature of Hinduism, both historically and in terms of the living tradition, is the impressive array of goddesses pervading its mythology, devotion, and worship. Hindu goddesses, furthermore, do not conform to a few stereotypes but represent a diverse range of beings that impress one with their many characteristics and functions. Some goddesses conform to social stereotypes for women, while others appear completely at odds with such models. There are goddesses associated with wealth and power, goddesses who are depicted as mighty warriors, and goddesses who are associated with death and destruction and who receive blood offerings. Some goddesses are associated with prominent physical features of the landscape, while others are strongly identified with particular villages, cities, or regions. Wherever one looks in Hinduism, there are goddesses.[1]

One of the most dramatic ways in which sacred female imagery pervades Hindu religion is the affirmation of and reverence for the earth itself (or the Indian subcontinent itself) as a great goddess. As the earth, she is known as Prithivi, and as India she is known as Bharat Ma (Mother India). To a great extent, Hinduism is a geographical religion, a religious tradition that is intensely associated with India itself. For Hindus, India is a sacred

[1]For an overview of Hindu goddesses, see David Kinsley, *Hindu Goddesses: Visions of the Divine Feminine in the Hindu Religious Tradition* (Berkeley: University of California Press, 1986).

129

place, and the reverence for the land of India as a goddess is a typical Hindu expression of this idea. In Varanasi, the sacred center of Hinduism, there is a temple dedicated to Bharat Ma. In most Hindu temples there is an image of the deity to whom the shrine is dedicated. Usually this image is anthropomorphic, depicting the deity in human form with appropriate symbols. In the case of this Varanasi temple to Bharat Ma, however, there is no anthropomorphic image in the inner sanctum. Instead, there is a large relief map of the Indian subcontinent. That is, the goddess is understood to be India itself.

The sacredness of the Indian landscape for Hindus is also seen in the many holy places, called *tirthas* or "crossings" (from the mundane to the spiritual, from the earthly to the heavenly), that dot the country. Frequently these places are associated with a particular goddess. All the rivers in India, for example, are thought of as goddesses in riverine form. The most sacred of all the rivers of India is the Ganges, which tumbles out of the foothills of the Himalayas and meanders across the vast northern plains, fertilizing and refreshing the land. The water of the Ganges is understood to be spiritually purifying, and a dip in the Ganges, particularly at such holy places as Hardwar in the north or Varanasi in the east, is believed to cleanse one of all impurities and is a ritual that nearly every devout Hindu would like to undertake at least once. The goddess who is the Ganges River, Ganga Ma (Mother Ganges), is believed to originate in heaven, from where she flows to earth, blessing and fructifying humankind and providing a tangible link between earth and heaven.

In many cases, sacred places in India are associated with a particular part of the goddess Sati, a deity who in Hindu mythology killed herself and whose body was subsequently distributed throughout the world—that is, throughout India. In this story, India is invested with the sacred power of the goddess and comes to be thought of as her actual body. As pilgrims travel from one sacred place to another, an underlying unity is often emphasized by means of this myth of Sati and her descent to earth. The myth reinforces the theme of India as a sacred female being by identifying specific places with particular parts of Sati's divine body.

Goddesses are also prominent at the village level. Nearly every village in India has its local goddess who presides over and protects that village from demons, disease, and disruptive outside forces. These goddesses are as numerous as the hundreds of thousands of Indian villages, and at the local level they are often the center of religious rituals and piety. They are deities whose power generally does not extend beyond the boundaries of the village, but they are also very approachable in the village context. They are, as it were, specialists in the locale, which in many ways they embody. Local villagers petition their goddess for daily needs and specific problems, none being too insignificant or trivial for her concern. Such goddesses are attentive to the local situation and therefore are often the most popular, responsive, and protective deities in the everyday lives of many Hindus. At village goddess festivals, all members of the village participate, regardless of their caste. These goddesses are protective of and partial to all villagers. Their field of power and concern is geographical, not social, political, economic, or caste related.

Of the goddesses who feature prominently in the Sanskrit textual tradition and who are known all over India, Durga, Lakshmi, Sarasvati, and Kali are among the most popular and impressive. Durga is a cosmic battle queen created by the massed power of the male Hindu gods after they have been defeated in battle by a demon who is invincible to all but a female. Durga usually is depicted having sixteen arms, each of which wields a weapon, and riding a fierce lion or tiger. This warrior goddess plays the role of protecting the cosmos from the disruptive influences of demons. She upholds the order of dharma by assuming a traditional male role and playing that role more effectively than any male deity. Durga is widely revered and worshiped in India and is known particularly as a goddess who rescues her devotees from exceptionally dangerous circumstances. In this role she plays the part of a savior to her devotees. One of the most popular, colorful, and lavish Hindu festivals, Durga Puja, is celebrated every autumn in honor of this mighty cosmic queen.

The goddess Lakshmi is the most popular Hindu goddess throughout India. She is associated with wealth, good luck, well-being, fertility, political

FIGURE 7-1 Woman propitiating the goddess Durga. (Courtesy of Hillary Rodrigues.)

FIGURE 7-2 Lakshmi holding an oil lamp. (From C. Sivararmamurti, *South Indian Bronzes* [New Delhi: Lalit Akademi, 1963], Fig. 96b.)

power, and royalty. Her image is found enshrined in small household altars, in shops and businesses, and in public temples and shrines all over India. She is often shown holding a lotus and seated on a lotus and is described as lotus eyed and lotus loving. The lotus is a particularly common and typical Hindu symbol for the organic world and the rhythmic and exuberant powers of fertility and growth that pervade that world. Lakshmi is manifest where growth, fertility, health, and well-being exist. As such, her presence is ardently sought after. She is often depicted with the god Vishnu as her spouse. It is fitting that the cosmic king Vishnu should be accompanied by Lakshmi, because the prosperity of kings is directly related to their ability to attract and keep Lakshmi at their side and in their kingdom. Should Lakshmi decide to depart, a king and his kingdom would fall into poverty, disease, infertility, and disorder. Lakshmi, to a great extent, is that mysterious, intangible, and undeniably powerful quality called "luck" or "fortune." Certain individuals seem to possess it, while others do not, and in the Hindu context it is Lakshmi's presence that makes the crucial difference.

Sarasvati, a goddess known throughout India, is associated with wisdom, knowledge, and culture. She is sometimes associated with Vishnu as his consort and so is often understood to be Lakshmi's co-wife. The two goddesses—representing quite different realities, blessings, and personalities—are often described as expressing impatience with each other, as co-wives are wont to do in much Hindu literature. Unlike Lakshmi, Sarasvati has no connection with fertility, and her blessings do not tend toward the material. Sarasvati's most typical places of worship are schools, musicians'

FIGURE 7-3 Lakshmi. (From C. Sivararmamurti, *South Indian Bronzes* [New Delhi: Lalit Kala Akademi, 1963], Fig. 68b.)

practice rooms, or the shrines of master artists and teachers—places where learning and art are cultivated. Iconographic depictions of Sarasvati emphasize her pure and ethereal appearance. She blesses those dwelling on the earth, but she is not of the earth in the sense that Lakshmi is. Her primary blessing is artistic, scholastic, and spiritual inspiration. She is often associated with refined speech, a primary characteristic of the civilized and intellectually superior person.

Sarasvati is also associated with the River Sarasvati that is mentioned in the *Vedas*, a river that has long since disappeared. She is often depicted with riverine attributes, along with Ganga Ma (the goddess of the Ganges River), on the door lintels of temples. Before entering a sacred precinct, it is important for devotees to become pure; the placement of Sarasvati and Ganga Ma at such locations suggests symbolic bathing in their purifying waters as the devotee enters the temple or shrine. In short, Sarasvati is a goddess associated with purity, intellectual and artistic inspiration, spiritual wisdom, and the refinements of culture in general. She therefore is revered widely in a culture that extols all of these things.

The goddess Kali has quite different associations from Durga, Lakshmi, or Sarasvati. Her name means "she who is black" or "blackie," and she is always shown as black, very dark, or bluish black, perhaps suggesting an affiliation with the dark-skinned tribal groups of India who live on the periphery (both geographically and culturally) of Hindu society. In Hindu mythology, Kali usually is mentioned in the context of fierce battles in which passions have reached great intensity. In these situations, it seems that she is the embodied wrath of the divine, which unleashes itself in a fury of violence and anger. Kali is often described as gulping down the hot blood of her victims and then dancing out of control, threatening to destroy the cosmos itself.

Iconography most typically shows Kali in the cremation ground. She may be seated on a corpse, standing on the recumbent Shiva, or standing on a body that is being burned on a cremation fire. She is accompanied by ghouls and jackals. Her hair usually is disheveled, whereas most other goddesses wear their hair braided or bound in the fashion of adult women. She is naked except for a garland of severed heads, a girdle of severed arms, and earrings of infant corpses. She has four arms and usually is shown holding a bloodied cleaver with her upper left hand and a severed head in her lower left hand and making the sign of "fear not" with her upper right hand and the sign of conferring boons with her lower right hand.

In appearance and function Kali symbolizes unrefined, uncontrollable, raw aspects of reality that not even the most heroic efforts of the gods or human beings can control completely: disease; untimely, violent death; the wearing down of all things by time; the inevitable process of decay; and the capricious violence of natural forces such as flood, drought, and storm. She represents the fragility of the order of dharma and, in so doing, awakens an interest in moksha, release from the bonds of karma and samsara. The boons that Kali bestows, suggested by her right-handed signs, pertain to the more realistic and wider vision of reality she grants when one finds the courage to face the darker, more painful dimensions of life that she symbolizes and the courage to reflect on one's own finite, fragile existence.

THE ROLE OF WOMEN

In the majority of written sources in the Hindu tradition, which all tend toward androcentrism (male centeredness), women are seen as dependent on and subservient to males. In the most famous and influential Hindu Law Book, the *Law Book of Manu*, we are told that young women are to be under the control of their fathers, married women under the control of their husbands, and widows under the control of their sons. Without male guidance and control, women are thought to be socially irresponsible and dangerous. Throughout this text, and in most others as well, women are viewed almost entirely vis-à-vis males. Their role in society is to serve, give birth to, and nourish males.

The four stages of life—student, householder, forest dweller, and world renouncer—apply primarily to males. For females, there usually are only three stages of life, and for the most part they are quite unlike the four stages so often described in Hindu writings. For females, the stages of life (although not formally prescribed) are: (1) unmarried young woman, (2) married woman, and (3) widow. The duties for each stage also bear little relation to the four stages that are meant to apply to males. In the first stage of her life, as a maiden, a girl is to learn the arts of being a good wife. She is to be obedient and subordinate to her parents and learn the arts of pleasing a man from them (particularly from her mother). In this regard, her model is the goddess Sita, the wife of Rama, the hero of the *Ramayana*. Sita is the ideal *pati-vrata*, the wife entirely devoted to her husband. For Sita, Rama's welfare, reputation, and well-being are the primary concerns of her life. In her unmarried state, the girl is to cultivate Sita's virtues and pray that she will be blessed with a husband as good as Rama. In her married state, which traditionally begins shortly after her first menstruation, she is urged to imitate Sita in all her thoughts and actions and to regard her husband as a god; by serving him she will realize worldly and spiritual fulfillment. She is to pray for sons, which according to most Hindu Law Books represent the fulfillment of a woman's life. One of her primary goals in life is to perpetuate her husband's lineage by giving him sons. When a female marries, she leaves her home village, moves to her husband's village, and assumes the identity of his lineage. In moving to this stage in her life, which

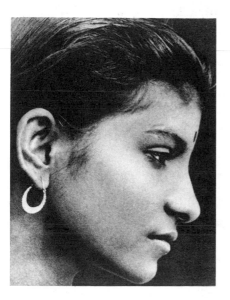

FIGURE 7-4 Young Bengali woman, Varanasi. (From Richard Lannoy, *India, People and Places* [New York: Vanguard Press, 1955], p. 156.)

is ritualized in the marriage ceremony, the Hindu female assumes a new identity that allies her strongly to her husband and his lineage. As a mother of sons, in which role Hindu females are revered in most Hindu scriptures, the female dotes on her sons and in return is adored by them. The intensity of the mother-son relationship in Hinduism is remarkable.

If her husband should die before she does, a woman enters a third stage of life, widowhood. According to most Hindu writings, she has lost her most important reason for living, even if she has sons. As a widow she is to lead an ascetic life, restricting what she eats to the simplest foods, dressing in plain clothes, and wearing no adornment. To some extent, especially in upper castes, she may be shunned as inauspicious and find her life greatly restricted socially. Remarriage for women is rare and is strongly opposed in most Hindu writings. In most circumstances and among most castes, the widow is an unenviable character.

> It is said that the "lines of misfortune" are written on her "white forehead" because it does not have the red dot (*tilaka*) any more [the mark of a married woman whose husband is alive]. Her tonsured head or flowing hair unadorned with flowers bespeaks her miserable status [the wife's hair is braided and adorned]. No jewels adorn her nose and ears, no chains her neck, no bangles her wrists, no rings her toes. Clad simply in a cotton sari of prescribed colour, often without a blouse, she as a rule goes about barefoot. Not only is she denied such enjoyments, but every other opportunity for pleasure (*bhoga*), such as participation in social gatherings, festivals, the partaking of rich food, indeed, entertainment or pleasures of any sort. So complete is the redefinition of her status and role from wife to widow that she bemoans the loss of her husband every moment.[2]

In some parts of India (particularly Bengal and Rajasthan) during certain periods the practice of widow suicide, or suttee, was practiced fairly widely by some castes. The logic of this practice was rooted in the depiction of women as subservient to, and socially defined by, males, particularly husbands. Without a husband, a woman literally is a nobody according to the male-oriented Hindu scriptures. Suttee was the final, quintessential act of a *pati-vrata*, a woman entirely devoted to her husband. Women who performed suttee were greatly revered, and there are shrines to them in many parts of India.

> For the woman who opts for *sati* [suttee], *sati* is like the performance of an especially solemn religious ceremony. Ideally her decision is immediate and without deliberation. She herself calmly orders the preliminaries of the *sati* rite and dons her bridal sari. Though others may implore her to reconsider

---

[2]Alaka Heijib and Katherine K. Young, "Towards Recognition of the Religious Structure of the Satī," paper presented to the American Oriental Society, 1978, cited in Katherine K. Young, "Hinduism," in Arvind Sharma, ed., *Women in World Religions* (Albany: State University of New York Press, 1987), p. 84.

her decision, especially for the sake of her children, she does not seem to hear them. She benevolently blesses them. She sheds not a tear, even though great lamentation may surround her, for she looks upon this moment as the most auspicious of her life. This is the supreme opportunity for self-sacrifice that consummates her life of dedication to her husband. As if departing on a joy-ous journey she prostrates herself before the elders and asks for their bless-ings. They then generously bless her and, reversing the usual norms of re-spect, prostrate themselves to her in return: they look upon her as the goddess incarnate. As she leads the procession to the cremation ground, where the corpse of her husband is awaiting cremation, she is joined by the people of the village, who come to witness this awesome moment.

After the performance of the preliminary rites, she bids final farewell with folded hands. . . . With perfect tranquillity, she climbs the ladder, sits down on the pyre and tenderly takes her husband's head on her lap. Optionally she may recline beside him. Even when the flames reach her, she maintains her composure. The crowd acclaims her as a good wife, a true *sati*, one who has brought immense dignity and honour to herself, her family, and the com-munity . . . they also express gratitude that they themselves had a chance to witness this noble sacrifice.[3]

In some cases, we can imagine that women were strongly encouraged, probably even forced, to kill themselves in this fashion and that the alter-native of living as a social outcaste must have weighed heavily in making such a dreadful decision. What is significant about this practice, however, is the way in which it represents a logical extension of the view that women only exist for males, which is a very common and strong theme in much Hindu literature.

Another theme in much Hindu writing, which we must always remem-ber was almost surely written by a small elite of high-caste males, is that women are inherently inferior to males in several ways. In many cases women are excluded from performing religious rituals or from assuming religious roles. In Vedic rituals, women are rarely allowed to take a direct part, although the presence of wives sometimes is required. In this role they are primarily passive observers of rituals performed by their husbands and male priests. Excluding females from rituals partly concerns attitudes to-ward their inherent impurity, which is linked directly to distinctive aspects of female sexuality, namely, menstruation and childbirth. Female sexual fluids are regarded as highly polluting, and during menstruation and im-mediately following childbirth, women are excluded from normal social contact and are banished from the kitchen lest they pollute the food. In many texts, women are included with the low castes as unfit to hear or read sacred texts, as too unclean to take part in a variety of rituals, and as lacking the spiritual maturity to qualify for most religious professions. They are also often said to be incapable of attaining moksha.

[3]Ibid., pp. 83–84.

Such, then, is the view of women in the vast majority of Hindu texts. Although not always misogynist, these tests usually regard women as in some sense marginal to religious and spiritual concerns. On the basis of these texts, one could easily conclude that Hinduism is primarily a religion for males with little place for females.

But such is not actually the case, as can be seen by anyone who spends a little time in India observing the everyday religious scene. Women are extremely active in almost every aspect of Hindu religion, and in many areas they dominate the scene. Although certain aspects of public Hinduism remain totally dominated by males, such as the temple priesthood and the priestly functions in a wide variety of life-cycle and home rituals, and although the vast majority of Hindus who renounce the world and take up the life of a sannyasi are males, females are intensely engaged in most aspects of Hinduism today and probably always have been.

Sifting through Hindu writings and history for a clearer picture of the actual role of women in Hinduism and of their religious experience has been underway for a generation, and a different picture from the male-centered view given earlier is slowly beginning to emerge. Historians, anthropologists, and religionists have begun to piece together a picture of women's spirituality that in many ways points out the stereotypical picture presented in the majority of Hindu scriptures written by males. Although this revised picture is far from complete, it is clear that there are at the present time, and probably always have been, a variety of female ways of being Hindu, ways that sometimes are shared with men but often are primarily or exclusively the province of females. That is, there are rituals, festivals, customs, and life-cycle rituals that are distinctively female-oriented and provide women with a satisfying and meaningful context in which to express their Hindu spirituality.

In addition to this, it is becoming increasingly clear that some women have assumed religious roles that are restricted to males in most Hindu scriptures. That is, we know of women who have been famous saints, teachers or gurus, monarchs with ritual responsibilities, healers, and priests. That males clearly outnumber women in all of these roles does not change the fact that some women have successfully challenged the high-caste male perception of the limits of women's spirituality.

To a great extent, the locus of Hindu women's spirituality, at present and historically, is the domestic sphere. It is the women of the house who perform daily worship to the household deities, who create the auspicious diagrams that adorn and protect the home from bad luck and evil spirits, and whose responsibility it is to create and maintain a source of auspicious power so strong that all those within the sphere of the home will be protected from harm. Hindu women create this source of power by cultivating the attitude of a *pati-vrata*, of whom the goddess Sita is the paradigm, and by performing special rituals call *vrats*.

The term *vrat* means "vow" and refers to a type of ritual that, while suitable for men or women, has become one of the mainstays of Hindu women's spirituality throughout India. In essence, *vrats* involve abstention from certain types of foods, indulgences, or pleasures in order to obtain the blessing or favor of a deity, usually for a member of the woman's immediate family. In this sense, a *vrat* is typically a form of asceticism or yoga, that is, concentrated self-control and self-denial. *Vrats* can be done seasonally, for special occasions, or weekly. Seasonal *vrats* are often elaborate affairs that take place over many days and may include festive public ceremonies undertaken by large groups of women together. *Vrats* done for special occasions take place when a particular need or crisis arises. Many women undertake *vrats* routinely, fasting or abstaining from particular foods or pleasures on certain days of the week. Several women I met in Varanasi observed such vows, and it was clear that they understood their entire life as the ongoing observation of rituals aimed at insuring the stability, safety, and vitality of their households. For them, and I suspect for a great many Hindu women, ritual and meditative restraint and self-control in the context of observing *vrats* are very much a part of the normal rhythm of their lives.

Vrats are often undertaken with the other female members of the household; aspects of the ritual that take place outside the house, on the banks of a river or tank or at a shrine or temple, for example, will be undertaken in the company of many other neighborhood women. The public parts of the ritual, furthermore, are sometimes undertaken without the help or presence of a male priest (although male priests sometimes do have a role). It is, for the most part, women's business.

One of the most popular *vrats* undertaken by women in Varanasi is called Jivit Putrika or Jiutiya. According to those who perform this *vrat*, and

FIGURE 7–5 Women performing a *vrat*. (Author's photograph.)

according to the pamphlets describing it that one can buy in the local ba-
zaars, this *vrat*, if properly done, prevents the untimely death of one's sons.
This is a seasonal *vrat*, undertaken each year in late September and early
October. A large number of women in Varanasi observe it, and the participants appear to be from all castes. In brief outline this *vrat* has three parts
or aspects. First, each woman who observes it must fast by abstaining from
foods that are not considered highly pure or sattvic ("pure" in this case
refers to the spiritual qualities of given foods), or abstaining from her favorite foods, or abstaining from all food. The severity of the fasting depends on the individual, but many women abstain from all food for an
entire day at some point during the observation of the *vrat*. Second, the
story concerning the origin of the *vrat* is recited by women observing the
vrat or read in a public forum (sometimes this is done by a male Brahmin
priest). The story of this particular *vrat* tells of women in the past who lost
their sons in battle, to sickness, or in accidents and how they regained their
sons' lives by performing the Jiutiya *vrat*, which was revealed to them by a
deity. Stories about the *vrat* also include cases in which women failed to
observe their fasts strictly and the fatal consequences to their sons. Third,
there is a public ceremony held at the Lakshmi temple in Varanasi, where
women come to make offerings to Lakshmi with the prayer that she will be
present in their households during the next year to bestow all her auspicious blessings.

The extent to which the well-being of the household and its individual
members is dependent on women's piety and spirituality is the subject of
many stories in Hindu texts and mythology. In a well-known Hindu myth,
the god Vishnu, who is known for his trickery and cunning, was unable to
defeat a particularly heroic demon. In desperation, Vishnu disguised him-

FIGURE 7-6   Women performing a *vrat*, Varanasi. (Author's photograph).

self as his adversary and approached the demon's wife. After having sex with her, Vishnu revealed his true identity. Although the demon's virtuous wife had been tricked into violating her loyalty to her husband, she immediately lost the power with which she had protected her husband from harm. The demon lost his aura of "luck" and was easily vanquished by Vishnu. As this story illustrates, a woman's protective power extends to the public sphere in the sense that all members of her household remain invulnerable to harm wherever they are. While remaining within the household sphere herself, within which she practices her piety, she extends her influence beyond that sphere by means of her devotedness, rituals, and piety. In this sense, women exercise control over a large area and win for themselves satisfaction that they are in control of their own lives and in control of the lives of those dear to them. While a skeptic might argue that women's domestic rituals are often done especially for the welfare of the male members of the household and that males rarely, if ever, perform such rituals for the benefit of women members of the home, it seems clear that *vrats* and other rituals undertaken by women in the domestic sphere express and create a feeling of women's religious space, in which they are in control of the most meaningful area of their lives.

WOMEN'S SPIRITUALITY

Although Hindu literature, which is strongly androcentric, gives the impression that women were excluded from many, if not most, types of religious spirituality—priestly, ascetic, monastic, mystical, and devotional—there is considerable evidence that women in fact were active in all of these roles, although in some more than others. Women's spirituality is rich and diverse in Hinduism despite the limitations imposed on women in the textual tradition.

Perhaps the area in which women's spirituality is most apparent historically is in the devotional movements of Hinduism. In these movements the role of priestly intermediaries (who are almost always male) is by and large irrelevant. The devotee, no matter of which caste, may approach the deity directly. The devotional language of these movements, furthermore, was usually not Sanskrit, which was only known by a small number of high-caste members, mostly male, but almost always was one of the vernacular languages of India. The devotional movements, then, were popular religious expressions of Hinduism and as such were open to full participation by women in many cases.

A typical theme in the devotion of female saints who were members of these devotional movements is their longing to marry the deity, often in preference to marrying, or remaining married to, a human husband. Indeed, devotion to God in the lives of many of these women involved the theme of marriage resistance, marriage refusal, or marriage denial. In a

FIGURE 7-7   Woman healer with male assistant, Durga temple, Varanasi. (Courtesy of Hillary Rodrigues.)

social situation where marriage represents the inherent destiny and fulfillment of women, not marrying, or finding release from an unhappy marriage, was extremely difficult. It seems from the lives of several women devotional saints that one way out of marriage was to live a life of devotion to a male deity who was adored and approached as one's lover or husband.

Mahadeviyakka (twelfth century C.E.) was forced into marriage to a local king against her will and eventually renounced the world, leaving her husband. She wandered naked through the land, legend says, and sang songs of passion and love for her true husband, the god Shiva. In some of her poems, which may have been written while she still lived with her human husband, she speaks of the impossibility of serving a husband who lusts after other women and lacks noble attributes. She expresses longing to be entirely devoted to her true husband, Shiva. Her poems are redolent with passion, and she often sings of a love for God that is intense and overwhelming, as in this poem:

> He bartered my heart,
> looted my flesh,
> claimed as tribute
> my pleasure,
> took over
> all of me.
>
> I'm the women of love
> for my lord, white as jasmine.[4]

Lalleshvari, who lived in Kashmir during the fourteenth century C.E., was also a devotee of Shiva and, like Mahadeviyakka, found herself trapped

---

[4]A. K. Ramanujan, trans., *Speaking of Śiva* (Baltimore: Penguin Books, 1973), p. 125.

in a difficult marriage. She was married at the age of fourteen, and her domestic life was extremely trying. Many legends tell of the harsh treatment she received from her mother-in-law and husband and extol her patience and forbearance. According to legend, her mother-in-law persecuted her unmercifully, while her husband was indifferent to her and refused to comfort her in her sufferings. At a certain point, about twelve years after her marriage, she suddenly left home and became a wandering religious singer. Precisely what incident prompted her to leave home is not known. Her difficult domestic life, however, must be understood as the background against which she rebelled and set off naked to sing songs to her beloved Shiva. It is likely that she had increasingly found solace in her devotion to God and that her final departure from her in-laws marked the end of her attempts to reconcile two worlds: the world of custom, duty, and social acceptance and the world of devotion to her Lord, which demanded the lifestyle of a wandering devotee. In renouncing her particular domestic hell, Lalleshvari found in her quest for union with Shiva an alternative to the normal expectations of society, namely, marriage and a life dominated by in-laws.[5]

The situation in the case of several female Krishna devotees is similar. Mirabai (1498–1546), a Rajasthani princess, was an ardent devotee of Krishna. Her in-laws objected to her preoccupation with joining a group of other Krishna devotees to take part in regular worship of God and sought to restrict her participation. Legend says that her in-laws were so displeased with her that they tried to convince her to commit suicide. Like the female devotees of Shiva mentioned previously, Mirabai eventually left her home and husband in order to live in Vrindavana, a town in northern India especially sacred to Krishna. There she doted on her god without the distraction of a difficult domestic situation. In her poems, which are famous throughout North India, the theme of marriage to and love for Krishna is central, and the overriding devotional metaphor is passionate married love. Many of her poems describe her desperate longing when Krishna is absent and bespeak an all-consuming passion for her god.

> *Without my beloved Master*
> *I cannot live.*
> *Body, mind and life*
> *Have I given to the Beloved.*
> *Fascinated by His beauty,*
> *I gaze down the road*
> *Night and day.*
> *Says Mira: My Lord, accept your servant—*
> *It is all she asks.*[6]

---

[5]For Lalleshvari, see David Kinsley, "Devotion as an Alternative to Marriage in the Lives of Some Hindu Women Devotees," *Journal of Asian and African Studies*, 15, nos. 1–2 (1980), pp. 86–87.

[6]A. J. Alston, *The Devotional Poems of Mīrābāī* (Delhi: Motilal Banarsidass, 1980), p. 63.

Andal, who lived during the sixth century C.E. in Tamilnad in South India, was the daughter of Perialvar, who was also a famous saint. Like her father, Andal was an ardent devotee of Krishna. Throughout her youth, father and daughter cultivated reverence and devotion for their god. Andal in particular cultivated the attitude of one of Krishna's milkmaid devotees (who are known as *gopis*). Like the *gopis* and Radha (the most famous *gopi* devotee) specifically, she developed a single-minded devotion for Krishna that expressed itself in terms of emotional, passionate longing for the beloved. Her affection for Krishna eventually turned into a desire to marry him. In her devotional hymns, Andal entreats Kama, the Hindu god of love and desire, to attract Krishna to her, to make him her husband. She pours out her frenzied emotions in which she sounds exactly like the lovesick Radha, who cannot exist without her Krishna.

When Andal reached marriageable age, her father raised the subject of marriage with her, and she told him that she could not bear to live if she had to marry a mortal man, as her only love was for God. "I intend to marry the Lord alone," legend tells us she told her father. So it was that her father escorted her to the temple one day and prayed to the image of Krishna that he accept his daughter as his wife. Legend says that thereupon the young Andal, dressed as a bride, went up and stood beside the image of Krishna. Then, to the amazement of all, she slowly disappeared from sight, never to be seen again. Her father, however, was told by Krishna in a dream that he had married Andal and that now Perialvar was Krishna's father-in-law. And so with Andal we have another example of a female devotee of God refusing marriage by pleading exclusive love and devotion for the divine. Devotion to God for Andal, as for Mirabai and many other female devotees, was an alternative to earthly marriage and all that that entails for a woman.[7]

The story of Gauribai (1815–65), a devotee of Vishnu from Gujarat, is somewhat different from those of the female devotees discussed so far in that Gauribai did not resist marriage nor seek to escape a difficult marriage. She was confronted with the unenviable position of being a child widow, who, as a member of a high caste, was not permitted to remarry. Gauribai was married at the age of six (not an uncommon event in traditional Hinduism among certain high castes), and barely a week after her marriage her husband died. Her family was grief stricken at this tragedy, but legend says that Gauribai herself did not indulge her misery but proclaimed that from then on God would be her master and that she would lead her life for him alone. As a widow she was expected to lead a chaste, almost ascetic life and avoid social contacts. This is what she did, cultivating a pious life devoted exclusively to worship of Vishnu in the form of Krishna.

The local ruler, himself a devotee of Vishnu, was impressed with Gau-

---

[7]For Andal, see Swami Ghanananda and Sir John Stewart-Wallace, eds., *Women Saints of East and West* (London: Ramakrishna Vedanta Centre, 1955), pp. 23–29.

ribai's ardent devotion and constructed a temple to Krishna in her honor. She was then invited to tend the image in the temple as its priest. At this point, Gauribai left her parents' house and became the full-time attendant of her god at the new temple. In effect, one might say, she set up house with the object of her devotion and entered into a "second marriage," a marriage to her god. Gauribai lived at this temple until she was about forty-five years old and then moved to Vrindavana, the place in India most sacred to Krishna. There she lived out the rest of her life. Gauribai is described as a beautiful woman who always dressed very simply in a white sari. She wore no adornments and was of modest demeanor, befitting a widow. She lived the outward life of a widow, but in many ways her life of devotion to Krishna was a religious marriage in which she was able to express her love in intense fashion.[8]

Considering that many Hindu scriptures say outright that women cannot achieve moksha without first reincarnating as a male, it is probably remarkable that any women have achieved the role of spiritual teacher, or guru, in which role they are qualified to lead others to moksha by example and teaching. Yet several women have achieved this religiously prestigious role. Two examples of this in recent times are Anandamayi Ma and Jnanananda Ma. Both of these remarkable women came to be known throughout India as enlightened individuals, and both came to form religious movements centered around themselves as gurus or spiritual masters.

Anandamayi Ma was born in 1896 in East Bengal (now Bangladesh) and given the name Nirmala Sundara ("perfect beauty"). Her parents were both religiously inclined, particularly her father, who was the son of a guru. Her father often would become intoxicated in his devotional moods and for days at a time would wander away in a mood of self forgetfulness. It is likely that Anandamayi Ma was influenced quite strongly by her parents' emotional and ecstatic style of piety. Nirmala herself is said to have been subject to trances and visions. She would talk to trees, insects, and animals and was considered by many to be either retarded or absent minded.[9]

When she was thirteen, her parents arranged her marriage to Ramani Chakravarti, whom Anandamayi Ma later called Bholanath. She stayed with his family for several years while he traveled about trying to find work. Their marriage was celibate, as Anandamayi Ma did not desire sex. Initially her husband thought this would be a temporary condition, but it turned into a permanent arrangement. When he would approach her with desire early in their marriage, her body would take on the characteristics of death, or in some cases she would give him electric shocks. Throughout this period, she heard voices that instructed her in different styles of meditation

---

[8]For Gauribai, see ibid., pp. 73–79.

[9]My discussion of Anandamayi Ma is based on June McDaniel, *The Madness of the Saints: Ecstatic Religion in Bengal* (Chicago: University of Chicago Press, 1989), pp. 193–202.

FIGURE 7-8 Anandamayi Ma. (From Richard Lannoy, *India, People and Places* [New York: Vanguard Press, 1955], p. 152.)

and yoga. During devotional singing, she would often fall into a trance, exhibit emotional frenzy, and take on the characteristics of the deities she was praising. People sometimes were healed by touching her body. Several attempts were made to cure her of what was thought to be madness. Such attempts were not successful, and at one point a doctor told her husband that Anandamayi Ma was not mentally disturbed rather she was intoxicated by God.[10]

Anandamayi Ma said that sometimes she would see deities come out of her body. She would worship these deities, which would then merge back into her body. For both Anandamayi Ma and her devotees her status was the subject of some question. Was she primarily a devotee who tended to assume the characteristics of the beings she worshiped, or was she herself divine, the Goddess in human form? While this tension persisted throughout her life, it is clear that many devotees approached her as a goddess in human form and that she herself, at times, thought of herself in this way. Once when she was in a trance, she uttered the following statements, which were written down by one of her devotees: "By Me alone are all created in My own image; by Me are all sent into this world and in Me all find final refuge. I am the final cause indicated . . . in the Vedas. . . . Devotion to Me is the cause of *moksha*. All are mine."[11] Once in 1925, while performing worship to the goddess Kali, Anandamayi Ma put the offerings meant for Kali on her own head, thus suggesting that she herself was Kali.[12]

[10]Ibid., pp. 195–96.
[11]Quoted in ibid., p. 197.
[12]Ibid.

During her life, Anandamayi Ma's spiritual life was expressed in a variety of different roles. She was an ardent devotee of several deities and often expressed the characteristics of devotional frenzy when worshiping. She also undertook long periods of silence in which she would speak to no one for years at a time. During these periods she would often fall into a meditative trance (samadhi) and experience union with the Absolute. She also played the role of a healer to many who sought her help. She was said to have direct access to the spirit world, often conversing directly with gods, spirits, and ancestors, and her healing powers were undoubtedly related to this shamanic ability to commune with spirits, who in Indian traditional healing are often implicated in sickness and healing. She also expressed her spiritual inclinations by undertaking pilgrimages to the numerous sacred places that dot the Indian subcontinent. During most of her life, she continued to travel tirelessly, refusing to spend long periods in any one place. In this respect her religious life was akin to that of a sannyasi, a world renouncer, whose religious discipline involves being constantly on the move. Finally, Anandamayi Ma played the role of a guru, dispensing spiritual guidance to a host of disciplines and devotees. In this capacity she was both a teacher, advising students on how best to realize the spiritual potential of their lives, and the object of reverence by her devotees, who wished only to be blessed by the sight of her.

Anandamayi Ma's teachings are not easy to determine, as she did not write anything of a systematic nature concerning her beliefs and ideas. In the sayings that have been recorded, however, it seems that she thought of her own spiritual path as involving an evolutionary process whereby at first one sees the divine or the Absolute only in a few select places, such as holy images in temples, and then gradually one's awareness of the divine expands. This expansion increases until one comes to the realization that the divine is everywhere and that to find it one only has to look within oneself. This understanding of the spiritual path, of course, is very similar to Advaita Vedanta teaching, according to which Brahman underlies and pervades all and according to which the realization that Brahman is one's own spiritual essence (Atman) precipitates enlightenment and moksha. Anandamayi Ma died in 1982 revered and mourned by millions of Hindus.

Jnanananda, whose official name is Her Holiness Satguru Swami Shri Jnanananda Saraswati, lives in Madras in South India. She was born in 1931 in Kerala. She belongs to the Nayar caste, in which lineage and inheritance are traced through the female line. Her father had an important position with the Southern Railway, and the family lived in relative luxury in Madras when she was young. She married and had five children. She officially took the vows of a world renouncer and became a sannyasini (female sannyasi) in May 1975. She was initiated by the Shankaracharya (the head religious teacher) of Kanchipuram, who is one of the most authoritative teachers of Vedanta philosophy in South India. She may well be the only woman to have been so initiated.[13] After this she and her husband ceased their con-jugal relationship. She did not study officially under any spiritual master and says that her knowledge is self-acquired. She also says that she has had mystical experiences in which she passes into samadhi, yogic trance, since she was a girl. She had been teaching students in the role of a guru well before her initiation. After her initiation she took up wearing the tradi-tional saffron robe of a world renouncer, cut her hair short, and did not wear any ornamentation. While very few sannyasis actually become spiri-tual masters who teach students, Jnanananda became a very popular guru in Madras.

Her style and speech have been described as "completely natural, homey, motherly,"[14] and she is said to have a wonderful sense of humor. Although her spirituality is routinely punctuated by extended periods of samadhi when she is completely absorbed in meditative bliss, she maintains a routine, intimate contact with many devotees who come to her regularly for practical and spiritual advice, which she gladly dispenses. Many of those who come to her are women, and she acknowledges that women might find her less intimidating than a male guru and that she is probably better at understanding many women's problems. In a given day, Jnanananda may be asked to provide help for a student about to take an exam, to give advice on whom to marry, to help a devotee find a job, to give medical advice, to interpret the experiences of a devotee's trance, and to advise students on their spiritual paths. When she is available for darshan, that is, when she makes herself available for people to see her and talk with her, there are always waiting lines. The relationship she has with her students is typical of guru-student relations in India. They are intense and personal and in-volve detailed knowledge of the student by the guru. Her teachings, accord-ing to Jnanananda herself, are not particularly remarkable and consist of several important Hindu ideas: truth, purity, doing one's dharma, and prac-tising noninjury to all beings. She also is inclined to the Advaita, or non-dual, philosophy, although she often speaks of the necessity, before all else, of completely surrendering oneself to God, which sounds quite theistic rather than monistic (Advaitan).

Jnanananda views the spiritual capacities of females and males as equal, although affirming their different psychological makeup. She has lit-tle patience with the view that women are inherently impure because of menstruation, although she thinks restrictions arising from menstrual ta-

---

[13]For Jnanananda, see Charles S. J. White, "Mother Guru: Jnanananda of Madras, In-dia," in Nancy Auer Falk and Rita M. Gross, eds., *Unspoken Worlds: Women's Religious Lives in Non-Western Cultures* (San Francisco: Harper & Row, 1980), pp. 22–37.

[14]Ibid., p. 24.

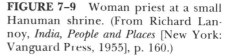

FIGURE 7-9 Woman priest at a small Hanuman shrine. (From Richard Lannoy, *India, People and Places* [New York: Vanguard Press, 1955], p. 160.)

boos may be a good way for women to get monthly relief from burdensome chores such as cooking. Her own life exemplifies the fact that, despite a strong androcentric bias in much of Hinduism's official scriptures and leadership, women can attain the most prestigious religious roles under certain circumstances.

Although temple priests are almost always male Brahmins, there are examples of women playing priestly roles at shrines and temples, usually ones of fairly modest size dedicated to goddesses. It is not uncommon for a priestly married couple, for example, to tend a shrine together, sharing the duties of daily worship of the image. In some cases, the only priest at a shrine may be a woman. A case in point is a small Kali temple in Varanasi, where the only priest is an elderly woman named Shanti Devi. Her mother, who was a Tantric practitioner, founded the temple when Shanti Devi was a little girl. She remembers that at that time the location of the temple was still forested and that wild animals lurked in the vicinity. Her mother used to cure people of a wide range of illnesses, and Shanti Devi herself remembers being called back from the land of the dead when she was very sick by the great healing power of her mother. Her mother used to keep many cats in the temple and came to be known as Billimai, "cat mother." Shanti Devi wears a saffron robe and sees herself as a sadhu, or holy person, in addition to being the temple priestess. She performs worship at the temple twice each day, from 4:00 to 6:00 A.M. and at 7:00 P.M. Several devotees attend the shrine daily and look after her needs.

FIGURE 7–10   Shanti Devi. (Author's photograph).

It is also the case that women play priestly roles in the context of many women's rituals, such as *vrats*. Although men do dominate priestly functions, the impression gleaned from Hindu scriptures that women are unfit to undertake priestly roles is exaggerated. There are many cases of women playing these roles in contemporary Hinduism, and this probably has always been the case historically.

Another area of Hinduism in which women play an important role is Tantrism. Many Tantric texts are partial to the feminine. Goddesses play an important role in Tantric imagery. Women often are revered and respected, and ill treatment of them is scorned in some texts. Some texts forbid giving daughters in marriage for money, advise the death penalty for rape, teach males to cherish their wives and never punish them for being unpleasant, and forbid the killing of female animals for sacrifice.[15] Women are said in many texts to be the image of the Goddess, and as such they are to be revered. Women also play an important role in Tantric ritual, and there are cases of women becoming Tantric teachers. The fact that Tantrism probably had its origins among lower-caste religious adepts and that it tends to mock Brahmanic pretense may account for its more liberal attitudes toward women. Tantrism, however, should not be considered a woman's preserve. It is clear that Tantric texts are written from a male point of view, that males dominate rituals, and that Tantric teachers and adepts are mostly males.

[15]Young, "Hinduism," p. 89.

CONCLUSION

It is easy to get the impression from Hindu scriptures that women do not figure prominently in Hindu religious life. The scriptures, for the most part, reflect a male point of view. They are written by men, about men, and for other men. Women, nevertheless, do figure prominently in almost every facet of living Hinduism, and this situation probably reflects what has always been the case historically in Hinduism. While women may not invest themselves in the same rituals and roles as males, it is clear that Hinduism is not a male religion with little or no room for women. The male-oriented scriptures may prefer to understand women in supporting roles, as adjuncts to and nourishers of males, but in actual practice women lead lives of their own that are religiously rich and distinctive.

8

Hindu Social Structure

INTRODUCTION

To a great extent the distinctive nature of Hinduism resides in its social structure, which is generally known as the caste system. This particular and unique social system native to India pervades day-to-day Hinduism; traditionally it was believed impossible to be a Hindu and live outside of India. That is, it was believed impossible to be a Hindu apart from the caste system. Historical migrations and new "portable" versions of Hinduism, as typified by recent movements such as the Ramakrishna Mission, Transcendental Meditation, and the International Society for Krishna Consciousness, have somewhat altered this situation, but basically for thousands of years to be a Hindu has meant to live in India and to be part of the caste system. For the vast majority of Hindus, life is lived entirely in Indian villages, and this means living the caste system every day of their lives.

Both the history and the present structure of the caste system are complex. In essence, however, it is a social system that is composed of closed, endogamous groups, most of which perform a traditional occupation and all of which are ranked in a hierarchical order. The system as it exists in Hinduism today seems to be the result of a historical blending of two social systems, the varna system, which dominates Vedic religion and the traditional Law Books, and the *jati* system, which is only vaguely described in Hindu literature but which dominates Hinduism at the village level. Both systems emphasize the importance of hierarchy and occupational specialization, but they are actually different in some respects.

In Vedic religion and in the traditional Law Books, the ideal social system is said to consist of four varnas, or social groups, each of which is said to pursue traditional types of occupations. The four varnas are: (1) the Brahmins, who are described as priests and scholars; (2) the Kshatriyas, who are said to be warriors and rulers; (3) the Vaishyas, who pursue commerce and trades; and (4) the Shudras, who are described as serfs whose duty it is to serve and support the three higher groups. The first three groups are called twice born because they alone are permitted to study the Vedic scriptures and perform the sacred-thread ceremony, the Vedic ritual of initiation in which the participant is reborn. The overall aim of society according to Vedic literature and the Law Books (which were written by Brahmins for Brahmins, it should be remembered) is to support the Brahmins at the head of society; their aim in turn is to perform Vedic rituals that insure the stability of the cosmos by nourishing the gods who control it. As described in the Law Books, these four varnas are closed groups, and intermarriage between them is forbidden. In some Law Books a fifth varna is described, the untouchables, who are beneath even the Shudras. The varna system as outlined in traditional Hindu texts, then, might be diagrammed as in figure 8–1.

Historically, the Indo-Aryans probably brought with them to India a tripartite social structure in which society was formally, but not rigidly, divided into priestly, military, and trading and agricultural functions.[1] Individual social mobility probably was possible in this system in its earliest Indian stage. The Aryans then added to this triple structure the Shudra varna in order to include in their view of the world the indigenous peoples of India, whom they subjugated and increasingly dominated culturally. It is possible, even likely, that the indigenous peoples had a society similar to the *jati* system, one of closed, endogamous groups based on occupational specialization, although we have exceedingly little information from this early period of Indian history. Eventually the varna system began to be characterized by attributes of the indigenous system, and by the time of the *Law Book of Manu* (around the first century C.E.) the four varnas were described in many ways like *jatis*. What took place historically, then, is that the Indo-Aryans imposed their social system on the indigenous peoples, while aspects of the indigenous system in turn began to characterize the varna system. The end result is the caste system as we see it in India today.

The *jati* system is difficult to study apart from the varna system be-

[1]The Indo-Aryan tripartite social structure is discussed in the works of Georges Dumézil; see *Les dieux des Indo-Européens* (Paris: Presses universitaires de France, 1952). For a discussion of Dumézil's theories, see C. Scott Littleton, *The New Comparative Mythology* (Berkeley: University of California Press, 1966).

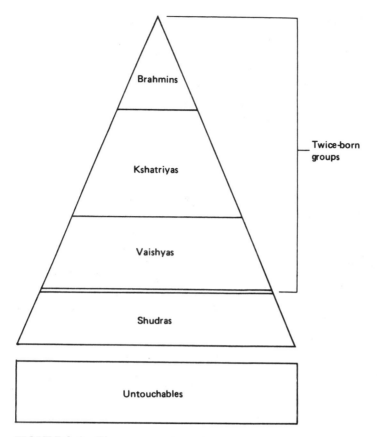

FIGURE 8-1   The varna system.

cause for centuries the two have been seen as complementary in the Hindu tradition, or in fact as one and the same. However, the *jati* system, the caste system proper as it operates at the village level, is quite different from the varna system as described in most traditional Hindu scriptures. The term *jati* means birth and is the proper term for caste. A caste is a group into which one is born and within which one must marry, and it usually is characterized by a traditional, specialized occupation. Unlike a varna, a *jati* is geographically and linguistically limited and in most cases has the characteristics of a large kin group with distinctive customs, dress, diet, and behavior. A *jati* is self-governing, being responsible for the behavior of its own members, and only mingles with other castes in carefully circumscribed ways. Sometimes it is also characterized by a particular type of religious affiliation or behavior. *Jatis* are ranked hierarchically vis-à-vis one another, and this ranking determines who may do what with whom under what conditions.

It is estimated that there are over two thousand *jatis* in India today, and among them hundreds of different occupations are pursued. By far the most common occupation is agriculture, but agriculture alone is not enough to define a *jati*, because there are hundreds of separate agricultural *jatis*, which are ranked very differently from region to region, village to village, and even within a particular village. The situation is similar for *jatis* that call themselves Brahmins. There are perhaps hundreds of Brahmin *jatis*, many of which do not occupy themselves with priestly functions, and all of them rank each other if the opportunity arises. A popular saying in India is that where there are seven Brahmins there will be seven cooking fires, as each of the seven Brahmins will believe him- or herself higher in the caste system than the others and thus will refuse to dine with them; such social contact would mean being polluted by someone lower in the caste system.

Lending daily force to the caste system is the Hindu preoccupation with purity and pollution. Whenever a high-caste Hindu has contact with a lower-caste Hindu, the former becomes impure in varying degrees depending on the intimacy of the contact and the relative ranks of the castes involved. Intermarriage involves the most intimate and therefore the most polluting contact, and for most castes it is held to be so polluting that purification is impossible and the guilty member may be cast out. Day-to-day life in Hinduism, then, involves a complex variety of carefully defined permissible intercaste contacts and a variety of rituals that seek to maintain caste purity, which is compromised periodically and almost unavoidably. The separation of castes typifies the caste system and maximizes the nature of castes as large kinship groups. Settlement patterns almost always insure that castes will live in carefully segregated quarters. Where social contact is unavoidable or a necessary part of the economic life of a village, a host of unwritten laws and customs regulate such contact to minimize the transfer of pollution. At a village council, for example, seating will be arranged carefully so that the higher castes are elevated above and distant from the lower castes (the higher-caste member may sit on a chair or a cot, whereas the lower-caste member may sit on the floor at a prescribed distance, for example). At village feasts and festivals, where a certain amount of contact between castes is unavoidable, a variety of rules will minimize socially awkward situations and insure that high-caste Hindus receive only manageable amounts of pollution, which later may be erased ritually.

Imposed upon this social system consisting of thousands of closed castes, each hierarchically ranked, is the varna system, which gives the village *jati* system a certain common pattern throughout India. The varna model of society is well known throughout India, and *jatis* typically will identify themselves with one or another of the four varnas or be classed in a particular varna by other *jatis*. This identification has to do far more with prestige and relative rank than with actual occupation or social function. It is quite possible, for example, to find agricultural Hindus belonging to every one of the four varnas. In recent years many castes have sought to elevate their relative status by identifying their *jati* with one of the higher varnas. The principal means of doing this are (1) imitating the habits (usually dietary) of the higher castes and (2) seeking to show historically that one's caste forefathers undertook an occupation traditionally associated with the varna in question. The large Maratha caste of Maharashtra, for example, which is an agricultural caste, has tried in recent years to elevate itself to the status of Kshatriya from the status of Shudra by demonstrating that caste forefathers fought the Muslims in the seventeenth and eighteenth centuries. Social mobility, then, is possible within the *jati* system, but for castes as a whole only, not for individuals. The *jati* system in combination with the varna system might be diagramed as in figure 8–2.

Precisely which varna a given caste is assigned to, and its relative rank vis-à-vis other castes, may vary according to different village informants, but

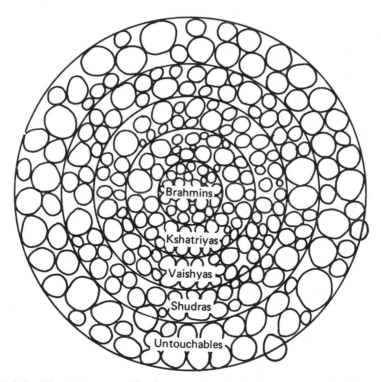

FIGURE 8–2   The *jati* system. The five concentric circles represent the four varnas and the untouchables. Each small circle represents a *jati*. The closer to the center a *jati* is located, the higher it is in the system. Some *jatis* are shown within two varnas to indicate the gradual shift of an entire caste in the overall system. The *jatis* that are shown overlapping the outer circle represent tribal groups that are in the process of becoming associated with the Hindu social system by adopting Hindu practices and beliefs.

usually there is general consensus concerning a caste's status by those both inside and outside the caste. Throughout India the pattern of castes differs greatly because most castes are limited regionally. Thus, in a particular village there may be very few Brahmin castes, no Kshatriya castes at all, and the bulk of the people will belong to castes identified with the Shudra varna. Elsewhere a village may be dominated by castes identifying themselves with the Kshatriya varna. Given the relative distribution of castes from village to village, it is also not unusual for fairly low castes to hold great economic and political power because of their numerical predominance.

A variety of justifications or legitimations of the caste system operate on both the all-India and the village level and tend to reinforce its closed, hierarchical nature. On the most general level, the need for order is affirmed to be basic. The world needs order, and to have it a great variety of social tasks must be undertaken faithfully. The world needs those whose occupation (and special privilege) it is to maintain a beneficial relationship with the gods, who nourish the world. It needs those who maintain civil order and administer justice. It needs those who supply goods and services. It needs those who raise food. It needs those who wash laundry, make pots, remove dead cattle, and perform a variety of types of manual labor and specialized services. Individual people also need order, which the caste system provides by placing each individual within an extended, closed group that provides economic, occupational, sexual, and emotional security. The caste system, to be sure, puts the order of society above the needs of the individual, but it rewards the individual with a secure place, a niche in society, that is ascribed at birth. Socially, it is unnecessary to undertake the often-taxing task of finding one's social role in a competitive society.

Another legitimation or assumption of the caste system is that people are different from one another. The term *adhikara* in popular usage means "predilection," and people are thought to be born with different *adhikaras*, which are determined for the most part by their previous karma. Religiously, *adhikara* means that different paths to spiritual fulfillment are available for people of different types. Socially, it means that different types of people are suited to different types of occupations. There are many stories that illustrate this idea and that seek to show the absurdity of certain types of individuals trying to undertake tasks unsuitable to their natures. The stories, which often use analogies from the animal kingdom, suggest that within the Hindu caste system the different castes are regarded as different species of being. The following story illustrates this belief well.

Once upon a time there was a potter who badly cut his forehead when he fell down on some broken pots. The wound healed slowly and left an impressive scar. When a famine occurred, the potter and his family went to another region, where he was seen by a king who admired his size and assumed from his scar that he was a brave fighter. The king put the potter in charge of his army. Shortly thereafter the kingdom was attacked, and as the warriors were about to leave for battle the king happened to ask the potter how he had acquired his scar. When the potter told him, the king was angry and sought to get rid of him. The potter, however, pleaded with the king to be allowed to demonstrate his martial qualities. Thereupon the king told the potter this story:

> A lion while hunting once came upon a fox cub, but it was so small that he pitied it and brought it to his wife, who had two cubs of her own. The three cubs were nursed by the lioness and grew up together. One day, while playing together, they saw an elephant pass. The lion cubs, seeing the hereditary enemy, roared and lashed their tails and were going to attack. The fox was afraid, and dissuaded the lion cubs from doing such a foolhardy thing and ran home, followed by the other two cubs. They all told this incident to their mother, who got the fox cub aside, and told him who he really was, and said, "Son, you are brave, you have learned all there is to learn; you are handsome, but in your line big game is not killed. Go away before my sons realize who you are."[2]

Having made his point, the king dismissed the potter. Potters are born to make pots. It is their nature, determined by their past actions. To pretend to be something one is not would be disastrous both for the potter and for the safety of the kingdom. It is similar for all castes. Karma and samsara insure that one is born into a situation appropriate to one's predilections, and to try to act like another "species" is unnatural.

Karma and samsara are also important underpinnings of the caste system by teaching that one's relative rank in the caste system is determined strictly by one's own past actions and that one's future social role is being determined in this life according to all one's present actions.

Proper actions, dharma, according to the caste system, are often relative. That is, certain types of actions may be forbidden to one caste and permitted to another. For example, strict vegetarianism may be fundamental to some castes (usually high ones), whereas eating meat may be allowed in other castes (usually low ones). In this situation, eating meat incurs bad karma for the vegetarian, whereas it does not for the nonvegetarian. Although there are several righteous kinds of actions for all castes—such as truthfulness, respect for elders, and generosity—the most important guideline for performing one's dharma is faithfully to perform one's caste duty, which is different from caste to caste. Inspired by the *Bhagavad Gita*'s teaching that disciplined action is the key to spiritual fulfillment and that each caste should perform the duty ascribed to it without desire for personal rewards, the caste system is further legitimized by the belief that any set of actions, any ascribed social role, may be performed in such a way that it is

---

[2]Irawati Karve, *Hindu Society—An Interpretation* (Poona, India: Deccan College, 1961), p. 72.

redemptive. Again, Hindu literature has many stories that make this point and that illustrate the possibility of low-caste Hindus outdoing high-caste Hindus in the performance of dharma. An example of such a story is found in the *Mahabharata*.

There was a Brahmin who was spattered by bird dung while meditating under a tree. The Brahmin was furious at the bird and burned him to ashes with the heat of his angry, fierce gaze. Feeling proud of this display of his spiritual powers, the Brahmin went on his daily rounds to beg food. Coming to the house of a certain woman, he called out to her to bring him food. The housewife answered that she was busy cleaning her dishes but would bring him food in a moment. At that point her husband came home. She immediately stopped her housework, washed her hands, and served him a meal. While he ate she stood by him attentively in case he desired anything. When he had finished his meal the woman remembered the waiting Brahmin. She brought him some food and apologized for having made him wait. The Brahmin was angry and began to harangue her about the proper way to treat Brahmins. The housewife replied calmly that as a wife her first duty was to her husband. She went on to say that Brahmins should not get angry and that he should not have killed the bird that dirtied him. The Brahmin, amazed that she knew of the killing, assumed rightly that she had acquired spiritual powers because of her great virtue in serving her husband. Properly humbled, the Brahmin asked her to tell him more about proper dharma. She told him to go to a distant city to seek out a certain butcher if he wished to be instructed in dharma. After a long journey the Brahmin finally succeeded in finding the butcher, and the butcher, after having shown his respect to his caste superior by bowing down at the Brahmin's feet, told the Brahmin that he already knew about the incident of the bird and the conversation with the housewife. Again the Brahmin was astonished at the spiritual powers of the butcher (a very low-caste occupation, as it involves intentional killing) and asked how he had acquired such extraordinary powers. The butcher then told the Brahmin that although he could not help his present social position, as it was the result of his past deeds, he performed his present occupation simply out of duty and with no attachment to the fruits of his actions. He instructed the Brahmin in the *Bhagavad Gita*'s teaching that any person may find release from the round of rebirth by acting selflessly.[3]

To Westerners accustomed to a fairly mobile social structure, the Indian caste system appears extremely oppressive. Individuals are locked into ascribed social roles from birth with no hope of changing their role and rank (except if an entire caste improves its rank through a gradual process). There are, however, certain personal compensations, such as security of

---

[3]J. A. B. van Buitenen, trans., *The Mahabharata*, 3 vols. (Chicago: University of Chicago Press, 1973–78), Vol. II: The Book of the Forest, chaps. 196–98, pp. 614–20.

occupation and the support of a group that is in many ways like an extended family. There are also a variety of justifications of the system from which low-caste Hindus in particular may take comfort. There are, too, certain built-in outlets for those who find the system too oppressive despite its compensations. Religious festivals and pilgrimages, in particular, often provide a social context in which certain restrictions are modified or held in abeyance or in which social roles may even be reversed. The Holi festival, held in the spring throughout North India, is a good example. During Holi, normally prohibited behavior is allowed, and people are encouraged to play the roles of their caste superiors.[4] On pilgrimages, in company with other spiritual sojourners, there is also a certain laxity about caste rules that allows Hindus to step out of their confining social roles to some extent and thus find relief from a low social position.

However, the most important way out of the restrictiveness of the caste system for Hindus is contained in the formula of the four stages of life. According to this system people must fulfill certain social obligations, such as learning the *Vedas*, if they are from a high caste, and, for all castes, parenting children. These obligations are met in the first two stages of life, those of student and householder. The third and fourth stages, the forest dweller and the sannyasi, involve essentially stepping out of society altogether in order to pursue the individual goal of personal release, moksha.

FIGURE 8-3   Nabani Das, a member of the Baul sect of Bengal. The Bauls are wandering minstrels who sing in praise of God. (From Richard Lannoy, *India, People and Places* [New York: Vanguard Press, 1955].)

[4]For a description of the Holi festival, see McKim Marriott, "The Feast of Love," in Milton Singer, ed., *Krishna: Myths, Rites, and Attitudes* (Honolulu: East-West Center Press, 1966), pp. 200–12.

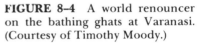

FIGURE 8–4 A world renouncer on the bathing ghats at Varanasi. (Courtesy of Timothy Moody.)

Entering the fourth stage, the renouncer is required to perform his or her own funeral ceremonies, erase all signs of caste identity, and leave family and village forever. Lending an air of both immediate and theoretical flexibility to the closed nature of the caste system, then, is the quite common appearance in an Indian village of these free-floating dropouts who wander through from time to time begging their food. Socially, these wandering renouncers are nobodies, having died to the social world. They are without village or caste identity and rank and thus may accept food from anyone and may be given food by anyone without any transfer of pollution. They are a periodic reminder of humanity's ultimate destiny to transcend the world and, as such, too, a reminder of the relativity of all worldly structures, roles, and habits. They remind Hindus still within the world and within the social system that they have another identity apart from their social one, and in this capacity the sannyasis represent the ever-present possibility of dropping out of society completely.

EXAMPLES OF THE CASTE SYSTEM

The Havik Brahmins of Mysore

In order to illustrate in concrete fashion both the underlying assumptions of the caste system and the specific ways in which it operates in daily life, we shall look in some detail at the life-style of a specific caste. In Mysore

State is located a high Brahmin caste of about two hundred thousand people, the Havik Brahmins. In a typical village the Haviks are both the highest caste in terms of rank and the dominant caste in terms of economic power. The other castes in a Havik village are usually classed either in the Shudra varna or as untouchables. Within the Shudra class there are many castes, each of them ranked in hierarchical order. The untouchables, too, are ranked into two divisions, left and right, the former being considered lower than the latter. The Kshatriya and Vaishya varnas are barely represented at all, so the general caste configuration is three tiered, with precise ranking among the Shudra and untouchable castes.[5]

The ranking of the castes in a typical village may be understood from two points of view, both of which reinforce each other. First, the castes tend to rank each other according to what anthropologists call an attributional theory of caste, in which a caste's occupation determines its status. So, for example, Haviks are ranked very high because they avoid work that brings them in contact with such polluting things as human filth, and they avoid labor such as plowing, which involves killing (albeit unintentional). The untouchables, on the other hand, are ranked at the bottom of the system because they do polluting kinds of work such as removing dead cattle, working with leather, and so on.

The attributional ranking of the castes is reinforced by what anthropologists call an interactional theory of caste. According to this way of looking at the castes, rank is determined by which castes interact with which other castes and by the amounts of pollution that pass from the lower to the higher caste when such interaction takes place. Among caste equals, for example, social interaction is very free, restricted only by family and kin ranking or by temporary states of relative purity, which we shall discuss later. The social interaction of a Havik with a member of a high Shudra caste is much more restricted because it is a relationship between two unequal castes in which pollution passes from the Shudra to the Havik Brahmin. High Shudra castes, however, are allowed into Havik houses, where they often work as servants, and their presence is not considered dangerously polluting if certain restrictions are observed. Haviks and untouchables are even more restricted in their social contacts, to the point where it is considered polluting to the Havik to touch the untouchable or sometimes even to converse directly with him or her. The interactional relations of the castes are seen clearly at a Havik wedding or other occasion at which a great feast is held for people of all castes. The Shudra castes will be fed outside the house on the porch, and they will be arranged there so as to reflect their status in relation to one another, or they will be served their

[5]My description of the religion of the Havik Brahmins is based on an article by Edward B. Harper, "Ritual Pollution as an Integrator of Caste and Religion," *Journal of Asian Studies*, XXIII (June 1964), 151–97.

food in a sequence that will reflect their relative ranks. Members of the untouchable castes are given the leftovers and usually are asked to eat their food in the street, outside the Havik family compound, or to take their food home. In hundreds of ways, as well, the social interaction between castes, or rather the lack of social interaction, determines quite precisely the relative rank of the castes. All these interactions are regulated by the amount of pollution that passes from one caste to another.

Among Haviks three states of purity are identified. The purest state is called *madi*. For a Havik it is only in this state of purity that he may worship the gods. The middle state of purity is called *mailige*, which is the normal state for Haviks because *madi* is easily lost in so many ways. For example, *madi* is lost when one eats, defecates, or interacts with lower castes or with other Haviks who are in a lesser state of purity. The lowest state of purity, actually a state better described as polluted, is called *muttuchettu*. For convenience we shall designate these three states at M_1 (*madi*), M_2 (*mailige*), and M_3 (*muttuchettu*).

These states of purity are to a great extent relative. For example, from the Havik point of view the untouchables are always in a state of M_3, and to interact or come in close contact with an untouchable is highly polluting, necessitating rituals to regain even the status of M_2. The Shudra castes are for the most part, from the Havik point of view, in a permanent state of either M_2 or M_3 and may never achieve the state of M_1. Within each state of purity there is further refining that reinforces sex and family ranking. For example, although a Havik woman must be in a state of M_1 in order to serve food to her family or guests (and thus must not eat until after everyone else has eaten, as the act of eating itself reduces one to a state of M_2), she cannot achieve the necessary purity within M_1 in order to serve the gods in household worship. She may worship the gods only through her husband. We may distinguish grades of purity, then, within each of the three states. Within M_1 we might designate the state of M_1A, the state of purity necessary to worship the gods and achievable only by Havik males, and M_1B, the state necessary for serving food to other Haviks and attainable by female Haviks.

States of purity are affected by receiving pollution, which occurs in various ways, and pollution is removed by certain purifying rituals, most of which involve bathing or drinking a mixture of certain ingredients. For Haviks, daily life is the process whereby they seek to remain in a relative state of purity and still be able to function fairly normally in society.

Pollution, although a very complex and intricate concept among Haviks, arises primarily from three types of sources. The first is from bodily excretions. Feces, urine, blood, pus, and saliva are highly polluting, and any activity or accident that involves contact with them reduces one's purity. The bodily excretions of different castes and different animals are further ranked according to the potency of their pollution. A whole host of rules

ıd regulations and very refined knowledge of precisely how much pollution is received cluster around this topic.

To exemplify how this system operates, we may consider the rules
concerning eating. Indians eat with their hands, and because the hands
touch the lips when eating, and therefore touch saliva that is transmitted
back to the food and hence back to the lips, the very act of eating involves
a certain amount of pollution. The act of dining together, partly because it
involves the risk of ingesting others' pollution in the form of saliva, must
be shared only among equals to minimize the transfer of pollution. Even
among caste equals, different seating arrangements are often called for because of the relative purity of the diners. It is typical, for example, for
Haviks to arrange themselves in "lines" that separate those of differing states
of purity. To be in the same line is automatically to share in the pollution
of other members of that line. So, among a group of adult male Haviks
eating together all in a state of M_2, different "lines" will indicate that they
refine M_2 among themselves into M_2A, M_2B, and so on. Removal of the large
leaves that are used as plates involves contact with the leftovers of others
or with one's own polluted leftovers and thus is hedged about with certain
rules. Within a family a woman is responsible for this polluting task, or a
servant from a lower caste. When a woman or lower-caste servant is not
available, the junior male member of the family may be asked to remove
the leaves. Certain types of food are also considered polluting. The Haviks
are strict vegetarians. Meat in any form is polluting for them, and certain
meats are more polluting than others. Beef is the most polluting of all.

Menstrual blood is another example of pollution from bodily excretions, and Havik women must observe many restrictive rules to insure that
others will not come in contact with them during their menstruation. For
five days, for example, a Havik woman may not serve food to her family or
even eat with them but must remain outside the house on the porch. The
clothes she wears during her menstruation are also very polluting and must
be handled carefully to avoid transmitting pollution to her family.

The second source of pollution is from kinship. The underlying assumption here is that one shares the pollution of one's relatives. The more
closely related one is to another person, the more intense the sharing of
pollution. The clearest examples of how this type of pollution works are
seen at birth and death, both of which are believed to involve pollution.
The death of a family member or even a kin member fairly far removed
automatically puts a Havik in the state of M_3, from which he or she cannot
regain a state of even M_2 for a certain period of time. The period of time
and the thoroughness of the rituals involved in removing the pollution of
M_3 at the end of the prescribed period of mourning vary according to how
close the kin relationship is. At the death of an immediate family member,
one's father, for example, the period is twelve days, but for a distant relative
it may be only thirty-six hours. During this period the Havik in question

must restrict contacts with other Haviks in order not to pollute them ar. may not worship the gods. When there is a birth in a family the pollutior. of the mother, which comes about because of the flow of blood, is shared by the immediate family. Birth takes place outside the house, usually on the porch where women are restricted during their menstruation, and for eleven days after the birth the woman is in a state of M_3; her near relatives remain polluted for as much as three days.

The third source of pollution is from people of other castes. As the Haviks are the highest caste in their village, all other castes are potential sources of pollution, because pollution passes, for the most part, only from lower to higher castes. Because the caste system is based on a principle of economic specialization and interdependence, it is impossible for Haviks to avoid contact with other castes altogether. Also, because Haviks will not perform certain kinds of polluting work, both occupational and household, periodic contact with those who do perform this work (such as washing clothes, cutting hair, and plowing) is unavoidable, and in the long run, beneficial in keeping Haviks in a relatively pure state.

Some social interaction between Haviks and the lower castes, then, is usual, desirable, and necessary, and many rules exist to make it tolerable. Most Haviks, for example, employ untouchables as laborers and will often work in the fields with them; such proximity while working is held to be only mildly polluting and can be gotten rid of by the simple process of bathing. To have physical contact with the untouchable, however, is more serious and generally avoided. Similarly, the untouchable as a family worker is often given food or water by the Haviks. The untouchable, however, will never eat with the Haviks, and when food or water is passed to an untouchable it will be done in such a way that pollution is not transmitted. For example, a Havik will pour water for the untouchable into a tin cup on the porch without actually touching the cup. The untouchable servant then drinks from it, cleans it, and sets it back in place. For any member of the Havik family actually to touch the cup used by the untouchable would mean transfer of pollution.

In ways such as these, social interaction is made possible between castes of different ranks without the higher caste incurring pollution or with pollution kept to manageable quantities. Much intercaste pollution undoubtedly takes place inadvertently, as when two members of different castes mistakenly touch or when a high-caste member unknowingly comes into contact with bodily excretions when walking along a street. To cleanse himself of such pollution, a Havik is in the strict habit of bathing once each day. The bath consists of pouring water over one's head and letting it spill down over the body. Running water is considered intrinsically purifying, and this simple act erases most kinds of pollution acquired during a normal day. Haviks also wash after defecating, urinating, and both before and after eating.

The removal of serious types of pollution may involve preparing and drinking a concoction of certain sacred elements or ritual bathing accompanied by sacred formulas (mantras). Among Haviks, as among most Hindus, cows are believed to be extremely sacred. They are held to be gods, or to "have more than a thousand gods residing in them,"[6] and are often worshiped by Havik women. The products of the cow (milk, dung, urine) alone or in mixture with each other or with other things such as honey and sugar are believed to be extremely purifying and are often used to rid a person or a house of pollution. A common practice to purify a house after the visit of a lower-caste person, or after the visit of other Haviks who are suspected of being less pure than those in the household, is to sprinkle some dried, powdered cow dung in those areas where the visitors have stayed.

Some pollution is thought to be so defiling that it may be removed only by casting out a member of the Havik caste. In this situation, the actual offender does not become pure but makes it possible for his or her kin to regain their purity. Only after the offender has died socially may his or her kin reenter Havik society without polluting other Haviks. Being an outcast is precisely a social death, since it involves the end of social interaction with other members of the caste. Taking food from an untouchable or fornicating with an untouchable are actions that are so polluting that casting out is the only solution. Intermarriage with a lower-caste person, although it rarely ever happens, also would merit casting out. Actual cases of casting out among the Haviks are extremely rare, in part because absolute proof of the act is required before conviction may be made. By far the most common cases involve the birth of children by Havik widows long after their husbands have died. As there is no doubt that illicit sexual relations have taken place, possibly with a lower-caste person, such widows may be cast out. The initiative must come from the widow's own family, however, and casting out is not necessarily automatic. Children born in this situation are assigned to the Maleru caste, which is composed only of such illegitimate children and their descendants.

Among Haviks, and among Hindus generally, there are a variety of acts that involve voluntary pollution in order to show respect to others or to the gods. A wife shows respect for her husband, who among traditional Haviks is her god, by eating from his plate (actually his leaf) after he has eaten, thus accepting his pollution. A world renouncer is shown respect when a Havik takes food from his or her leaf, or when a Havik touches the renouncer's feet. The lower half of the body is considered less pure than the upper half, and the feet are the least pure part of the body. By touching another's feet, then touching one's own head, one demonstrates respect by showing that the person's feet are more pure than one's own head. The

[6]Ibid., p. 182.

FIGURE 8-5 A South Indian Brahmin. (From Richard Lannoy, *India, People and Places* [New York: Vanguard Press, 1955].)

practice of worshiping the feet of another is extremely common among Hindus and is the usual way of expressing relative rank between castes, between family members, and between men and women. A servant typically will perform this act each year when he renews his contract with his or her Havik employer. In turn, a Havik will perform the same ceremony when the caste guru visits his or her house.[7]

For Havik Brahmins the overall aim of the caste system is quite clear. The whole system—with its ranked castes, ranks between men and women, and varying states of ritual purity, which are determined by personal and intercaste interaction and the amounts of pollution incurred or avoided—is intended to permit select members of society to attain a sufficiently pure state (M_1A) so that the gods who oversee society and the world generally may be served. For Haviks it is humanity's fundamental responsibility to serve and nourish the gods, who in turn nourish the world, and this can be done only by those who approximate the gods in purity. Daily worship of the gods traditionally takes place in every Havik household, and a male member of the family must be in the state of M_1A. Worship (puja) is clearly a form of symbolic service in which the god is bathed, fed, and otherwise tended. To perform this service in a state other than the most pure involves polluting the god. If the god is polluted, he or she is insulted, and the wel-

[7]Ibid., pp. 181–82.

are of the household, and theoretically the world, is in danger. At a minimum, the god is believed to depart his or her household shrine if polluted,
and at worst will inflict punishments on the guilty party and his family.

The state of M_1A is achievable only in the context of the caste system
as a whole. Certain actions necessary to the functioning of society are so
polluting that to perform them means the impossibility of becoming pure
enough to serve the gods, who of course are always in a state of purity much
higher than that of humans. Plowing, washing clothes, cutting hair, and
many other necessary actions must be avoided by those who would be pure
enough to serve the gods, and so these chores are relegated to others (lower
castes) to enable certain members of the highest caste (male Haviks) to perform the equally necessary task of nourishing the gods. In this sense, society
in a Havik village has a unified aim, and theoretically all members of society
ultimately benefit from the worship of the gods by the Havik males.[8]

The world of the divine as understood by the Haviks is also ranked
according to innate states of purity and as such is to some extent a reflection of the logic underlying human society. The gods worshiped in household shrines by Haviks are almost always gods of the Sanskrit tradition (for
example, Shiva and Vishnu). These gods are innately purer than Haviks and
therefore must be served only by Havik males in the purest possible state
or in specially restricted conditions by lower castes in specially pure places,
such as large temples, by specially purified officiants.

Another class of deities is related to local traditions. These deities,
often village goddesses, have specific associations such as disease and fertility. They may be worshiped more casually by Hindus, and though they
may be polluted and thus angered, they are generally thought to be in a
less-pure natural state than the higher, Sanskritic gods.

An even lower class of divine beings, spirits, is also recognized. These
are usually malevolent spirits that must be avoided. They are generally
thought to be in a state of M_3 relative to the higher gods.

Unlike the logic of human society, however, the higher gods are not
thought to be polluted by the lower gods. It appears that the higher gods,
especially the Sanskritic gods worshiped by the Haviks, have a strong "field
of purity"[9] that cannot be penetrated by the lower gods and that also protects them from many kinds of pollution from humans.

Similarly, certain human beings have an almost inviolable field of purity vis-à-vis the spirits. The spirits may attack only those who are relatively
impure among the Haviks (and of course those of other castes, all of which
are more impure than Haviks). Havik women and children, for example,
are more likely to be attacked by spirits than are adult male Haviks. Adult

[8]Ibid., pp. 151–52.
[9]This is Harper's term.

males are versed in the sacred scriptures, and the very possession of such knowledge is thought to provide a field of purity against which the spirits are powerless. Only in states of M_3 are such Haviks possibly vulnerable to these spirits.

So it is, then, that the caste system as practiced and understood by the Havik Brahmins of Mysore aims at maintaining the order of the cosmos for the welfare of all. The whole system is geared to preserving continued contact with and service of the gods, without which cosmic order would be impossible. Although the Havik males play the most dramatic role (as the ones who actually serve the gods in daily worship), each caste has a part to play in making this system possible. The system does not rule out the possibility of lower castes worshiping the gods in special circumstances, of worshiping lesser divinities on a regular basis, or of achieving a high spiritual state in terms of the logic of the *Bhagavad Gita*. In day-to-day life, however, it is the service of the gods by the Haviks, which is only possible within the context of the caste system, that lends that system its logic and force.

The Pilgrimage to Pandharpur

Among Hindus in the State of Maharashtra in Southwest India a religious cult known as the Varkari movement is very popular. The movement dates back to at least the twelfth century and has been a prominent, sometimes dominant, feature in the religious lives of Marathi-speaking Hindus of this area. The movement is highly devotional, and the deity adored is Viththala (also called Vithoba), a regional name for Vishnu. The place most sacred to Viththala is a temple in the sacred city of Pandharpur, on the west bank of the Bhima River in southern Maharashtra.

The history of the Varkari movement centers around several extraordinary saints, whose writings form the most important and popular literature for all Varkaris. The earliest saint of the tradition was Jnanadeva (sometimes written Dyanadeva), who lived in the thirteenth century. Jnanadeva wrote a commentary in Marathi on the *Bhagavad Gita*, several theological tracts, and many hymns of praise to Viththala. Although a Brahmin, he was critical of certain aspects of the caste system and stressed both devotion and disciplined action as the best paths for achieving spiritual fulfillment. For centuries he has been one of the most revered saints of the Varkari movement.

The saints who came after Jnanadeva continued to emphasize devotion as central to religious life, and many of them were highly critical of the caste system, empty knowledge, and habitual ritualism. They stressed that a person's true worth is determined solely by devotion to God and that ascribed social roles are irrelevant to the devotional relations between God and his devotee. Many Varkari saints came from low castes, and the saint Chokhamela was from the untouchable Mahar caste of Maharashtra.

Perhaps the most popular of all Varkari saints is Tukarama, who lived in the seventeenth century. Tukarama came from a poor Shudra family, and at several points in his life he was harassed by Brahmins. Once they forced him to throw all his writings into a river. Tukarama wrote hundreds of hymns to Viththala, and they are among the most loved by Varkaris today. Many of his hymns stress the centrality of simple, ardent devotion to God and make fun of elaborate rituals, erudite knowledge, and those who take pride in their high-caste status. Although Tukarama never advocated the overthrow of the caste system, many of his hymns contrast people's spiritual worth with their status in society. High caste, wealth, and power are no reflection of a person's worth in the eyes of God, and to equate worldly prestige with spiritual status is wrong. Implicit in Tukarama's hymns, and in the hymns of many other Varkari saints, is a criticism of the belief of many Hindus that birth in a high caste represents spiritual superiority.

The vital center of the Varkari movement for centuries has been the pilgrimage to Pandharpur, which takes place twice each year. Indeed, to be a Varkari is to make this pilgrimage as often as possible. The basic idea is that living devotees on their way to Pandharpur represent the traditional saints of the movement, who also made their pilgrimage to God at Pandharpur. The pilgrimage represents, as it were, a river of devotion converging on the holy city of Pandharpur, and to be involved in this devotional river is especially sacred and purifying. On pilgrimage a Varkari not only joins thousands of other present-day Varkari devotees, he or she also joins with all Varkaris from the past, who are believed to be spiritually present during the pilgrimage, and particularly with the great saints of the movement, who are plainly represented and worshiped, as we shall see.

Pilgrimage is always made in groups, and each group carries with it a portable shrine with an image or symbol of a particular saint from the past. The groups come from different geographical areas, some hundreds of miles distant from Pandharpur, and the saint whom they revere has been prominent in their region and usually died in that locale. The portable shrines are called *palkis*, and the term refers to the individual group as a whole as well. The symbol of the saint housed in the *palki* is called the *paduka*, which means "foot," and in fact the most common symbol of the saint is a pair of metal feet. This symbol reinforces the idea that the pilgrims are actually making the pilgrimage with their particular saint from the past.

On a pilgrimage there will be between twenty-five and thirty groups, or *palkis*, each beginning its journey from a different part of Maharashtra. As it is necessary for all groups to converge on a particular, auspicious day just outside the city of Pandharpur, and from there to enter the city in one huge stream, the individual *palkis* must begin their journeys on different days because of the differing distances. It is traditional to this day for the pilgrimage to be made on foot, and for some groups the journey takes sev-

eral weeks. Each group follows a specified route, which has varied very littl.
over the centuries, and as it slowly moves through villages the numbers are
swelled by those who join the *palki* en route. The long procession that finally enters Pandharpur numbers over one hundred thousand and takes
hours to pass through the city gates.

Each *palki* has an appointed leader—or in the case of larger *palkis*, an
organizing committee—who is responsible for making preparations for the
pilgrimage. A truck or several bullock carts accompany each *palki* to transport baggage and food, and a host of details must be arranged and anticipated. The progress of the *palki* also must be carefully timed so that it ar-
rives on the right day, and it is these kinds of details that are the
responsibility of the leader.

The pilgrimage itself is dominated by two physical acts of devotion:
walking with or in the footsteps of other devotees, past and present, particularly the saints, and singing the devotional hymns composed by the saints.
Walking in the path of the saints is held to be particularly sacred, and many
songs emphasize the sacred nature of the road itself, which has been and is
being walked by the saints. A poem of Tukarama, for example, says:

> *I should like to become the small pebbles*
> *or the big stones, or the dust*
> *of the road which leads to Paṇḍharpūr.*
> *Thus would I be under the feet of the Santas* [saints].[10]

The hymns themselves express a variety of devotional sentiments and
frequently ask Viththala to protect the devotee from harm and to ease personal sorrows. In many songs of Tukarama, Viththala is addressed as a
mother and is invoked to look after her children like a loving mother. The
songs are all well known to the pilgrims and are sung communally as the
procession winds its way along. This singing encourages a strong feeling of
community in which the normal world to a large extent drops away and the
pilgrim feels in the midst of a special family. The procession makes periodic stops during the day, and at these times the pilgrims sit in groups and
share details of their personal lives with one another and often reveal secret
griefs and sorrows. Strong friendships are made quickly in the unified, devotional context of the pilgrimage. Indeed, the last few miles of road near
Pandharpur are referred to by the pilgrims as the Weeping Plateau, as it is
at this point that goodbyes are said just before disbanding the *palki* inside
the city.

The evenings are spent in worship of the saint enshrined in the portable shrine, in singing hymns, and in popular religious recitations, which
are sometimes spiced with double entendres, much to the delight of the

---

[10]G. A. Deleury, *The Cult of Viṭhobā* (Poona, India: Deccan College, 1960), p. 76.

rowd. Villagers join the pilgrims each evening, and a festive atmosphere surrounds the *palki* as it progresses from village to village. Each village makes an effort to put up decorations and signs of welcome and to accommodate the weary pilgrims. Although this must be a considerable burden to some villages, as the number of pilgrims is often in the thousands, each village seems to take pride in outdoing the others in its hospitality. Most pilgrims sleep outside or, when it rains, in makeshift tents. The daily hike is wearying and nightly accommodations simple, often crude, all of which tends to reinforce the spirit of community. Generally, grumbling is discouraged as inappropriate to the religious atmosphere, and most pilgrims seem cheerful throughout these physically difficult days on the road.

The spirit of solidarity and mutual joy of the pilgrimage is described by Irawati Karve, an anthropologist from Maharashtra, who joined the *palki* of Jnanadeva originating near the city of Poona.

> So, I was getting to know my Maharashtra anew every day. I found a new definition of Maharashtra: the land whose people go to Pandharpur for pilgrimage. When the palanquin started from Poona, there were people from Poona, Jannar, Moglai, Satara, etc. Every day people were joining the pilgrimage from Khandesh, Sholapur, Nasik, Berar. As we neared Pandharpur, the pilgrimage was becoming bigger and bigger. All were Marathi-speaking people—coming from different castes, but singing the same songs, the same verses of Vārkari cult, speaking to each other, helping each other, singing songs to each other.... I witnessed how the language and culture of Maharashtra had spread among its social layers. The fine poetry of five centuries was recited daily. That poetry embodied a religion and a philosophy. People speaking many dialects sang the same verses and thus learned a standard language.... Every one was laughing and joking during the march. Nobody pressed people to join the pilgrimage. No public announcement of the program was made, and the outside world might just as well not exist. The pilgrims were intoxicated with happiness; anyone who had a heart, who had the insight, could have the same joy.[11]

The hymns of the saints sung by the pilgrims help create and reinforce the feelings of solidarity and community by emphasizing love and a person's inner worth. In a hymn of Chokhamela, the untouchable saint, it is said: "Chokha is uncouth, but his devotion is not uncouth. Why judge him by his exterior?"[12] In all, the shared hardships of the road, the communal singing of hymns all well known to the pilgrims, the feeling that all are devotees of Viththala journeying to pay him homage, and the words of the hymns, which often stress the meaninglessness of exterior qualities, combine to create an atmosphere in which there is relaxation of caste exclusivity.

---

[11]Irawati Karve, "On the Road, a Maharashtrian Pilgrimage," *Journal of Asian Studies*, XXII, no. 1 (November 1962), 22.

[12]Ibid., p. 21.

The pilgrimage to Pandharpur is a good example of a religious even‹ that works to alleviate the confining strictures of the caste system. Maharashtrian society, like society elsewhere in India, is dominated by the closed caste system. Despite the teachings of the saints, society is divided into numerous ranked castes that normally have very little social interaction with one another. There is a large Shudra caste, the Marathas, and many large untouchable castes in Maharashtra, and in everyday life the divisions among them, especially between untouchables and other castes, is very strict. On the pilgrimage to Pandharpur, however, all castes are welcome, and many rules concerning intercaste contact are suspended temporarily.

Nevertheless, it is interesting to note the extent to which certain aspects of the caste system persist among the pilgrims. Pilgrims belonging to any given *palki*, no matter how strong the feeling of solidarity, do not mix with each other indiscriminately. In the first place, each *palki* is divided into smaller subgroups of about one hundred pilgrims known as *dindis*. Although some of these subgroups are made up of a religious teacher and his or her disciples, most *dindis* are determined by caste affiliation. So, for example, in the large *palki* of Jnanadeva that originates in the Poona area, there may be twenty or more *dindis*, most of which are identified by caste or family ties. There are *dindis* of tailors, merchants, village agriculturalists, and so on. On the road, people walk only within their *dindi*, and when there are stops along the way the pilgrims almost always choose fellow members of their *dindi* to converse with. The *palki* organizer or the organizing committee determines the order in which the *dindis* will proceed. Positions closest to the portable shrines are the most desired, and the order of the *dindis* varies each year so that each one in turn may occupy a position close to the shrine while on the road. Within the long line of any *palki*, then, there is a precise order of *dindis*. Furthermore, while on the road, the *palki* as a whole does not sing the same hymn at once, except perhaps at the beginning of the route of smaller *palkis*. Each *dindi* has its own song leader, who determines which hymns will be sung. Therefore, at any one time there may be twenty or more hymns being sung by the *dindis* as the *palki* makes its way along the road.[13] An individual pilgrim's strongest identity, then, is with his or her particular *dindi*, which consists of his or her own caste members. It is obvious on the pilgrimage that a feeling of general community and mutual helpfulness exists, but the basic structure of the *palki* does maintain a certain amount of caste separateness.

It is also clear on the pilgrimage that certain basic caste rules are not breached. Next to intermarriage, eating together is the surest way of conveying pollution between castes, and in normal life interdining prohibitions are very strictly observed by almost all Hindus. When the *palki* stops

---

[13]Deleury, *The Cult of Vithobā*, pp. 83–85.

or meals, separate kitchens are set up, and the *dindis* dine separately. If by chance there is more than one caste represented in a *dindi* because a particular caste could not muster enough pilgrims to form its own *dindi*, there may be a further proliferation of kitchens. The feeling of brotherhood and community generated by the pilgrimage may ease caste exclusivity, but it is not strong enough to break down this fundamental taboo, which reinforces caste separateness in everyday life.

Irawati Karve, an educated and modernized Hindu who had little patience with many aspects of traditional Hinduism, was often troubled by the persistence of caste exclusivity and caste observance on the pilgrimage to Pandharpur in which she took part. She herself made a point of visiting with, and sometimes dining with, lower castes, but her behavior was the exception. She was particularly irked one day when they arrived at a village in which the well was far from their camp. She was complaining about not having enough water to a fellow pilgrim from a low caste and was delighted when he later brought her a large container of water from the well. For Karve as a Brahmin it was a fundamental violation of caste law to use this water for any other purpose than bathing. However, she used the water for cooking and drinking. Her caste sisters, fellow Brahmins, refused to do so. They insisted on using only water brought by themselves, preferring to suffer thirst before accepting water given by a lower-caste Hindu. In Karve's eyes, restrictive caste rules prevented her Brahmin companions from appreciating an act of service. The *dindi* she was a part of contained both Brahmins and Marathas, and throughout the pilgrimage many barriers remained in force. She comments on this:

> Every day I regretted the fact that one and the same *dindi* was divided into these two sections. All of the people were clean, and ate their food only after taking a bath. Then why this separateness? Was all this walking together, singing together, and reciting the poetry of the saints together directed only towards union in the other world while retaining separateness in this world? This question was in my mind all the time. Just as I had become friendly with the Brahmin group, the Maratha women had also taken me to their heart. As I could not bring them together, I joined now one group and now another, trying to construct a bridge, at least as far as I was concerned. After I had taken my meal with them, I felt that they were more friendly. Many of them walked alongside of me, held my hand, and told me many things about their life. Toward the end, they called me "Tai," meaning "Sister." A few of them said, "Mark you, Tai, we shall visit you in Poona." And then one girl said, "But will you behave with us then as you are behaving now?" It was a simple question, but it touched me to the quick. We have been living near each other for thousands of years, but they are still not of us and we are not of them.[14]

One more example of how caste exclusivity persists in the pilgrimage, despite strong tendencies toward a feeling of general community, is the

---

[14]Karve, "On the Road," p. 19.

traditional prohibition against untouchables entering the temple of Vi-
thala in Pandharpur itself. Until independence in 1947, at which time the
new Indian government prohibited the practice, nearly all temples that ca-
tered to high-caste Hindus prohibited untouchables from entering temple
precincts. At Pandharpur the situation was no different. Varkari pilgrims
from untouchable castes were not permitted inside the temple to see the
holy image of their god, the ultimate goal of every pilgrim. They had to
remain outside the temple precincts and be content with worshiping an
image of Chokhamela, the untouchable saint, who in his lifetime was similarly excluded from the temple.

In India today there is considerable legislation that seeks to ease traditional caste divisions, and in an increasingly industrialized society, particularly in cities where intercaste contact is necessary, many traditional
taboos are being breached or modified. Nevertheless, the caste system is
such an integral part of the Hindu tradition and world view that it is unlikely to be fundamentally altered until Hinduism itself is fundamentally
altered or disappears. The caste system is not an entity unto itself but part
and parcel of the Hindu vision of reality, and as such it is not surprising
that it persists strongly to this day and has resisted all but the most minor
and gradual changes.

9

Symbols and Structures: A Concluding Analysis

The distinctive nature of Hinduism resides in its simultaneous affirmation that people have an obligation to uphold the world, on the one hand, and to transcend the world, on the other hand. Although traditional Hinduism has formulated solutions to this double emphasis, the essence of Hinduism lies not so much in these compromises as in the clear demand that both obligations are absolute. Over the centuries Hinduism has been characterized more by a desire to push each obligation to its limit than by the desire to reconcile the two and risk compromising either of them. It is the tension between dharma and moksha, then, that characterizes Hinduism and lends it its special appeal.

The Hindu scriptures often tell stories that deal with the tension between dharma and moksha, and the mythologies of the three most important Hindu deities, Vishnu, Shiva, and the Great Goddess, all exemplify how this tension may be appreciated without compromising either obligation. These stories and myths capture vividly the distinctive nature of Hinduism and serve to impress on those who hear them the importance of acknowledging more than one perspective in humanity's spiritual sojourn. The stories and myths often juxtapose one perspective with another and in so doing remind the reader or listener that to remain locked into one perspective alone is to miss the extraordinary richness of being human. By shifting perspectives the Hindu stories and myths invite us to expand our awareness to a more complete understanding of who we are and what the human venture is about.

Many cherished Hindu stories delight in juxtaposing the perspective of the world renouncer (the moksha obligation) and the householder (the dharma obligation). The stories generally aim, not at reconciling the two perspectives, but at showing what the consequences may be if one is not tempered with the other. Implicit in most of these stories is a criticism of one extreme in light of the other. The *Mahabharata* is a treasure house of such stories. Two tales from this epic exemplify the way in which one perspective functions as a corrective to the other. The first story emphasizes the importance of dharma and contains an implicit criticism of world renunciation, whereas the second does just the opposite.

Once upon a time there was a formidable ascetic named Jaratkaru. He wandered the land, refused to call any place his home, and was attached to no one and nothing. He slept wherever he happened to be and undertook rigorous asceticism to dry up the sap of life within himself. It is said that he was so heroic in his austerities that he abstained from food altogether and existed merely on air. Having abandoned the world, he quested for final release. In his travels he came one day to a cave, where he beheld a remarkable sight. He saw many men hanging upside down, suspended above a chasm. They dangled by a single thread of grass, and Jaratkaru noticed that the rats that lived in the cave would nibble on the thread from time to time and that it soon would break, sending the unfortunate men plunging into the chasm. He asked them who they were and what he might do to help them in their distress.

They told their sad tale. They all belonged to the same lineage, which was in danger of becoming extinct. Because their lone living descendent had not met his obligation to society and his ancestors to produce progeny, his forefathers had fallen from heaven and been reduced to this pitiful plight. When their descendent died childless, they would die too. The grass string, they explained, was the thread of their lineage, now nearly worn out, and the rats gnawing on the string represented time. They went on to tell Jaratkaru that their lone remaining descendant, their last possible hope from being hurled into the chasm of oblivion, had neither wife nor kin and had renounced the world in order to practice asceticism. They lamented his folly, saying that the greatest merit is earned by him who marries and produces offspring. They cursed their descendent for abandoning his ancestors to this plight and pleaded with Jaratkaru to tell their ascetic descendent of their situation should he happen upon him in his travels. Their descendent, they said, was famed in the world by the name of Jaratkaru! In this way Jaratkaru was awakened to his obligation to uphold the world. Ashamed and grieved at the condition of his ancestors, he set out in search of a wife.[1]

---

[1]J. A. B. van Buitenen, trans., *The Mahabharata*, 3 vols. (Chicago: University of Chicago Press, 1973–78), Vol. I: *The Book of the Beginning*, chap. 41, pp. 103–5.

By juxtaposing the perspective of the world renouncer with that of those he has renounced, the story tempers the ascetic ideal by teaching that if all people renounced the world, if only the moksha extreme dominated their vision of their destiny, there soon would be no people to have visions at all. Jaratkaru, confirmed in the moksha obligation, is chastened when confronted with the neglect of his dharma obligation. The story, however, does not seek to reconcile the two obligations. Typically, it leaves intact a lively tension between them.

The second story features a righteous householder named Mudgala. Mudgala had a wife and sons and made his living by gleaning rice. He was truthful in all things, generous, and never became angry. Although his own resources were meager, he always treated guests with great hospitality and preferred to go hungry himself rather than see a guest go unsatisfied. He also observed traditional rituals and regularly made offerings to the gods from his scarce supplies. The fame of Mudgala spread through the heavens and the earth, and a particular sage named Durvasas decided to test the householder's generosity and hospitality. Disguised as a naked madman, Durvasas appeared one day at Mudgala's house and announced that he wished to be fed. Mudgala invited him in with all customary respect and provided him with food. Durvasas was not easily satisfied and kept requesting more food until Mudgala's supplies were exhausted. Mudgala showed no sign of irritation throughout. Durvasas returned five more times, and each time he behaved outrageously, eating all the food Mudgala had on hand and leaving Mudgala and his family destitute. At no time, however, did Mudgala lose his equanimity. He was generous and hospitable every time Durvasas tested him.

Durvasas was greatly impressed and announced to Mudgala that he had never seen such meritorious conduct, either in the heavens or on earth. The gods, too, were impressed and sent a messenger with a chariot to transport Mudgala to heaven. Arriving at Mudgala's humble house, the messenger praised Mudgala's great deeds and announced that his merit had earned him bodily entry into heaven. He invited Mudgala to mount the chariot and return with him to the realm of the gods. Mudgala hesitated, however, and asked the messenger what heaven was like. The messenger replied that only those of good deeds dwelt there. Beautiful nymphs inhabited heaven, and wish-fulfilling trees were everywhere. There were pleasure parks; there was never excessive heat or cold; there was no disease, old age, sorrow, or death; there were only pleasing smells and sounds; and all heaven-dwelling creatures were beautiful and luminous and wore unfading garlands. All these delights, the messenger said, had been won by Mudgala's good deeds.

When pressed by Mudgala for further details, however, the messenger had to admit that the joys of heaven did not last forever. Eventually, he said, the merit earned by good deeds would become exhausted, and it was necessary for all heaven-abiding creatures sooner or later to reenter the world. They would reenter the world in situations of high birth and status because of their past merit, but if they acted in unmeritorious ways they would be reborn in lower positions or even possibly have to reap the results of bad actions by sojourning in hell for a time.

Mudgala politely refused the messenger's invitation to enter the chariot, saying that such heavenly joys held no attraction for him if after experiencing them he must again be reborn in the world. Dismissing the heavenly messenger, Mudgala gave up gleaning rice. He occupied himself completely in meditation and became indifferent to the world. Gold and clay became the same to him. Praise and blame became the same to him. Through meditation he gained spiritual strength, insight, and detachment and finally achieved the imperishable goal of release from the cycles of karma and samsara.[2]

The story is an implicit criticism of the logic of actions undertaken to gain rewards, the logic that underlies most people's support of the world. Support of the world in and of itself only leads to the perpetuation of the world and the eternal recycling of individuals. Supporting the world, the story suggests, necessarily involves acting according to the logic of reward and punishment. Worldly order is based precisely on this logic. In this world, with its heavens and hells and rebirth, all actions reap results, either good or bad. The good results may be heavenly, indeed, but they are temporary. If a person accepts the rewards—that is, if he accepts the logic that his deeds arose from a desire for rewards—he continues to be subject to the implacable laws of karma and eventually must exhaust any excess of merit and be reborn. Good deeds do not lead to moksha. Moksha is won only when, like Mudgala, one becomes indifferent to reward and punishment and drops out of the merit game of the world. Heaven is no ultimate release from karma and samsara, and Mudgala saw it as simply an extension of the normal world, a kind of way station where one enjoys certain pleasures before plunging back into the world of cause and effect, merit and demerit, reward and punishment, and perpetual rebirth.

The great deities of the Hindu pantheon also concretely express the tension between dharma and moksha, between the householder and the renouncer, between support of the world and indifference to the world. As symbolic representations of the essential vision underlying Hinduism, they embody in their complex personalities and various deeds both emphases within the Hindu tradition.

Vishnu is preeminently the creator and maintainer of the world and typically is depicted as a heavenly king who descends to the world from time to time in various forms to uphold dharma by rescuing the world from demons. Said to be present in all kings who uphold the order of dharma,

---

[2]Ibid., Vol. II: *The Book of the Forest*, chaps. 246–47, pp. 701–5.

he has as his consorts the goddess Lakshmi, the goddess of wealth and abundance, and Bhudevi, the goddess Earth. Vishnu oversees the world and as the guardian of Earth herself is attentive to worldly stability and prosperity. On the other hand, Vishnu's mythology also emphasizes the eternal perspective of moksha. Vishnu is often described as lying on the serpent-couch Shesha, the cosmic serpent, in the middle of the limitless waters of chaos. As he lies there, universes emerge from his every pore. That is, Vishnu creates this world of ours, but it is only one among countless other worlds that, from the perspective of eternity, come and go with the fleetingness of bubbles on the surface of the ocean. Our world, so precious and seemingly eternal, is the spontaneous, ephemeral reflex of the great god Vishnu, who grows universes as effortlessly and naturally as we grow hair. Vishnu, too, is the destroyer of the worlds. At the end of each cosmic cycle he inhales the world, and it resides within him in embryonic form, where it is renourished, or recycled, prior to its next creation. Vishnu exhales universes every time he breathes, as it were, and destroys them every time he inhales. From this perspective, our world is reduced to insignificance, and the truths of moksha are illustrated. Life, with its joys and sorrows, dreams and longings, disappointments and tragedies, is only a sigh of the god Vishnu.

The world-attentive aspects of the god Shiva are best seen in his most popular symbol, the lingam, or phallus, and in his creative cosmic dance. In Shiva temples, the central image is the lingam, which traditionally is set in the yoni, the female organ, and typically Shiva is shown with an erect penis. This emphasis in Shiva's mythology underlines the truth in Hinduism that Shiva is embodied in the very sap of existence. He is the creative, vigorous power that pervades all life and without which there would be no life. The many images of the dancing Shiva also emphasize his creative role. They convey an orderly, refined, rhythmic grace that suggests universal order and refinement. The alternating rhythms of Shiva's dance are said to reveal themselves in the rhythms of the seasons and the biological processes. Shiva's dance is the orderly dance of life, nature, and the physical cosmos generally.

Indifference to the world is equally vivid in Shiva's myths. His great cosmic dance eventually and invariably includes a particularly wild sequence in which the world is burned to ashes. Descriptions of this step describe his whirling arms and flying feet smashing worlds into smithereens. Shiva is also the divine model of yoga and is often pictured in isolated meditation. In his trance he is oblivious to the world and is angered when distracted by it. One of the most popular Shiva myths tells of his destruction of the god of lust, who sought to distract Shiva from meditation with thoughts of women, spring, and sex. In fury, Shiva burnt him to ashes with the heat from his eyes. Shiva is also described as an antisocial madman in many myths. He roams the world naked, haunts cremation grounds, and is surrounded by a weird entourage of ghouls. He wears a necklace of skulls,

FIGURE 9-1 Dancing Shiva. (Courtesy of Air India.)

his hair is tangled and matted, and he is often intoxicated with hemp. In these aspects, dwelling on the periphery of civilization, Shiva beckons one out of the world of social roles and dharmic order to the ultimate goal of release.

The Great Goddess of Hinduism has a great many forms. Indeed, she is said to be the source of all goddesses and to be present wherever there is a woman. Her benign forms are many, and in these forms she protects and nourishes her devotees and the world. She is often depicted as a fierce warrior who, like Vishnu, is attentive to the well-being of the world and assumes various forms for its protection. She is often described as an eternally wakeful mother who jealously guards the world as a mother guards its young, and as the mother of the world she is said to be the primordial source from which all life springs. Two manifestations of the Great Goddess in particular underline her role as world guardian: Annapurna, the one full of food, who appeared during a severe drought and nourished the world with food that grew from her body and tears that flowed from her eyes, and Jagaddhatri, the world nurse, who suckles all creation.

The Great Goddess also illustrates the perspective of the moksha tradition in her destructive, bloodthirsty manifestations, which underline the inherent painfulness of existence. The most vivid example of the Goddess in this aspect is the goddess Kali. Kali is typically shown with a sunken stomach signifying her insatiable hunger and thirst for blood. She lives in the cremation grounds as the symbol of the all-consuming power of death.

ne is sometimes said to wear infant corpses as earrings and to drink blood from a skull. Jackals and goblins accompany her, and her appearance is unkempt and fearful. She has large, sharp fangs and fills the world with terrifying roars. She vividly illustrates certain inevitables of human existence, such as sorrow, sickness, and death, and reminds humans of the fragility of their life and its inevitable end. In her terrible appearance and loathsome habits she is enough to turn people away from the world toward their eternal destiny of moksha, complete release from embodied existence with its inevitable sorrows.

A vision of the Great Goddess by the nineteenth-century saint Ramakrishna is a dramatic example of how she reveals both Hindu tendencies, to affirm and support the world and to reject and gain release from the world.

> In this vision he saw a woman of exquisite beauty, about to become a mother, emerging from the Ganges and slowly approaching the Panchavati [the steps for bathing leading into the river]. Presently she gave birth to a child and began to nurse it tenderly. A moment later she assumed a terrible aspect, seized the child with her grim jaws, and crushed it. Swallowing it, she reentered the waters of the Ganges.[3]

From the temporal perspective, from the point of view of dharma, the world may indeed appear warm, nourishing, and beautiful. As such it is worth supporting, protecting, and refining. From this perspective, the world may become a fit and habitable place for humans, a place where with the help of other people one may carve out an orderly, secure destiny for oneself and one's children. From the eternal point of view, however, the fragility of the world becomes clear, as do the inevitable shortcomings of finite human existence. The Great Goddess gives perpetually and unstintingly, the ever-creative source of life. She also, however, must be renourished. She is ever fertile and ever hungry and reveals dramatically the truth that life must feed on death.

A final tale from Hindu mythology, which moves dramatically from the dharma to the moksha perspective and back again, is a fitting conclusion to this book.[4] The tale illustrates what it is like to be a Hindu, for whom the double obligations of dharma and moksha temper each other in such a way that one is constantly reminded that one is both a social animal with worldly duties and an eternal sojourner in an infinite drama whose goal is ultimate release. The tale features the god Indra, who is often called king of the gods and who is famous in Vedic mythology for slaying the demon

[3]M. [Mahendranath Gupta], *The Gospel of Sri Ramakrishna*, trans. Swami Nikhilananda (New York: Ramakrishna-Vivekananda Center, 1942), pp. 21–22.

[4]The story is taken from *Brahma-vaivarta Purana* 4. 47. 69–161; see Rajendra Nath Sen, trans., *The Brahma-vaivarta Purana* (Allahabad, India: Sudhindra Nath Vasu, 1922), Pt. II, pp. 308–12. The story is also told in Heinrich Zimmer, *Myths and Symbols in Indian Art and Civilization* (New York: Harper & Row, 1962), pp. 3–11.

FIGURE 9-2 The goddess Kali.

of chaos and stabilizing the world. The story begins just after the defeat of the demon and pictures Indra feeling very proud of himself indeed.

Swollen with the pride of victory, Indra decided to have a palace built befitting his position as world creator and summoned his divine architect, Vishvakarma, the All-Maker. He commissioned the architect to build the most splendid structure he could manage. Vishvakarma set about the task with relish, and soon a fabulous palace was underway. Indra, happening by the construction site one day, however, and looking over what had been built and the plans for the remaining structure, expressed disappointment, wondering if his architect could think of something grander to befit Indra's exalted position. Vishvakarma, accepting the challenge, set out again, draw-

FIGURE 9-3 The goddess Durga slaying the buffalo demon. (Courtesy of Timothy Moody.)

ing up a whole new set of plans for an even more fantastic palace. Again, Indra happened along one day before the palace was completed, looked it over, and urged his architect to build something even more elaborate and grand. This happened once again, and Vishvakarma soon realized that he had an insoluble problem on his hands, namely, Indra's hopelessly inflated view of himself. Indra was convinced that no being in the universe was greater than he, that he was the center of the universe, and that he should be surrounded by unsurpassed grandeur suitable to his lofty position. Vishvakarma realized that nothing he could envision would satisfy Indra's exalted view of himself. Indra had a very bad case of maya, imagining himself to be the sole focus of the cosmic processes, the be-all and end-all of existence.

Vishvakarma was desperate and decided to seek help. In this story Vishnu is affirmed to be the highest god, the real source of the universes, and so it was to Vishnu that Vishvakarma went in search of relief. The great god listened sympathetically and assured the frustrated architect that he himself would remedy the situation. The next day a handsome youth appeared at Indra's half-completed palace and asked to see the self-styled king of the gods. Indra invited the lad into his splendid throne room and entered into conversation with the boy. While they talked Indra grew impatient, as the boy had said nothing about Indra's splendid palace. Finally,

Indra interrupted the youth and asked him point-blank what he thought of the place. "Isn't it grand?" Indra asked. "Of course I have remodeling plans that will make it even more sumptuous, but tell me, what do you think?" The boy, who was none other than Vishnu in disguise, looked around and then said, "Well, it isn't bad for *an* Indra." Indra wasn't quite sure he'd heard the boy correctly and wanted to know what the lad knew of other Indras. Surely, there was only one Indra, ruler of the cosmos, and he himself was that Indra.

The boy set out to enlighten Indra on the great cosmic cycles lasting billions of years, during which the world is created and destroyed over and over endlessly, and of the infinite reaches of space, which contain infinite worlds just like this one, each with an Indra as its ruler. Indra began to have inklings of self-doubt about his preeminent position, and as he fidgeted there suddenly appeared in the throne room an immense army of ants. Rank upon rank they streamed through the room, thousands and thousands of them. The boy looked at the teeming masses of ants and laughed softly. Indra wished to know what amused the boy about this invasion. The boy hesitated, wondering aloud if Indra was god enough to know the truth concerning what amused him. Indra, in godly fashion, puffed out his chest and demanded to know the truth that had provoked his guest's laughter. "It has just been revealed to me," the youth said to Indra, "that each one of these ants streaming through your palace was in some past life also an Indra."

So Indra was humbled. Granted a vision of eternity by Vishnu, realizing the truth that he had only assumed his lofty position through countless previous lives and that eventually he would fall from it and cycle endlessly in future births, Indra called off the construction of his palace and announced to his wife that he wished to renounce the world. Indra's severe case of maya was remedied by his realization that in the infinite future he might well be reduced to the status of an ant, like countless Indras before him, crushed by the vastness of the cosmic cycles and the unalterable laws of karma and samsara. However, when he consulted his palace priest concerning his wish to renounce the world and achieve release from the endless merry-go-round of lives, he was instructed to remain at his post. It was not fitting, he was told, to abandon the world. Without its Indra this world would return to chaos, and all other creatures would suffer needless disruption, pain, and misery. An Indra's duty is to stay at his post and guard the world from chaos. Indra, we are told, did as he was instructed. He stayed at his post, fulfilling his obligation to dharma, but with a chastened view of himself. Acting with detachment, he realized that as Indra he was only fulfilling one of the world's necessary functions and that like all other creatures his temporary role should not be confused with his essential identity and ultimate destiny.

The Hindu solution to grasping the distinctive essence of being human is to affirm the fundamental importance of dharma while not losing sight of moksha. Dharma without moksha risks reducing humans to artificial social roles, to mere masks. Moksha without dharma, however, risks reducing humans to mere ants in an ocean of whirling galaxies and denies their distinctive nature as cultured beings who are capable of creating dazzling worlds of their own. For Hinduism we are all Indras, creators and conquerors of our own particular worlds, which are carved out with courage, resourcefulness, and imagination. That these worlds are only part of a much larger scheme, however, is also affirmed and must be appreciated for us to be fully human.

Glossary

adhikara   Predilection or inclination, the idea that different people have different abilities and tendencies.

ahimsa   Noninjury, nonviolence.

ananda   Bliss or joy, a characteristic of self-realization.

ashrama   A stage of life, such as the householder stage; a hermitage or sanctuary for meditation.

Atman   The eternal self or soul.

avatar   A descent or incarnation; the god Vishnu has ten avatars.

bhakti   Devotion.

bija   (lit. "seed") The root syllable of a deity or sacred formula.

Brahman   Ultimate reality; the eternal, unchanging essence that underlies all things.

Brahmin   A member of the highest class, traditionally a priest.

darshan   The act of having a view or sight of a holy image, place, or person.

dharma   Proper social behavior; virtuous behavior; social duty; acting in prescribed ways; the proper way of things.

dig-vijaya   A tour or journey in which a person triumphs over opponents either militarily or intellectually.

Garbha-griha   (lit. "womb room") The innermost sanctuary of a temple.

gopura   A gateway in the form of a towering structure, most dramatic feature of many South Indian temples.

guru   A spiritual master.

Jainism   An indigenous Indian religion dating back to the sixth century B.C.E. in which there is a heavy emphasis on asceticism.

jati   A caste or closed social group into which one is born and within which one must marry.

jiva   The life source of an individual.

jivanmukta   One who is liberated while still living.

kalpa   A cosmic era consisting of 4,320,000,000 years.

karma   The moral law of cause and effect by which one reaps what one sows.

karma-yoga   Disciplined action whereby one acts without desiring the fruits of one's actions.

karma-yogi   One who has mastered karma-yoga.

khadi   Native or homespun cloth; a symbol of economic independence from Britain during the Indian independence movement.

kirtan   Singing praises to a deity.

lingam   (lit. "mark") A stylized phallus, the most common symbol of the god Shiva.

loka-samgraha   Supporting the world by performing one's ascribed social duty or dharma.

mandala   A symbolic rendition of the cosmos; a stylized diagram of the world.

mantra   A sacred formula or verse.

maya   Appearance; that which prevents one from seeing things truly; illusion.

moksha   Release from bondage to karma and samsara and the goal of the spiritual quest in much of Hinduism.

mudras   Hand gestures used in rituals to express complex meanings or emotions.

nirguna   Having no qualities, a term often used to characterize Brahman.

palki   A portable shrine housing an image of a saint used on pilgrimages to the city of Pandharpur in Maharashtra; also, a group making the pilgrimage.

pancha tattva **ritual**   A ceremony in left-handed Tantra in which one partakes of five normally polluting things.

pati-vrata   A woman who is completely devoted to her husband.

prakriti   Material reality; nature; that from which one seeks to disentangle oneself in the practice of yoga.

prasad   (lit. "grace") Food or some other offering given to a deity and then returned to a devotee as a blessing.

puja   Worship, usually of a deity or the image of a deity.

pundit   A teacher, usually of traditional subjects such as grammar, philosophy, or logic.

purusha   (lit. "male") In yoga and later Hinduism the spiritual essence of an individual, which is eternal and unchanging.

rishi   A sage or visionary, the name given to the poets of the Vedic hymns.

saguna   Having qualities; a lesser or lower form of the divine according to Shankara; a personalized form of the divine as opposed to *nirguna* Brahman, unqualified divinity.

samadhi   A trancelike state sought in yoga in which the yogi transcends the limitations of prakriti.

samsara   Rebirth; the realm of individual existence generally.

samskara   Life-cycle rituals such as marriage and funeral ceremonies.

sannyasi One who has renounced the world and wanders about begging one's food.

satyagraha (lit. "seizing the truth") The term used by Gandhi to describe his method of nonviolent opposition to social and political injustices.

satyagrahi One who is adept in the methods and philosophy of satyagraha.

shikhara A soaring tower above the sanctuary of a temple.

suttee The suicide of a widow by burning herself alive on her husband's funeral pyre.

tirtha (lit. "crossing") A sacred place of pilgrimage.

untouchables Members of the lowest castes, whose traditional occupations are believed to be highly polluting by the higher castes.

vahana The vehicle of a deity, usually an animal of some kind.

varna A social class, of which there are traditionally four in Hinduism: Brahmin (priest), Kshatriya (warrior), Vaishya (merchant), and Shudra (serf).

vrat (lit. "vow") Rituals often done by women to protect their households and family members.

yajna A sacrifice, a term that refers to most Vedic rituals.

yantra A schematic diagram used as an aid to meditation.

yoga A system of physical and mental exercises that aims at disentangling the adept from the bonds of material existence; also the name of a school of Hindu philosophy.

yogi One who practices yoga.

yoni The female organ.

yuga An era or age consisting of thousands of years, of which there are four of different lengths in the history of each world system.

Bibliography

GENERAL INTRODUCTIONS

HOPKINS, THOMAS J. *The Hindu Religious Tradition.* Encino, Calif.: Dickenson Publishing Company, Inc., 1971.

ZIMMER, HEINRICH. *Philosophies of India.* Ed. Joseph Campbell. Bollingen Series XXVI. Princeton, N.J.: Princeton University Press, 1951.

GENERAL HISTORIES

BASHAM, A. L. *The Wonder That Was India.* New York: Grove Press, 1959.

MAJUMDAR, R. C., H. C. RAYCHAUDHURI, and **K. DATTA.** *An Advanced History of India.* London: Macmillan & Co., Ltd., 1960.

VEDIC RELIGION

GONDA, JAN. *The Vision of the Vedic Poets.* The Hague: Mouton & Co., 1963.

GRIFFITH, RALPH T. H., trans. *Hymns of the Rig Veda,* 2 vols. Varanasi, India: The Chowkhamba Sanskrit Series Office, 1963.

KEITH, A. B. *The Religion and Philosophy of the Veda and Upanishads.* Cambridge, Mass.: Harvard University Press, 1925.

RADHAKRISHNANA, S., trans. *The Principle Upanisads.* London: George Allen & Unwin, Ltd., 1953.

YOGA

ELIADE, MIRCEA. *Yoga: Immortality and Freedom.* Trans. Willard R. Trask. New York: Pantheon Books, Inc., 1958.

WOODS, JAMES HAUGHTON, trans. *The Yoga-System of Patañjali.* Harvard Oriental Series, vol. 17. Cambridge, Mass.: Harvard University Press, 1914.

EPIC LITERATURE

GOLDMAN, ROBERT, et al. *The Rāmāyana of Vālmīki: An Epic of Ancient India.* 7 vols. Princeton, N.J.: Princeton University Press, 1984– . (Incomplete.)

HILTEBEITEL, ALF. *The Ritual of Battle: Krishna in the Mahābhārata.* Ithaca, N.Y.: Cornell University Press, 1976.

HOPKINS, E. WASHBURN. *Epic Mythology.* Varanasi, India: Indological Book House, 1968.

ROY, PRATAP CHANDRA, trans. *The Mahabharata,* 11 vols. Calcutta: Oriental Publishing Company, 1927–32.

SHASTRI, HARI PRASAD, trans. *The Ramayana of Valmiki.* London: Shantisadan, 1953–59.

VAN BUITEN, J. A. B., trans. *The Mahabharata,* 3 vols. Chicago: University of Chicago Press, 1973–78. (Incomplete.)

THE LAW BOOKS

BUHLER, GEORG, trans. *The Laws of Manu.* Sacred Books of the East, vol. 25. London: Oxford University Press, 1886.

KANE, P. V. *History of Dharmaśāstra,* 5 vols. Poona, India: Bhandarkar Oriental Research Institute, 1930–62.

LINGAT, ROBERT. *The Classical Law of India.* Berkeley: University of California Press, 1973.

THE PURANAS AND MYTHOLOGICAL LITERATURE

DIMMITT, CORNELIA, and J. A. B. VAN BUITENEN, ed. and trans. *Classical Hindu Mythology: A Reader in the Sanskrit Purāṇas.* Philadelphia: Temple University Press, 1978.

KINSLEY, DAVID R. *The Sword and the Flute: Kālī and Kṛṣṇa, Dark Visions of the Terrible and the Sublime in Hindu Mythology.* Berkeley: University of California Press, 1975.

O'FLAHERTY, WENDY. *Asceticism and Eroticism in the Mythology of Śiva.* London: Oxford University Press, 1973.

WILSON, H. H., trans. *The Vishnu Purāṇa,* 3rd ed. Calcutta: Punthi Pustak, 1961.

ZIMMER, HEINRICH. *Myths and Symbols of Indian Art and Civilization.* New York: Harper & Row, Publishers, Inc., 1962.

GODDESSES AND WOMEN'S SPIRITUALITY

BHATTACHARYYA, NARENDRA NATH. *History of Śākta Religion.* New Delhi: Munshiram Manoharlal Publishers, 1974.

HAWLEY, JOHN, and DONNA WULFF, eds. *The Divine Consort: Rādhā and the Goddesses of India.* Berkeley: Berkeley Religious Studies Series, 1982.

KINSLEY, DAVID. *Hindu Goddesses: Visions of the Divine Feminine in the Hindu Religious Tradition.* Berkeley: University of California Press, 1986.

YOUNG, KATHERINE. "Hinduism." In Arvind Sharma, ed. *Women in World Religions*. Albany: State University of New York Press, 1987. Pp. 59–103.

SOCIAL STRUCTURE

DUMONT, LOUIS. *Homo Hierarchicus: The Caste System and Its Implications*. London: Paladin, 1972.
KARVE, IRAWATI. *Hindu Society—An Interpretation*. Poona, India: Deccan College, 1961.
MANDELBAUM, DAVID G. *Society in India*, 2 vols. Berkeley: University of California Press, 1970.

TANTRISM

AVALON, ARTHUR, trans. *Tantra of the Great Liberation* (Mahānirvāna Tantra). New York: Dover Publications, Inc., 1972.
BHARATI, AGEHANANDA. *The Tantric Tradition*. London: Rider & Company, 1965.

PHILOSOPHY

DASGUPTA, SURENDRANATH. *A History of Indian Philosophy*, 5 vols. Cambridge: Cambridge University Press, 1952–55.
HIRIYANNA, M. *Outlines of Indian Philosophy*. London: George Allen & Unwin, Ltd., 1967.
SHARMA, CHANDRADHAR. *A Critical Survey of Indian Philosophy*. Delhi: Motilal Banarsidass, 1964.

TEMPLES

KRAMRISCH, STELLA. *The Hindu Temple*, 2 vols. Delhi: Motilal Banarsidass, 1976.
MICHELL, GEORGE. *The Hindu Temple: An Introduction to Its Meaning and Forms*. London: Paul Elek, 1977.

ART

GOETZ, HERMANN. *India: Five Thousand Years of Indian Art*. New York: Crown Publishers, Inc., 1959.
ROWLAND, BENJAMIN. *The Art and Architecture of India*. Baltimore, Md.: Penguin Books, Inc., 1970.
ZIMMER, HEINRICH. *The Art of Indian Asia*, 2 vols. New York: Pantheon Books, Inc., 1960.

DEVOTIONAL MOVEMENTS

ALLCHIN, F. R., trans. *Tulsī Dās, The Petition to Rām*. London: George Allen & Unwin, Ltd., 1966.
DIMOCK, EDWARD C., and DENISE LEVERTOV, trans. *In Praise of Krishna: Songs from the Bengali*. Garden City, N.Y.: Doubleday & Co., Inc., 1967.
MAJUMDAR, A. K. *Caitanya, His Life and Doctrine*. Bombay: Bharatiya Vidya Bhavan, 1969.

POPE, G. U., trans. *The Tiruvāçakam of Māṇikkavācakar*. London: Oxford University Press, 1900.

RAMUNUJAN, A. K., trans. *Speaking of Śiva*. Baltimore, Md.: Penguin Books, 1973.

MODERN PERIOD

GANDHI, M. K. *An Autobiography or the Story of My Experiments with Truth*. Boston: Beacon Press, 1957.

FARQUHAR, J. N. *Modern Religious Movements in India*. New York: Macmillan, Inc., 1924.

M. [MAHENDRANATH GUPTA]. *The Gospel of Sri Ramakrishna*. Trans. Swami Nikhilananda. New York: Ramakrishna-Vivekananda Center, 1942.

MAHARISHI MAHESH YOGI. *The Science of Being and Art of Living*. New York: Signet Books, 1969.

Index

The letter f following a page number indicates a figure.

The letter n following a page number indicates a note.